DRUGS, RAINBOWS & DIRTY WORDS

For Agnes and Walter and their example that hard work pays.

The Days

DAY 1 1

DAY 2 5

DAY 3 16

DAY 4 25

DAY 5 34

DAY 6 45

DAY 7 61

DAY 8 76

DAY 9 87

DAY 10 99

DAY 11 107

DAY 12 121

DAY 13 129

DAY 14 130

DAY 15 131

DAY 16 133

DAY 17 138

DAY 18 138

DAY 19 138

DAY 20 142

DAY 21 146

DAY 22 149

DAY 23 158

DAY 24 158

DAY 25 159

DAY 26 159

DAY 27 163

DAY 28 163

DAY 29 169

DAY 30 170

DAY 31 175

DAY 32 176

DAY 33 183

DAY 34 186

DAY 35 191

DAY 36 197

DAY 37 203

DAY 38 214

DAY 39 221

DAY 40 235

DAY 41 254

DAY 42 271

Drugs, Rainbows & Dirty Words

Ken Piaskowski

Mayopia Productions, LLC

mayopia.com

Acknowledgements

I would like to thank Santa Claus, Judy Miller, Molly Walter Burnham, Ph.D., and Robert W. Piaskowski and Mom and Dad for their help and accommodations in the early years of the making of this book. And especially my genius wife, Lorie, my soulmate, without whose help this book would never have been published, and special thanks to Heather Macleod for her editing and Milburn Mehlhop for his cover designs on all the projects of the past ten years and his patience with WORD and ACROBATS. I would also like to thank Henry Miller, John Steinbeck, Kurt Vonnegut, Jerzy Kosinski, Jim Beam, King George IV, Herman Hesse, gods and the American Experiment of Freedom, unfailing sources of inspiration.

This is the month *Hey, Diddle Diddle—Blood is the Riddle*, a fact-based novel, is being published. *Dust, Rainbows and Dirty Sox* was published in 2001: another fact-based novel where the names have been changed and some situations are out and out lies—IT'S A NOVEL! We wanted to reissue *DUST* in a different format and found out we would need a new ISBN number. This got me to thinking I might as well do an overhaul and make a few things more confusing than *DUST*. *Drugs, Rainbows and Dirty Words* is virtually the same book as *DUST*—but as I write this prologue things have changed: Rupert still drives a taxi and likes to rhyme but no longer does drugs that haven't been prescribed or sold over the counter. *DUST* was written on typewriters and now there are computers and cell phones everywhere (including my studio).

Ronald Reagan was elected in 1980 and that was the beginning of major changes in the good ole USA. He busted the unions, subverted the Constitution and got an airport named after him instead of being impeached. We have become the military industrial complex that Ike warned us about. Clinton was impeached because of a blow job in the oval office. That should be somebody's platform. We've just gone through nearly eight years of arguably the most evil administration in the history of the United States UNDER THE GUISE OF GOD IS GOOD, GOD IS GREAT, LET US THANK HIM FOR OUR FOOD AHGHHH-MEN. The Vice President directly profited from the Iraq War because of his connections with private industry (you know, like using them to generate federal energy policy). Bush holds hands with the Saudis and probably played in the sandbox with the bearded fella that supposedly was behind blowing a hole in the Pentagon, and I still don't know shit— only the bullshit they tell me. Hitchhiking is a thing of the past and we don't really know if there are any good guys left anywhere.

What I do know is that MDMA was legal at the time the original *DUST* was written; we called it Easy Now in the book and Mellow Yellow on the street. It became illegal in 1985 and now a similar molecule is used in the antidepressant Effexor and MDMA is called "Ecstasy"–though I have yet to actually seen a pill from the Ecstasy era. Johns Hopkins Hospital in Baltimore is conducting clinical trials with psilocybin mushroom—administered to human subjects, as used to be done in dorms and deserts—with positive results. It is an election year and a conservative win would continue to rewrite the Constitution in favor of the wealthy few and big business at the expense of the huddled masses.

The land of the free and the home of the brave has become the land of total joint replacement and the home of the multi-national corporation. The 42 days in the book is the actual time it took to write the first typewritten draft and the events of those days are true. The fourteen days along coastal highway 1 are also pretty much accurate, from the perspective of the writer, as are the events leading there.

Sullivan who?

September, 2008

Foreword

Forty-two days of solitude--with breaks.

AIDS was not yet part of the everyday lexicon. Some drugs were still legal. "Classic Rock" was not yet a genre. Nobody had named an airport after Ronald Reagan—he was the new president who just survived being shot. And Sullivan Duda went to a cabin to reflect and write the story of his Journey to the west, when his adventures had culminated in a mystical experience. Now he faced the ultimate question: "To be or not to be?" What do you do after you become God? And when do we eat?

Rupert on the other hand, likes to rhyme. Lalalala lalala.

— Heather Macleod 2001

The nerve of some people—I wrote that little blurb, Forty-two days of Solitude, when *Dust, Rainbows and Dirty Sox* first came out in 2001. [**Spoiler alert!**] First of all, Sullivan obviously didn't shoot himself—yet. And now he asks me to write another blurb to go inside the new edition: *Drugs, Rainbows & Dirty Words*. Can't he just let it go? What am I supposed to do? Talk religion? Talk politics? Talk about the bums of Cannery Row—talk about the thousands and thousands of homeless people there are now in a country that could feed the world from its dumpsters and house the poor in its tanks and Hummers, or even set them up in shelters that would withstand tornadoes and hurricanes for a change? And did the CIA create crack cocaine and spike Ecstasy with something vile that kills people?

Really, you fooled us with that "42 days of solitude with breaks"—it's really more Jack Kerouac than Gabriel Garcia Marquez. (But is it true that *Hey, Diddle Diddle—Blood is the Riddle* is supposed to be an homage to *Love in the Time of Cholera*?) Whew—it's a strain to reintroduce a work that needs no introduction.

— Heather Macleod 2008

DRUGS

DAY 1

Rupert likes to rhyme.

> Hideehi Hideeho
> I'm a dreamer don'tcha know?
> Can't ya tell? Can't ya tell?
> Might as well, might as well.

* * *

There's a hollow point on my table. There's a box of hollow points on my table, made by Remington. My thirty-eight special is within my reach, fully loaded. The emblem on the gun is similar to that of Mattel toys. It is in my eyes—I'm very nearsighted. This, however, is not the story of my impending suicide, though it's not out of the question. It is a question of balance. Let's call the gun my initiative. Do it or die: there is a choice. At the moment my choice is a Sweetheart cup of white wine to my left and a cup of hot coffee with honey and chemical creamer to my right.

There's a story in my head; hopefully my fingers can find the way to push the correct keys of my portable typewriter without losing too much to time. The hollow points would make such a mess. Nature's given me enough holes in my body. Who am I to fuck with nature? I'll leave that to them, whoever they are. The gun does add a touch of drama to the situation. Isn't that what handguns are for, drama? Oh, illusion, see how I am. I forgot they're to kill people. I killed a man once, with my initiative. I watched them take the body away. That sucker's still with me, but I won't get into that just yet. I'm here to tell the story of my journey, my journey to the west.

If only Rupert were here, things would be much easier. His rhymes amuse me. But then I wouldn't get any work done. How can I keep my nose to the grindstone when someone is tickling my feet? I'd much rather have Ermonie tickle my fancy. She's not here either. I very much doubt if she'll ever speak to me again. I brought mementos of past loves to this cabin in the woods. Those other loves are mere shadows compared to my love for Ermonie Hunter. She told me she didn't want me around; I told her to go fry an egg. Sweet goodbyes are such a trauma.

There is a Santa Claus. He drives a cab. So does Rupert occasionally. Rupert introduced me to Santa Claus. The cabin I'm in belongs to Santa Claus. Santa Claus has long white hair and a long white beard; he has a big round belly and carries a gray tattered Bible on the dash of his cab. He quotes from his Bible often and sings gospel songs to his customers and fellow drivers. He once scared off a would-be robber by saying, "Jesus loves you," and singing "Shall We Gather At the River?" Santa Claus believes in Jesus. He claims that's all there is. Whatever gets you through the night. He is letting me use his cabin, rent free. I've been driving a cab for the past eight weeks. It really sucks. I can understand why Santa Claus needs Jesus. Rupert, on the other hand, likes to rhyme:

> I've got taxi fever--My head's off the receiver
> Seems like I've been in this cab for thirty years.
> As my head goes through the ceiling
> I get a crazy feeling
> I'd better take a night and drink some beers.
> Purgatory
> It's still the same old story--You hang out there
> In limbo as you drive. You can't make any money
> And still it's rather funny
> You always make enough to just survive.
> Copulation
> Sure beats masturbation--If the meter's running
> It's okay. If you get your rock off
> Or someone knocks your block off
> The only thing that matters is they pay.
> It's all distorted--My windshield needs a wipe
> I'll let it go and watch the show
> And just sit here and gripe.
> If I didn't have my weed--Or the other drugs I need
> I'd run myself right over with my hack
> So what my brain is burning--So long
> As I am earning

Enough to buy some drugs and give it back.
Sometimes it seems so hopeless
But only when I'm dopeless--You see
The drugs they come on with the turf
I am told for my existence
I'll always need persistence
Or so it seems my role in life is just a serf
So my hands are on the wheel
As I try to make a deal--To keep illusions flowing
All around me
Cause the chain has wrapped me tight
And it's drained me of my fight
So I simply watch the stars and they Astound me.

I've asked Rupert on several occasions why he continues to drive a taxicab. He always says, "Some people are meant to be cab drivers." The hollow point that sits on my table is quite an interesting object. On its former box it is described as a semi-jacketed hollow point, designed for greater shocking power, improved handgun efficiency. Power can be shocking--especially to those it's inflicted.

Rupert's ambition is to live on an island and write sayings for greeting cards. For now he drives his taxi and writes his rhymes. "Sullivan," he says, "everything in its own time. When the time comes as the time comes. And time always passes." No one has been in this cabin for a year; there's rat shit everywhere.

This is my first day here. I've done some cleaning and some writing. I walked in the woods behind Santa's cabin and came upon a wooden tree house hovering above the earth. It's used for stalking deer. I've never shot an animal. I only kill people.

Here I am in the woods. I'm fortunate to have the time to take my time; there's always the gun. Everyone should have one, it seems almost natural. It's probably the most easily obtainable vehicle of death over life for the common man. I've heard everyone is equal. Why shouldn't everyone taste a touch of power? Kill a human today—see what makes the generals tick. I really must be careful not to get hung up on such things. After all, this is the story of my journey to the west, one of the two times in my life when I became God.

Santa Claus claims to have built this cabin in two days, with his helpers, of course. It's not the North Pole; still, the western panhandle of Maryland is quite chilly in April. I must thank Rhoda Apple. Rhoda Apple is the owner of the Hope Springs Eternal Hotel in Grantsville, Maryland. She loaned me an electric space heater. There is still warmth in the world. The Hope Springs Eternal Hotel is where my journey began. That's where I met Ermonie Hunter.

* * *

There are eight beds to choose from in this one-room shack—threebunks, a rollaway and a couch that expands. The condition of two top bunks makes it evident that they're already occupied by mice or some sort of unsettled spirits with the runs and a craving for munching on mattresses. We are not alone. Perhaps I'll sleep on the floor.

The ceiling is wavy masonite with three bare light bulbs holding it up. My role as a hermit writer is taking hold in this cave-like structure with two of the four windows broken and covered with Hefty trashcan liners to block out the wind and the light. There is truth in darkness, though it seems weird. Perhaps it's only weird because there is so little truth around anymore. What can be more honest than an outhouse with a bucket? The bucket was empty when I arrived; I have time to figure out what to do with it when it becomes full. Maybe I'll stop eating. Then again, there's always my thirty-eight with the hollow points. If I shoot enough holes in the bottom of the bucket, it may drain. I am not here to play.

* * *

I had been working on my first attempt at a novel at the Hope Springs Eternal Hotel. The hotel houses a bar on its bottom, where such things have a purpose. I was a former manager of the Ease On Inn. Rhoda Apple was my boss. She plays classical piano and translates Russian for the CIA. She's an anarchist and hard core capitalist—call that Republican. Dear Rhoda is the reason I'm addicted to coffee. "Would you care for a cup of coffee?" she says, instead of "Hello." I would ask for the time of day and she would answer, "Would you care for a cup of coffee?" That plump little blonde haired blue-eyed Jewess must have stock in Maxwell House.

She believed I was working on a story entitled "Forty-two Steps to Overthrow Your Local Government and Then Some." She furnished me with room and board and enough money to keep me high in exchange for working in the bar on weekends. I look at one of my mementos from a past love. It's a jagged stone with the words "Love is merely you" inscribed on its face. The story I was working on at the time was about my experiences at the Ease On Inn and my love for the woman who gave me that stone. She was a lesbian. I took her from a woman and lost her to a man. It wouldn't have hurt as much had I lost her to another woman. My masculinity and ego wouldn't have felt abused if she had continued to prefer women— stimulated, perhaps, but not abused. The stone has a jagged edge. That is another story. It's filed away with time and as confused as my concept of ego and lesbians.

DAY 2

I woke up this morning watching my breath. I'm alive. I do have a companion. She's a three-legged Dalmatian belonging to my dear friend, Damien Rumsford. The dog is wrapped in blankets and lying in front of the space heater. She seems very comfortable.

I chose a bunk on the bottom. I wrapped my body in a black satin sheet, a blanket and a sleeping bag. I kept warm, no thanks to the space heater.

Damien is a regional distributor, traveling sales representative and a staunch supporter of unions, women's rights and indoor soccer. "Power to the people," he says. We met when I was manager of the Ease On Inn beneath the Hope Springs Eternal Hotel. He stopped in one day looking for a restaurant. I directed him to a Mennonite restaurant down the road though I had never been there myself. He returned after his meal and seemed delighted and eternally grateful. It seems the restaurant I had directed him to served deep-fried calf's brains. He claimed not to have had them since his childhood. Damien was from a large family and many times buckets of calf brains from a kind butcher were all they would eat for days at a time. Damien returned frequently to the restaurant and to the Ease On Inn; we became very close. "Poverty sucks," Damien always says.

Damien Rumsford makes a perfectly good living selling drugs, yet he's very unfulfilled. He's always on the lookout for a new cause or business scheme for easy money. "Rumsford has a better idea." Of course, he's never followed through on anything. Why should he? He has the best drug on the market, Easy Now.

Easy Now promotes a tremendous feeling of well being and oneness with the universe. Where acid takes me away whether I'm ready or not, Easy Now shows me the way and allows me to be here, wherever I am at the time. Of course, it's only an illusion enhancer. It remains an underground mind-expanding drug, and since it isn't sold over the counter or handled by some major pharmaceutical company, it's only a matter of time before they make it illegal. Put your faith in the Powers that be and the hereafter, and your money in big pockets and the collection plate. That's real. That's what we're here after.

I've heard on the radio a spacecraft is being launched today. It's a manned shuttlecraft. Ronald Reagan sent a message to the astronauts that all America is proud of them and American technology. Hey, I don't know them. I didn't vote for him. That's for them, not me. I'm still here. Don't speak for me without asking. I'm proud of my friends and the technology that produced Easy Now. So are the people who have experienced the drug. Many of my friends work hard at menial tasks or for large companies that control their lives. Their free time is theirs. It's good that Easy Now is underground, isn't it?

* * *

Though the cabin itself is far from a palace or even a tenement, it is in a beautiful setting. I stuck my head out the door a few moments ago and listened to a woodpecker. A rooster crows in the distance; a brook is babbling at the foot of the knoll on which the cabin rests. It all beats any drug. I find it hard to appreciate completely, since my program of asphalt and neon and television has all but covered the earth.

Ermonie Hunter appreciates the earth. There is no asphalt or neon or television in her valley. A dirt road snaking through the mountains is the only way in. Ermonie's Valley is long and narrow with a flowing creek and lush, green pasture between soft, stretched-out long, leg-like mountains spread apart. Life is fun on Buffalo Run. Buffalo Run oozes through Ermonie's Valley and empties into the upper Youghiogheny River which flows northward through Friendsville, a town of five hundred country folk on the other side of the mountain. Kayakers and white water rafters play on the upper Yough. The river eats canoes.

I've always been a city person, caught up in the fast lane, digging on the asphalt and neon, fucking and sucking every woman I could get my mood into and having the favor returned. Life is give and take.

Rupert says, "Fucking is a very important part of life." Rupert has the fingernails of a grease monkey. He claims it improves his tips driving a taxi. He says people are afraid to accept any change once they've seen his tarred and feathered hands.

* * *

It's a dog's life. My trustworthy companion, Tripod, has eaten her breakfast of Purina Dog Chow and is once again curled up in her blankets in front of the space heater. I had Raisins, Rice and Rye with evaporated milk and three cups of coffee and a glass of white wine. I'm reading a book on fasting for when my supplies run out.

Sweet Ermonie, out on the farm-I've never been so much in love. It really doesn't matter that she's ten years older than I am, and has four daughters. I'm ready for a lifelong commitment. Rupert says, "Commitment is a very important part of life."

I remember the first time I met Ermonie. She was with Ethel Much for the weekend and they were visiting the Ease On Inn. Ermonie's estranged and alcoholic husband was dry and entertaining the kids. I wrote all week and on weekends I tried to recapture what had been when I was the full time manager of the Ease On Inn.

Ethel Much had been my neighbor across the hall at the Hope Springs Eternal Hotel, back when I could afford an apartment and lived the material I was attempting to write about. Ethel studied lips in motion whenever they were acting as a springboard for words. She studied them in such a way I often found myself knocking on her door to ask to borrow a cup of flour when, in truth, I never did any baking. Ethel is a dear, sweet lady and always reminds me of chicken soup.

Rupert says, "Chicken soup is a very important part of life." It was a little over a year ago, near the end of March. I felt my first attempt at a novel was really taking shape. I thought I had something to say. I had been living in one room alone for nearly three months saying it. It was all new to me, saying it in such a way, on paper. The weekends provided me with a welcome relief and a taste of the familiar. I was very suicidal. Some things never change.

Yes, I was involved in writing a story of love won and lost, so I had no desire for new love, especially since I still maintained hopes for the old love. Yes, I thought the gay girl would return for me once she realized what she was giving up. But my desire for sex is ever present. Ermonie aroused this desire all the more.

Her beauty and manner gave her a foundation for sex that only age and experience can bring. I felt she knew something I didn't. I remember trying to convince her that my only hope for survival was the pleasure of her womanly ways, which only she possessed above all others. I was very drunk at the time, which accounted for my being so forward. She handled my advances like a good accountant keeping everything in its proper column. She held her glass of white wine as if it were something of value and not once let me know I was making a fool of myself. It was a very private introduction. She accepted the little boy in me.

Ethel allowed it. Ethel and I had become buddies back when I was full-time manager at the Ease On Inn. We had the opportunity to witness one another's imperfections. Ethel was another displaced city girl. She had appreciated the Ease On Inn and the social reality it provided at a time when there was a need, being single in an area where alcohol was still drunk from mason jars out back with the boys. This was fine with her but she kept trying to make them talk right and this didn't go over that great with the locals. The Ease On Inn filled a gap in the stories of lost souls and dissatisfied city folk.

She knew I wouldn't get too far out of hand with Ermonie. She also knew Ermonie could handle herself on most occasions. The Ease On Inn hadn't always been easy.

Attitude and atmosphere is what we tried to present. Of course, there were always a few who may have seen things differently; that was okay. Rhoda presented me with a challenge when she first called me to the Hope Springs Eternal Hotel; she also offered me a cup of coffee. Damien Rumsford, on the other hand, offered me Easy Now; that's when things began to develop along pleasant lines. All I did was direct him to a restaurant that served calf brains and I didn't even know they had all of that to offer.

The Cannonball Inn was the challenge and one of the reasons Rhoda changed her name to Apple from Applebaum; that's what the bar used to be called, Cannonball. She had a bad attitude. She was bare and hollow without more to offer than a hangout and a cheap high. Her only allure was as a rabble-rousing troublemaker. It wasn't just the emotional trouble that a little excessive alcohol sometimes brings; it was the violent kind. I guess Rhoda called for me at about the right time in my life. I had a hang-up about violence. I really disliked it. I thought I was above it—like a good cop. I also had a knack for running bars and a need to carry a gun, a fascination with the cool steel, my thirty-eight special—like a detective. It gave me a longer arm, a bigger member. I didn't want to do it again, but I knew there was always that possibility; get them before they got me, whoever they were.

A few well-placed rumors that a killer was in charge at the bar soon made those who were simply interested in a bar-room brawl disappear. They didn't want to die. Things began to evolve from there. The music was changed and things rearranged and Damien introduced me to Easy Now. The bawdy little broad named Cannonball became Ease On, where joviality, merrymaking and illusion prevailed. Yes, I was there for a year and a half before Rhoda fired me. I was becoming too involved with my self-importance and power and issued Rhoda the ultimatum that one of us had to go. I felt certain she would leave. She didn't even like to drink. I was eliminated.

I ran off to Key West, had an affair with an informer, dined on mangoes, walked on air. Came back to Baltimore (my home), firmed up my relationship with Damien Rumsford, decided I had something to say —and Rhoda invited me back to the Hope Springs Eternal Hotel for the winter where I began working on my first novel and met Ermonie Hunter.

Though my initial reason for returning to the Hope Springs Eternal Hotel was to write, the lure of the Ease On Inn was pulling me to familiar territory and I enjoyed it. I felt myself once more gradually taking over since no one else seemed to do much more than talk about things to do. Rhoda felt it also, and didn't like it. Once more I was asked to leave the Hope Springs Eternal Hotel while spring and new growth showed promise on the pictures of trees that had survived the winter. I left in early April to stay with my folks in Baltimore and sell some drugs to finance my writing.

* * *

I walked around Santa's cabin this morning. The knoll is covered with leaves and weeds and trash and other signs of neglect. It's a mess. It's like a vagrant with a sordid past and no hope for tomorrow. A definite challenge to fill my spare time--It'll keep me from shooting myself when my thoughts run dry.

Rupert says, "Fame is fleeting; litter is annoying." Ah, and then I left the knoll. The ferns were feeling the earth like scouts, sending signals that it's safe for the rest of the troops to roll in. It's nearly the time of year when I first visited Ermonie's Valley—a place like no other place I've ever known, where dreams and fantasies are free to grow and become real as spring creeps in and then explodes with no limits but time, and time always passes.

I'll never be welcome there again.

Rupert says, "Love is like a freight train: whether it's coming or going it always makes a lot of noise."

I earned a few hundred dollars the week I spent in Baltimore. Easy Now is easy to sell. I met up with Damien Rumsford; he stays with his sister whenever he's in town in search of a new picket line or simply delivering a batch of Easy Now.

Damien's got the smile of the Cheshire cat and a stubby little body his head seems to balance on, only because he parts his hair down the middle. His heavy brow and handlebar moustache seem only to enhance his balance.

We gathered at Dogs, an eastside neighborhood bar, with Rupert. Rupert wasn't driving a cab that Saturday night. He had his first taste of the drug. When Rupert is high on something he likes, he looks like an owl. I may have given him too much. All night long his grin with gaps on either side flashed. His eyes glowed, drawing stares and causing people to back away. "Who," is all he said, "Who! Who!" Damien went about gathering converts, void of any paranoia, passing out little gifts wrapped in tiny patches of toilet paper. As the night wore on, a gathering of grins commenced. The music from the jukebox expanded and there was dancing.

I called my mother at home to see if there were any messages. "Ermonie—out on the farm," she said, and gave me the number to call.

* * *

As messy as it still is, my little knoll feels nice today. I was in the cabin contemplating suicide, so I moved my typewriter and work outside.

Rupert says, "Moving outside is much better than suicide inside."

The highs are so high and the lows are so low. I'm simply trying to tell the story of my journey to the west, when I became God. The hollow-point and the loaded thirty-eight speak to me as I write. For lunch I had a combination of refried beans, jalapenos and tomatoes, peanuts, olives, bamboo shoots, water chestnuts, and chunks of pineapple all mixed together. Maybe that's why I'm thinking of shooting myself. It was rather tasty, sopped up with whole wheat pita bread and washed down with white wine and a shot of cheap brandy.

Tripod seems content, basking in the sun as motionless as a rug. I hope she isn't dead. Damien would be really angry. I often wonder what it would be like to be a dog—without all the explosions in the mind, content to just be, doing whatever's necessary to survive; coming into heat every once in awhile to make use of the extra parts besides for pissing, basking in the sun and frolicking all the other times.

It's not that way. I'm meant to change and grow and love and be confused until I get it right. I'm meant to be pushed to the edge, always with a choice and learning by my mistakes, only to make new mistakes when I'm overcome with my self-importance and forgetfulness. My hollow-point stares at me and laughs. It's too windy to burn leaves. I'm too lazy to gather the empty cans and bottles strewn about. I must improve my vocabulary.

I'll never forget the first time I heard Ermonie's voice over the telephone. "Hello," she said. It was a husky, sultry, oddly businesslike hello. It was the hello you'd hear from a high-class brothel. I was so turned on by her hello, I stammered momentarily trying to gain my composure.

"Er-Er-Er-Monie, this is Sullivan Duda. I got a message to call," I said.

She asked if I could come and stay in her valley. Her husband had gone completely berserk. He had flown to England on a whim and totally freaked out. He realized he was losing control. He cried—screamed—for help by making threats. He returned to New York and called Ermonie. He threatened her and the lives of their children. He screamed he was coming home—to kill her. He was coming by bus.

Ermonie's lover had joined the Marines to be rebuilt as a man ("The Marines build Men"), so he was no help. Besides, he had been her husband's best friend and his guilt made him powerless. Especially since it was stronger than his desire, I thought. She thought of running, she said; she didn't know where to run or who to run to. Her other friends had their own responsibilities and feared Oscar also—the law needs more than threats to get involved. So I was called after being recommended by Ethel Much, my former neighbor at the Hope Springs Eternal Hotel.

"I'll be there Monday," I said. "If you need me sooner, I'm three hours away." Oscar had told her he'd be a few days. And so it was: I had a purpose. I was immediately transformed from a vagrant, drug-dealing, all-talk writer, into a knight in shining armor, off to defend the existence of the beautiful matron and her four defenseless daughters against the demon rum and the freight train carrying heavy explosives—in this case a Greyhound Bus.

My intentions were strictly honorable. It also provided me with a much needed escape from the city. After the phone call, I rejoined Rupert and Damien at the bar. Dogs has a bar the length of the room with mirrors providing depth where, otherwise, there is none; Dogs is long and narrow. Still, there's room enough for entertainment among friends who gather there, and that Saturday night, thanks to Damien and his gifts, there was much enjoyment.

I knew there wasn't any great hurry to get to the valley outside Friendsville. I was anxious anyway. If there was that much anger in Oscar that he wanted to kill, surely he would find enough reason to kill someone on the bus trip from New York or at least in the bus station. A verbal threat from a long distance provides an ample buffer zone unless you're a nuclear-armed country. I began mentally preparing for anything.

Rupert says, "A good doctor makes his necessary rounds; so must a seeker follow his necessary path, accepting what is." I also thought the Valley would be a perfect place to finish writing a story I was really involved in, about the young madman falling passionately in love with the beautiful lesbian barmaid in a honky-tonk saloon. There was action, there was beauty and love and romance and some hard-core pornography. Talent, on the other hand, was the unknown factor—some ability to manipulate words to tell a story and keep the attention of the reader for a period of time and maybe even say something of value occasionally. . . What the fuck. There was, however, a touch of violent passion and much confusion.

There's always confusion—except for Rupert. He always sees things clearly. We shared a reflection from the mirror behind the bar and excitedly I began to relate my phone conversation with Ermonie.

"Who," he said, his face glowing as if he were either blessed or insane.

"Ermonie," I said.

"WHO!" he said.

"Ermonie—out on the farm," I said.

"Who are you?" he said.

I realized that he had taken too much of the drug. Knowing it would wear off, I humored him. "Sullivan Duda," I said.

"That's all that matters," he said and handed me a decorative napkin with his tribute to Dogs on it.

> The roaches crawl up the bathroom wall;
> The mice run across the floor.
> But the drinks, they feel nice so I never
> Think twice about having a drink or two more.
> The company's fine and the music is mine
> I may have a shot, if it's free.
> My money is low, I may soon have to go
> And remember you're you and I'm me.

Rupert is one of the lucky ones. He's never lost control while under the influence of any mind-altering substance; sometimes he gets a little weird, but he's never lost control. He claims to have tried everything. Ermonie's husband wasn't so lucky. He was a violent paranoid drunk who didn't know who he was or why. He blamed it on the bossa nova and anything or anyone else he could. He couldn't accept the responsibility of his own being. Sometimes neither can I, so the hollow point sits on the table and laughs and waits. I haven't even begun the story of my journey to the west, a story that must be told.

* * *

I've located a spring with fresh water for drinking and coffee. The brook at the base of the knoll is adequate for washing and cleaning. On the other side of my bathing area, there sits another cabin. No one is there. I hope they never come, whoever they are. Tripod and all the noises of the forest are all the company I want for now; I've temporarily lost myself and I want no one to find me before I do.

My gun isn't a Saturday night special; it's capable of working any time. One need only squeeze the trigger and the semi-jacketed hollow point does the rest. Try it sometime. Anyone can obtain one. Ronald Reagan was shot while I was driving a cab. None of my customers were particularly upset about the near-destruction of the mandate of the people. Neither was I. People can adapt to anything.

Rupert says, "Life is indoctrinating, accepting and adapting. You are what you eat. Blame it on the bossa nova."

* * *

I possessed no vehicle at the time; Rupert became the pilot for the evening, guiding us along our seemingly predetermined path in Damien's '58 Austin Healey. Rupert gazed at the now and then city as if he had never seen it before, marveling at the sights and sounds of an inner city Saturday night. I enjoyed the company and the ten-cent tour, which only an experienced cab driver can give. Damien enjoyed the ride, along for the ride, in his vehicle. We were led to a face in Mount Vernon Place, where a concrete man with fire in his eyes and a scream on his lips held up a building. He had pillars for shoulders and no hands for his time, but his scream wasn't for help. He was singing. I think it was opera.

Rupert likes to travel on the back streets and alleys, preying on their honesty and rhythm, keeping his own beat as only one who knows can, not missing a beat, making his own music. Rupert says, "There is always a beat and there is always music."

My own composition was slowly developing as I prepared myself for yet another change of scene and role as the bodyguard. We parted in the wee small hours of the morning, smiling at one another and the world. I spent Sunday tying up loose ends, packing and visiting with friends. I had no idea what to expect from Ermonie's husband Oscar, so on Monday, my mind conditioned for my role, I purchased a box of 50 semi-jacketed hollow points, possibly to kill with—for no other use. Handguns are for killing people. I called it a deterrent but was aware of its purpose and knew I would make use of it if the need arose. Now that's premeditation. Anyone who owns a handgun knows this but few admit it. Bang— shoot him in the knee. Bang Bang Bang, shoot him in the other knee. Sure and he'll be back to get you later. That same box sits on my table—minus six cartridges. Five are in my gun and one hollow point sits on the table and laughs at me.

For now, I laugh back.

DAY 3

This is my third morning in Santa's cabin. I have been formally introduced to the mice, two of them anyway. One danced for me in the beam of my flashlight. The little fucker didn't run. He stood there and danced. His insolence will be justly rewarded—he was dancing on one of the two D-Con mouse baits I've planted in dark corners. The other mouse was checking out the morning coffee on top of the stove.

Last night I nearly finished reading a book on fasting. A pot of rice simmers on the front burner of the electric stove. I'll mix it with my leftover Chinese-Mexican mishmash. The first thunder storm of spring rages outside; I'm surprised and happy to say the roof of the cabin doesn't leak. Maybe the snakes will come and eat the mice.

I don't feel very suicidal this morning. In fact, I feel rather content in my environment. I'm not sure about Tripod. At the first crack of thunder she hid under my chair. She's also afraid of mice. Earlier, Tripod saw a mouse and ran under one of the bunks.

I must be the slowest typist in the world. This damn book is going to take forever. The strangest thing, I was looking through one of my thirteen containers of possessions; I came upon a decorated bar napkin. There are drinking jokes printed on it; there's also a handwritten message etched across a picture of a martini. The message reads, "If I never finish this, the sculpting and the process of it is worth the pain. LOVE GOD." It figures.

Rupert says, "It ain't what you're doing, it's how you do it."

I arrived in Grantsville, Maryland, late Monday evening, confident I was ahead of Oscar. I had been in touch with Ethel Much, the grand dame of speech therapy; she assured me of the safety net of time. Oscar had called Monday afternoon and said he was still on his way to kill Ermonie. He called from a bar in Philly. I was on the last bus of the day.

As a former stutterer, I have found my relationship with the overly dramatic Ethel quite rewarding. I'd had the opportunity to witness her work on occasion and sensed she was doing the right thing with her pupils, though my observations were brief because I always found myself intimidated by the young stutterers. I don't know what to say to them. Ethel, however, finds it quite frustrating to pursue her work in a bureaucratic, suppressive public school system where the individual is classified and grouped. In Catholic school they tried to put me in a special school for speech problems but my parents abided by my wishes not to be thrown into a group of others like me. I remained with others who were different and witnessed speech that was not disruptive.

I always carry enough baggage for any occasion. I had with me two suitcases, a large army-type duffel bag, my portable typewriter and, of course, my thirty-eight special. In this case I had the full intention of killing Oscar Hunter if he decided to attempt to carry through on his threat to Ermonie. I have a very strong distaste for woman-beaters; Oscar fit the bill. Killing is a matter of attitude, atmosphere and mood. I had gotten the impression that Oscar disliked women and used fear tactics to gain control as if he were at war. I was called to the front.

Ethel Much is a big, buxom woman with a childlike face, capable of changing its expression from innocence to the infliction of death. A pleasant smile of relief was in her eyes; a touch of apprehension showed in her thin lips, for once not knowing what to say. Her bright flowering long dress over her large body made words unnecessary, and we greeted each other with a warm hug, after which I promptly kissed her hand.

Ah, the sweet joys of life. I never get my fill of kissing ladies' knuckles. It's so sexual under any circumstances. If only I could speak as easily as Ethel usually does, maybe there would be no reason to hide and write and speak only to Tripod.

Rupert says, "Rupert says, 'Communication is a very important part of life. But words aren't always necessary.' "

* * *

Ah, April showers bring May flowers and drown the bloody mice. They'll never wash away all the empty rusted cans and broken jars and bottles. Only man can clean the mess he's made. If only I weren't so lazy. How lucky I am, to listen to the trees make music by the rain. Up until my time in the Valley, my closest encounter with nature over any extended period of time had been my trial at the Hope Springs Eternal Hotel.

I thought I was in the country at the time, being surrounded by trees and mountains to look at as if they were pictures. But my entire reality was focused on the illusion of the Ease On Inn. It had to be that way to fulfill its purpose as an escape for others, a place to gather, meet new people, expand horizons and get shit-faced drunk. It's quite a pleasant experience to stand on the stone step of the cabin in the rain and piss. Perhaps if I look in the mirror and stick the loaded gun in my mouth, I'll get some work done.

I believe the angle in suicide is very important. Some angles definitely look as if they would be more effective than others. I'd hate to screw up and become a vegetable. I believe it's my Catholic upbringing that gives me all of my guilt and my need to confess. I was an altar boy and I also made good my nine first Fridays of the month with Mass and Communion. I feel a certain sense of security that no matter what I say or do a priest will greet me on my deathbed and grant me Extreme Unction. I can't remember if that's canceled out with suicide. I still remember the Pope's phone number, Et cum spirit 2 2 0.

* * *

I believe it was part of a plan for me to arrive in the Valley during the daylight hours so I would receive the full impact of its magic and beauty. Ethel took me to her comfortable cottage where everything was in its proper place. In fact, the only thing that seemed out of place in that wonderful woman's home was the handcuffs on the coffee table.

I didn't ask. Other than handcuffs, everything, even Ethel's bed, was related to speech therapy. Above the pillows the words "SPEAK AS YOU FEEL" were hand carved in the maple headboard.

She prepared a late snack and filled me in on my duties just to be around. Ethel knew I was a killer; I figured that was one of the reasons I was called in as the bodyguard. She also knew I had no particular fear of Oscar, or of dying for that matter. It was apparent to me that Oscar had not only emotionally and physically brutalized

Ermonie, but he also had collected a toll from her caring friends. Fear of Oscar also pushed Ermonie's lover, Andrew, to join the Marines. That I couldn't figure out.

I was invited to sleep with Ethel for the night after a lecture on how I should behave with Ermonie. I was told I shouldn't let my sexual curiosity get the best of me and to be a gentleman at all times. I was also told that I would be posing as Ethel's lover so Oscar wouldn't get the idea I was sleeping in his bed if he showed up. After all, if I was going to kill him it had to be in my role as protector—not as a burglar caught in the act. The pretense was also meant to make Andrew feel a little more secure in his passion. Ermonie needed to be in love and saw a future with Andrew—he played her like a fiddle. I had no emotional ties at the time. My love for the gay girl had been finally put in its place—away.

Since I was supposed to play a part, I attempted several sexual advances, but never managed to get beyond a little freelance groping. Looking up at her headboard, I said, "Ethel, if I'm supposed to be your lover, shouldn't we?" I was perfectly serious. "I can't fake an orgasm."

She looked at me with kind eyes and said, "Sullivan, neither can I."

* * *

This fucking gun, I've never had the nerve to carve a notch in it. Yet they gave it back to me and I still keep it. It fits my hand so perfectly. The first time I was God, I became the gun. The power I felt being all things! Will I feel the same power when I look in the mirror and pull the trigger? The hollow point looks at me and says, "Forget it, sucker. You don't have any say." There are gunshots outside. I wonder, should I shoot back? Whoever it is has a rifle. Ah, I have my hollow points. I wish Rupert were here. I have his book, his book of unpublished rhymes.

Rupert says,

> As it feels--So it continues,
> Never really ending--Never really beginning
> Always changing--Always remaining the same.
> She too--Continues through her daughters
> And so ON--Always changing--Always remaining
> the same. Quenching thirsts--Replenishing the land
> With strength and beauty allowing life to blossom
> Around her and in her. Sweet woman,
> You are the River.

Rupert likes to rhyme.

* * *

Sweet Ermonie, when I visited your Valley was the first time I felt peace in my life. Is that why people contribute to charities—the plight of another makes them feel better? Or is it the Offering.

On Tuesday morning I dropped Ethel at her school and continued in her Volkswagen to the Valley. I followed the directions carefully until I came to the mailbox with the rainbows on either side. It had been a rough winter and the dirt road was pitted and parts were melting into the ditches on either side. Ermonie and her four daughters had spent it alone, without much help; Oscar had the gall to threaten, and Andrew, Ermonie's lover, had the urge to join the Marines.

I believed I was the bodyguard. I knew if Oscar would show his threatening face, he should surely die. I was also ready to make Ermonie's lover do the duck walk at gunpoint, the fucking asshole. Then something strange happened as I reached the valley and continued towards the farmhouse.

I noticed children's toys strewn about in some sort of loose epilogue of enjoyment. I had driven over under overcast skies; now the sun was like a floodlight for an encore waiting for a bow. Ermonie and her three year old twins, Jennifer and Star, were over by the enormous chestnut barn—waiting. I switched off the clanking motor of the VW.

The sound of Buffalo Run, applauding the sun, eased my mood. A gentle breeze caught Ermonie's long soft skirt and pressed it against her thighs. She approached me with bare muddy feet and a welcome-here smile. Her body danced above the earth as it moved for her. A few subtle lines were like quotation marks for the clarity in her straightforward blue eyes that met mine without reservation, without question. She seemed far from a woman in fear of her life, but rather a queen at home in her kingdom; I was a stranger who had once propositioned her in a bar.

"We're going for a walk. Would you care to join us?" I, the beast, was knocked over by some feeling of acceptance. There was no doubt in my mind that I would be the perfect bodyguard. I left my

luggage and gun in the VW and kicked off my shoes and any preconceptions I had about how to act. We walked to the river, followed by several sheep, an affectionate goat, two playful dogs, and a cat that looked like Damien. We met on a soft spring day with tulips blooming. It was a dream. It must have been a dream.

Sweet Ermonie, is it because I fell in love with you that you no longer ask me to go for walks to your river? I don't understand. Have I become part of some malignant disease by wanting more than I deserve? I want to love you and give to you not strangle your life—or is it confused in me? Do I need to be eliminated like a cancer? Like my victim? Am I my victim? Life was so sweet in your Valley, only because you were there.

That fucking semi-jacketed hollow-point keeps laughing, knowing it belongs to me. The balance, I mustn't forget the balance and my journey to the west. That's my only salvation—to recreate the time when all I came into contact with lived for me alone. I'm sworn to no secrecy. I have a need to share. My only obligation is to die--When the time comes. For now I still live, as I've always lived, testing the waters and then learning to swim or at least tread water—swallowing enough to drown an alligator.

The water with Ermonie was fine and deep and moving enough to devour a kayak if one didn't have a paddle. But why be careful? Why be bored? You never know unless you try. Life can be so exciting, even watching yourself in the mirror with a loaded gun in your mouth. It's quite sexual. For the gun to be fulfilled it must cum.

It has cum before, now it's back to a little freelance groping. Like the sex act itself, it needs a cooperative partner to be complete.

I've never forced myself sexually on anyone. I'd rather be celibate or masturbate in a world of fantasy—except for when I was the gun and I raped the life of another man. The gun wants more. It looks to me to masturbate in my own mouth with the hollow point acting as the sperm, giving me life in the next dimension, yet another uncharted course, with the risk that there is nothing else. There is always a risk.

The twins, Jennifer and Star, quickly shed their clothes, uninhibited by the presence of this strange man. They perched on a large flat rock overlooking the River. They were witnesses, but were on display, on this little stage, for all they witnessed and for anything witnessing them. Jennifer and Star, with a bond I had never seen before between sisters, frolicked like two little pixies, splashing in a stream, with complete innocence, enjoying without fear, without expectations,, all that was offered on an unusually warm spring day in their yet tiny circle, extending to the total oneness of the universe. Ermonie not scolding, allowed them the full experience of their existence and innocence.

* * *

My wine is still white; I've switched from California Chablis to Gallo White Port. My first experience with Gallo White Port was on Monastery Beach, south of Monterey, California. It was July, a Thursday evening. I was hitchhiking on Coastal Highway 1, with $4.82 in my pocket. I had eaten a bagel in San Francisco that morning. My destination was LA, where Damien Rumsford was looking into female mud wrestling as a possible business venture. My incentive was the promise of a plane ticket back to the east coast.

I had been hitchhiking for nearly two weeks and my luck had been planned by God or some other creator of fiction. I carried a large army surplus duffel bag with clothes for every occasion and my leather briefcase packed inside. I also had my portable typewriter by my side.

I had been at the mercy of discriminate drivers since Eugene,

Oregon; all whom I had come into contact with were exactly the right ones. I was sunburnt and high and happy, accepting everything as a gift. WHOA! Can I speak of the climax of an evening without first sharing the foreplay of the day? Let me begin with the bagel and the freshly ground coffee.

Ramona preferred the blackest beans for the richest coffee. Thanks to the hospitality of her friends and her trusting nature, I had spent Wednesday evening in a warm bed after a hot bath. Ramona graciously washed my back. As I gently fell off into a deep sleep, she played the record with the words she had constantly sung to me since our meeting on Monday.

> TRUCKIN' with the doodah man
> Who once told me you've got to play your hand
> Sometimes, your cards ain't worth a dime
> If you don't lay 'em down. . .
> Sometimes the lights all shinin' on me
> Other times I can barely see
> Lately it occurs to me
> What a long strange trip it's been.

And now I'm thinking of suicide. Santa will be greatly upset when he finds his cabin a bloody mess.

* * *

After our bagel and coffee on Thursday morning, Ramona donned her favorite Grateful Dead tee shirt over a long flowering dress and strapped her ukulele over her shoulder. I wrapped a red bandana around my neck, and we wore our tweed slouch caps. She carried my portable typewriter and I my green surplus duffel bag. We left the Mission and hopped a bus to an entrance to the freeway.

We rode the bus in silence, standing, but taking up more space than we were supposed to, smiling constantly as we looked into one another's eyes, knowing we would never cross paths again and cherishing the brief moments we shared when nothing else mattered but here now. I was on the road and Ramona was preparing to return to her home in Australia after five years of seeing the world through rose-colored glasses.

We left the bus and Ramona Pearl walked with me to a block ahead of an on-ramp where we hugged and I kissed her hand and doffed my cap, with tears matching hers. We shared a wave and her turned head until the corner came and she disappeared. Sweet Woman, you are the river.

I waited two hours for a ride. Ramona had drawn me a sign on a folder from my briefcase. One side said "SOUTH," the other, "L.A." LA. Lalalala lalala. While I was waiting for the right ride, I had three brief encounters.

The first was with two black men, ragged and jivin', bumming money for a bottle of wine. I contributed 35 cents to the cause. "Ride on Bro, it's such a nice day. We jus' wanna catch a buzz and fuck it away," one of the men said. Sure sounded good to me.

I held up my sign to the air when a well-dressed man crossed in the middle of the block and passed close by. He seemed very mysterious, not cracking a smile but reading my sign and saying in a low monotone without losing stride, "You know, if I were going to L.A., I'd take the BART over to Oakland and hop the 3:30 freight. You'll be there in the morning. That's what I would do." He disappeared. It sounded like a good idea.

I'd never hopped a train before. I used the excuse of my heavy bag and typewriter to talk myself out of it. After a while longer I was joined by three black children who amused themselves with me in turn entertaining and amusing me. They danced and played and decided I needed help and took turns holding my sign and sticking out their thumbs. They had walked out of the house in front of which I was standing and became my hosts. A portable radio reiterated their movements, keeping time until an old Ford panel truck stopped.

The truck had been reconditioned and was rather sleek. It looked like Peter Fonda was driving and Henry was the passenger. Peter climbed from the driver's seat to unlock the back doors, letting me climb into the rear compartment. Henry had been visiting and was headed to the airport to return to New York. I kept silent while they compared cities as you would compare artichokes and apples.

I have always enjoyed the work of both actors, so the fact that there were no windows in the rear made no difference. The movie was fine. They dropped me at the entrance to the airport where Peter Fonda once more climbed from his seat to unlock the back doors and let me out. I thanked him and crossed a median strip to reach the outgoing traffic, and I waited in the glaring sun, stashing my slouch cap in my bag.

* * *

The birds sing and the brook babbles and so do I. I need initiative. Have you ever put a loaded gun in your mouth and watched your eyes in the mirror? Try pulling the trigger. I just did. I took the bullets out first. Let's call it a dry run. Even if it was loaded, I'm sure I would have the same look of conviction—Conviction of myself. After all, it must come from the EYE.

DAY 4

And so it is, the beginning of the fourth day in Santa's cabin, with fresh coffee and Gallo White Port for breakfast. The day is gray and dingy. Tripod ran off looking for rabbits to run away from; I'm smoking like a fiend. I'm surrounded by Number 25 Virginia tobacco, Swisher Sweets with tips, and Pall Malls. The store didn't have any Philip Morris Commanders. Prince Albert also keeps me company— he's in a can. Maybe I should let him out before he suffocates. He may have something to contribute; he traveled with me. Don't misunderstand my pipe tobacco, I roll my own.

The gang on Monastery beach had a communal can of Tops cigarette tobacco. The only thing I find wrong with rolling and smoking pipe tobacco is that it cuts a red callused tunnel through your lips. I always hold whatever I'm smoking on the right side of my mouth. Pipe tobacco leaves a dark red impression if you smoke it constantly. It really is strange looking. I hold my lips together; there it is, that callused red tunnel leading to the one rotting tooth. I had the same tunnel from smoking Prince Albert on my journey. It was miraculously healed at the hot springs at Orr. It returned a day later.

* * *

A large gray step-van driven by a round man with a smile stopped on its way from the airport. I saw the same smile constantly on my trip down the west coast. It was a smile that said, Easy Now, isn't life wonderful? The round man had been delivering cleaning chemicals at the airport hotel; the step-van was empty except for a half-dozen or so five-gallon containers. They were so full they weren't sliding around. There were three large boards across the width of the truck between the containers and the driver's seat. Joe had his sliding door propped open for air, and his was the only seat.

* * *

I just dumped the remainder of my Chinese-Mexican mishmash in the weeds. I hate to be wasteful, but it was in its third day and the refrigerator doesn't work. I promised Santa I would have it fixed. I will—at the moment, I'm emotionally involved with my life and death. It's a question of balance. Maybe some animal out there is into spicy gook.

The balance, that was why I had to help Joe that day—to fulfill a basic need. Nothing but good had happened to me on my entire journey. I felt I had to repay someone; Joe presented the opportunity for me to fulfill my selfish desire. I sat on the boards as we pulled off. Looking back, I think that sly devil with his disarming smile set me up.

We introduced ourselves and cruised on to 101.

"I'm going as far as San Mateo," he said, bouncing in his seat.

"Fine," I said, ignoring splinters and not really knowing where San Mateo was. I was truly in a state of mind where I knew everything was in perfect order; I need only agree.

"Unless you're in a hurry. I have to stop over in Newark across the bridge; then I'm going to San Jose," he said with none of it making any real sense to me. I took it for granted it was farther along in the direction I was headed. "Why not?" I said.

I related my story of who I was and how I got to where I was and how my path had been one continuous rainbow, casually mentioning I was nearly broke. He told me who he was and how he was enjoying his life, casually mentioning he was driving to Newark to a salt factory to take on 3,000 pounds of coarse salt to be delivered to the San Jose Hyatt Regency. He worked for an industrial cleaning chemical distributor, and the owner of the company didn't mind if he used the truck to pick up some extra money on the side.

In my solitude, I am driven, but on my journey I flowed. It takes searching to learn not to search. I sat and studied my map, while Joe and a factory worker loaded the 50-pound sacks of salt on the truck. The heat was unbearable. The salt air did help. Joe insisted I relax. I was trying to decide whether to continue to LA by way of Highway 101 because of lack of funds or to head for Coastal Highway 1, the scenic route. I was told 101 would be much quicker. When you're on the road, such decisions are often made for you.

Rupert says, "Whenever you try to rush, you screw up anyway, so what's the hurry?"

Joe and the factory worker toiled mercilessly in the upper 90-degree heat, stacking the tight but arching sacks to maintain a balance of weight in the rear of the van.

* * *

Tripod is lying in the wet grass just outside the cabin door. I've picked up a public radio station originating in Pittsburgh. It's bombarding me with kultcha and classical music and tidbits of news from the BBC and all things are considered. There are distractions everywhere. The music reminds me of Rhoda Apple and the news is telling me never to leave the forest. I'd get a lot more work done if I didn't pace so much, up and back and in circles, trying to collect thoughts and reconstruct feelings and attempting to get my point across; there is no point. Only the hollow point which sits on my table and stares with its regal crown of soft lead bored out to explode into fragments on impact and pushed by its semi-jacket of glimmering copper and meant to continue on a course gathering pieces of flesh and bone and any material in its path, looking very carnivorous. It is certainly not a vegetarian.

It is a matter of life or death. All that's left of the Gallo White Port is in my Sweetheart cup. I have a bottle of Thunderbird. We drank Thunderbird—or, as my hosts called it, "Thunderchicken"—that night on Monastery Beach.

* * *

On the way to San Jose I suggested to Joe that I might help him do what he had to do with the salt.

"I couldn't pay you. I never carry cash," he said.

"Buy me a cold beer and we'll call it even," I said.

"I don't even have any change. I can get you all the Coca-Cola you can handle," he said.

I explained that since everyone had been so good to me, I had to help someone. In the back of my mind I thought he might be holding out on me. A few dollars sure would have come in handy, especially since he had mentioned he received $60 for his effort. And an effort it was. When I volunteered, I had no idea what I was letting myself in for.

We parked a good hundred feet from the door of the Hyatt so as not to block the entrance for the paying customers. Joe led me through a wooden gate and explained the task, showing me the two very large water softening tanks to be filled with the coarse salt.

Joe acquired a hand truck and we took turns hauling and dumping. At first, he hauled three bags at a time on the cart while I dumped the individual bags of the dried crystals into the head-high container hooked up to the hotel's water filtering system. Joe's puffy cheeks turned red in the scorching sun, but he never lost his smile.

I must admit, thoughts of being used crept into my mind from time to time; I reminded myself constantly that I had volunteered, so I continued. After the first thousand pounds we drove around to the Employee's Entrance and helped ourselves to cup after cup of ice cold Coca-Cola in the Employee's Lounge, which seemed to be another country. There were Mexicans everywhere. They work cheap, I was told. I was working for a few cups of Coke. After a 10-minute break we returned to the salt. I hauled while Joe dumped. We filled the two tanks to their capacity and drove to a garage area where we filled another tank and stored the remainder of the salt. The fat but nimble Joe worked like a man possessed, showing me he was quite capable of doing it all himself. The industrial cleaning chemicals he normally delivered kept him in top shape. I did my share. The job completed, we returned to the lounge to replace the lost fluids and wash up a bit. We didn't drink the water. It was after three in the afternoon when Joe dropped me at the on-ramp to the freeway. On the short ride I mentioned once more that a few dollars sure would come in handy.

"I only have checks," he said with his ever present smile, as he reached in his pocket and pulled out a handful of checks. "Never carry cash," he added while he stopped to let me off.

"It's been a pleasure, thanks for the ride," I said. I don't know why I said that. Actually it had been a pleasure, but he never thanked me. I suddenly felt very confused.

He chuckled a little bit and cocked his head and smiled. "Sure, anytime," he answered and the battleship gray step-van disappeared within seconds, leaving me at the fenced-in on ramp.

The confusion was immediately replaced with a focused anger that I had been seen and taken for a sucker. Some sort of tense hatred welled up in my gut and each new thought began striking out at a man who had actually been my benefactor in a tough free-ride market. He was trying to earn a living and I was on the road and had nearly 400 miles to travel with less than five bucks in my perspiration-soaked pocket. I had taken on a strong odor. He could have gotten cash at the Hyatt, I thought. He lived in the area, I thought. He could have gotten a check cashed anywhere, I thought. "The greedy motherfucker," I thought. I was hungry and began feeling very sorry for myself.

Suddenly, like a flash of piercing white light, came a different voice—a voice that had been keeping me company on my entire journey. "Easy Now," I laughed out loud, feeling fresh and clean, and I carried my typewriter to a spot on the freeway that said, "HERE." I waited for my next ride.

Maria came to me, quiet and unassuming, providing me with her visual beauty and a moment of peace for my soul. We were silent after exchanging names. She was Mexican and may not even have spoken English. Music from her tape deck, by the English group Pink Floyd—*BREATHE* filled her battered Mustang with sound; I glanced at her dark eyes as often as I could without being rude. She watched the road and allowed me to tell her how beautiful she was. It was rush hour and the traffic was becoming close and cramped and heavy, but the mood with Maria was easy and comfortable. The only words were the words to the music, something about breathing and running and making a lot of money and dying. I didn't care; I didn't listen. It was just a soundtrack for the vision of Maria—that was the only conscious message I heard.

She dropped me a quarter mile before the Gilroy exit. Gilroy was there. Sweet woman, you are the river. I was left with no ramp to protect me from the law, at the mercy of the sun, but no longer feeling a victim. They arrest you in California for hitchhiking on the freeway. I was hoping for a quick ride and I kept constant watch for the law, though there was no escape other than a ride. I observed a car pulling to the center median strip with smoke pouring from under its hood. It came to a stop a little farther down the road. There was nothing I could do to ease his overheating though I discussed it with myself for a moment.

"I got no tools. I got no water. I certainly got no advice."

I looked back at the oncoming traffic, reminding myself of the train I didn't take. The vehicles were so bunched together the flow became like unfocused hostility, sporadic in its dispute, in a hurry but having to slow down. I spotted a bubble coming towards me, almost hopping. I attempted to conceal my sign, thinking perhaps the cop would assume I was waiting for a bus. He saw me, but continued past to where the overheated casualty sent up a smoke signal for help. I knew it was only a matter of time before he returned to take me away.

It didn't happen. A starship came for me before he had a chance. It was baby blue and rust with a cleft palate, like a giant scoop gathering cosmic debris. It had scooped up eight cylinders pumping and belching with a chrome breather. There seemed uncertainty as to whether it was display or disarray. It was manned by two billed-capped Prunedalians. They were headed back to their native planet after a search and destroy mission. They informed me that they had found nothing to destroy but had managed to greatly alter their consciousness in their searching.

They were heavily armed. My compartment was in the rear where my ticket granted me an in-flight movie. It didn't take me by surprise when the flow changed as I observed from within. We jockeyed for position and soared past the casualty and the cop. The cop smiled. The Prunedalians cursed him just the same. And a soundtrack came up as the movie began: *Highway to Hell*.

Where I sat it was like wearing enormous headphones. Two speakers from someone's living room filled the rear shelf while AC-DC made them move. There wasn't much I could say and there was no need. There was no question of my destination; I was going where they were taking me. I was immediately drugged with hashish and given a quart of Miller High Life for my thirst. NO DEPOSIT, NO RETURN.

Traffic thinned and Gilroy wasn't there anymore. The Prunedalians spoke in a strange tongue and used hand signals with jerking head movements as if they were stalking. The needle on the control panel shot up to 80 and higher whenever there was something to overtake. I thought of death; I was ready. If they could deal with it so could I. I sucked on a beer, inhaled the smoke and enjoyed the movie.

Han Solo seemed like an able pilot though a bit cocky and irregular. His hairy partner, Chewbacca, was an alert navigator, knowing what to look for and able to shave the blonde Lebanese hash into fine slivers, keeping the pipe circulating. I saw nothing past the windows once my interest became divided between the two. They saw for me anything that was a threat or just a passing fancy. They were familiar with the territory, its dangers and its pleasures, and they didn't intend to return home with a loaded magazine.

We were zooming through the Milky Way dodging asteroids and slower traffic. Chewbacca emptied his quart of Miller High Life, and cleared his line of fire by draining his window of glass. He spotted something ahead that I didn't see. Han knew instinctively what to do, becoming calm and deliberate, glancing at Chewbacca making ready. Han took evasive action, swerving from left to right and back and zeroing in on the target, back to the right. Chewbacca cocked his arm and let loose with the missile. We must have hit an air pocket with the starship wobbling momentarily; Han regained control quickly. Their expressions told me it was a miss. I didn't know what they were shooting at. I sucked on my beer.

"Amenahead," Chewbacca blurted out. I took it to mean, "Don't worry, we'll get the next one." I was silent but secretly rooting, hoping my pilots would get them before they got us--Whoever they were.

"Closer," I heard. The gunner prepared and cocked his arm, fully loaded with a missile. I once more inhaled deeply from the pipe. The gunner nodded. The starship swerved to the right, leaving gravel and stone in its wake. The gunner let loose—another miss. Chewbacca turned and looked at me.

I thought I was about to be shot as a spy. My missile was still half full. From the muttering and the pointing, I soon understood. I was to lift the tattered carpet on the floor of the cluttered rear compartment. I discovered that's where the extra ammo was stored.

There were four missiles left besides mine, two ready and two with beer, needing attention. I passed everything forward. The Prunedalians had a mission. Who was I to stop a Prunedalian from accomplishing his mission? Though who the enemy was sure beat the hell out of me.

I was rather enjoying my ride to the outer limits. It was all for my benefit. It happened on the fourth shot. The gunner found his target. There was a celebration and another bowl was filled. The Prunedalians slapped hands like football players after a touchdown. We didn't slow down. They both turned and looked at me. I smiled and said, "Yeah."

We soon arrived in Prunedale where they left me off. The pilot said, "We have a good time. Have a good trip."

"Yeah," I said. Once again I was on the freeway at the edge of another planet waiting patiently with my thumb extended, stoned out of my gourd.

I've just now come back from a walk with Tripod down to the muddy road leading from Santa's cabin, where I am, to an asphalt road, where I've been. There's a house near the asphalt road with

an entire forest between me and it. I'm sure someone lives there. The property is well kept. Indeed, I am a lucky man. Why I should feel so fortunate beats the hell out of me. I came here to kill myself. Kicky. About a year and a half ago, I read *Cannery Row* by John Steinbeck. That's when I decided to become a writer of novels. No matter what it takes I will become whoever I am meant to become. Why not?

* * *

Time passed. And as Rupert says, "Time always passes." I'm not really sure how much time passed, standing there on the outskirts of Prunedale, digging on whatever was handy, tugging on the little star that dangled from my left ear. A cowboy stopped and gave me a ride into Salinas on his Pinto pony. He was a country western singer, decked out in his boots and cowboy hat. His guitar was in his back seat. He was on his way to perform in a bar that night, trying to save enough money to cut a demo tape.

"Country music, that's where the money is," he said.

"Yeah," I agreed.

"This here is Steinbeck country," he said.

"Wow, how's he doin'?"

"He's dead, but they made a shrine of his house," he said.

"Yeah?" I said.

"Yup," he said. "If yeh get the time, yeh can swing over to Monterey and down the Coastal Highway. Yeh shouldn't miss Big Sur. Ah heard o' people getting' lost for days and enjoyin' ever' minute of it."

"Why not?" I said.

He dropped me at the edge of Salinas on Route 68, headed for Cannery Row. The air was beginning to chill; I donned my slouch cap once more. An old gray school bus filled with migrant workers towing an outhouse passed while I waited. "What do they do when the bucket is full?" I wondered.

My next ride took me all the way to Carmel, south of Monterey. The vehicle was a Toyota driven by a student of international business. We discussed briefly: multinational corporations, stock fraud, bank investments, the distribution of wealth and the manipulation of the masses.

"What's the problem," I asked. "What's the question," he answered.

Rupert said, "What do they do when the bucket is full?"

DAY 5

I went to sleep last night with the idea of starting a fast today. I also intended to quit smoking tobacco and dope. I haven't much alcohol left; I guess I'll quit drinking in the near future. I haven't had a good bath or shower in a week.

Tripod shot out of here like a bullet this morning. I'm burning candles and incense to ward off evil spirits. It's become a common practice to stick the gun in my mouth at different angles while looking in the mirror. That seems my only regular break from smoking tobacco, smoking gun.

The fog began to roll in as I stood there on the side of the road. There was a traffic signal a city block from where I stood. It was the only traffic signal until San Simeon. The international business major had mentioned Carmel was one of the wealthiest areas per capita in the country.

Tripod has returned for breakfast. She's eating outside in the rain. I read somewhere that lecithin helps a burnt out brain regroup. I've been eating four capsules a day; I don't think it's helping. The air is chilled this morning; Santa's cabin is shrouded in fog.

I'm quite miserable.

* * *

My first month in the Valley was sheer ecstasy and positive movement in my soul; it was the best month in my entire adult life. I didn't think I was God. I felt like an honest and good human being. Everything was simplified. I had nothing to prove, no obligations to fulfill. So what if I slept with my 38 under the pillow. That didn't take away from the simple existence of no pressure. I didn't even feel a great need for sex. I wanted it, but I could do without it.

There's something tremendously exciting about getting to know new people in an unpretentious environment. Nature never pretends. There was no television, only communication and soft warm hugs. It was a time when I even grew to know and love dear Ethel much more than I thought was possible. It was a time and a place where I learned that everything was possible.

Ethel is all the television anyone could ever need. She spent quite a bit of time in the Valley, posing as my lover in case anyone asked what I was doing there. We couldn't very well say I was there to shoot Oscar if he showed up.

Ethel should have been an actress, exploding into tears at the loss of a kitten or describing a past experience or the plight of an acquaintance, putting you right there as a witness. I got no writing done—there was too much excitement—counting the stars and watching spring come into focus like one of Ethel's stories, blossoming with beauty and sometimes tears. And Sweet Ermonie, I never would have believed a woman of 40 could look and act and remain like eternal spring, after suffering so many of life's indelicacies. Such moments we shared, mending fences and shearing sheep. I milked my first cow and mucked out my first stall.

Ethel had her teaching job, so much of my time was spent alone with Ermonie and Jennifer and Star. We went on long walks and picked wild flowers and asparagus. After school when we met Catherine and Heather, the nine- and seven-year-olds, the school bus at the top of the road seemed as though it was from a different era. The elder, Catherine, torn between wanting to kill her father for beating their mom and just wanting her father back, leaned more toward the ball-busting thing. Heather, on the other hand, would have forgiven Attila the Hun. They all actually trusted me. I was there alone on a farm with six females. The cat was the only other distinguishable male in the vicinity besides the roosters. Sex was put out of my mind.

It was the closest I'd ever been, watching a mother and her daughters living the natural bond between them. I slept alone in a side room, never feeling lonely, and was put to sleep by the sound of the river each night though more and more my thoughts were focused on Ermonie and her children. I thought it might have been the newness of the experience that excited me; in my solitude I now understand it was the experience itself, for every day is new. We experienced each other's lives by communicating and sharing many special moments and much laughter, dwelling in the laughter. There was always something to do with no time being lost or wasted, even in an afternoon nap. Of course, I confessed my murder, self defense no less, but still murder in my eyes. I still carried a gun.

* * *

I stood on the outskirts of Carmel, knowing my evening had already been planned. Just like every other evening on my journey to the west. For nearly two hours I waited for the right ride; there was very little traffic from which to choose. At the time, and on my entire journey, it was never my choice to make. I was at the delicate mercy of the intricate mechanism that keeps stars from colliding and, for the time being, the sun from exploding. I needed only to allow things to happen.

I was finally chosen by an old rusted Ford station wagon with three angels in the front seat. I watched as they drove by; one of them yelled something from the window. I waved and smiled and flashed my LA sign. Lalalala lalala! The wagon came to a stop a quarter mile down the road and turned around. Once more they drove past in the opposite direction. Lalalala lalala!

They reached the intersection with the traffic signal and did another loop. Lalalala lalala! They drifted to a stop as they approached me. I am not throwing stones because I am not what you would call clean cut. These dudes looked like vagabonds from a parable. I'm very nearsighted.

Crazy Tom was sitting in the window seat and did the introductory speaking. "We ain't goin' too far; if ya got the price of a bottle of wine, we'll take you a ways and feed ya. We got plenty a food," he said. He had short hair and big ears, with a thin, bony face and ozone eyes.

"Sounds good but my money's kinda tight," I said, forgetting for a moment I was supposed to agree to everything.

"Shit, a bottle a wine don't cost much," he said like he was selling me a used car.

I felt myself being carefully scrutinized; I was doing the same to them. The station wagon had no back seat. Its rear deck was cluttered with an old tire, a pile of what looked like clothes, and a cardboard box decorated with pictures of apples and bananas. The driver was wearing a Hawaiian shirt and a ruddy face in contrast to his deep blue eyes. He looked at me from a distance, but spoke not a word. They called him Woody. Red sat calm and peaceful in the middle, correcting Crazy Tom when he said the wrong thing.

* * *

My time in the Valley prepared me for my godlike status, just as everything is preparation for the next step. Seven years before was also my preparation. How can one experience extreme love without also experiencing extreme hate? God is extreme, and everything in between. How can I continue to speak of love without also speaking of hate and its power? The godlike status I felt, watching a man's eyes as he knew I was his executioner in the split second where his raised knife meant his own death but he kept coming. His own anger consumed his will to survive. My fear became power to act. Bang—bang bang bang. And I was marked for life. He was only dead. If I ever carve a notch in the handle of my gun, it will be for me. There is already a notch in my soul to remind me of the pain God endures; my semi-jacketed hollow point sits on my table and laughs hysterically.

Rupert says, "It's a question of balance and a matter of priorities."

Rupert says,

> It was early Sunday morning--Fast midnight
> In the town in a noisy little tavern where
> The air was smoky brown. There were
> Two crazy people both under the light
> One would die forever--One would die that night
> Listen to my story--It's one that must be told
> The reasons aren't important--For destiny is cold
> I still see a bloody body beneath my feet
> Besides the wall--The missiles cut his mind out.
> The giant had to fall.

Rupert likes to rhyme.

"What do you do when the bucket is full?"

* * *

Oscar never made an appearance the whole time I spent in the Valley. So I never got to shoot him. Besides, Ermonie found my gun while being kind and straightening things for me. She was upset. I sent the gun away. Then, the physical threat of Oscar became irrelevant when he sought help in a program for alcoholics.

That's when the Marine appeared on the scene, when the risk of confrontation was tucked away in a hospital. Andrew and I sat and stared at one another one evening while Ermonie prepared for an evening out. I'm sure part of my sense of loss comes from the fact that he deemed me the babysitter and took me for a fool—and from my misplaced anger.

My purpose had been explained to him; in my eyes, he wasn't fulfilling his purpose, to grow in love with one who loved him. He was seen as a spiritual feather in the wind—searching. I see him, like Oscar, a conscious manipulator of women, gaining control in different ways. My jealousy amuses me. Or perhaps like myself—a piece of me, anyway—thinking about it—fighting it—the game that men and women play.

My presence in the Valley, where I couldn't write, but could linger with a smile, became accepted and my time with Ermonie will always be cherished. After several weeks of getting to know one another, growing closer, close enough to find peace in one another's arms, we became lovers. And we danced together. FUCK.

The Marine was stationed on the west coast by choice, once more proclaiming the great love he expressed for Ermonie, setting the hook, with her believing every word. I found myself in a situation to fulfill the needs of a very sexual woman, having my needs fulfilled in the process. If I could put it in its place: as a connection for the moment, a very pleasant experience and a convenience, there would be no pain. But I fell in love and wanted much more; I cannot put that away.

Ethel and Ermonie and the children had planned their own journey to the west for the summer. I was to remain and take care of the farm and the animals—and write. How perfect it would have been with the music of the river and the Valley and the afterglow of love without all of its distractions.

Quite possibly I could have written a very beautiful, mellow book of poetry. It was my destiny to become God again. God is honest, regardless of the pain that can cause. He has no qualms over a tornado or a volcano. He also gives us spring. Rupert gives us rhymes. Beans give you gas.

* * *

The morning is barely over and already I've broken my fast. It's okay. It's okay. I keep telling myself it's okay. It is okay, isn't it? Say, it's okay. Eureka! I believe I've become a vegetarian. I've cooked too much; perhaps there will be guests for dinner. I'm running low on candles. Is there any truth in advertising? Is this all a prelude to a suicide that will never be? I'm not quite sure of the angle yet. Maybe I should try it in the ear? No, it's more sexual in the mouth; we do live in a world of sex.

It's a shame, sometimes it's so controlling. Now, I have no control. I need a woman, NOW! Not just for sex, but for completion. Woman, you are the river. The river wasn't the same after Ermonie and Ethel and the children left the Valley for Oregon.

If I have no tobacco, I will not smoke. If I have no booze, I will not drink. If I have no dope, I need not be drugged. If I have no food, I'll starve. If I have no hope I need not be. If I have no will power I'll never finish anything—nor start for that matter. If I have no money— I have no money. Oh. Now that's a real problem.

I do have my gun. This is the story of my journey to the west. My newly adopted family were on their way to a summer camp for children with speech defects. None of Ermonie's children had speech problems. She was going to run the art program.

Ethel, of course, sought the environment, so different from the constriction of public school. Frustration breeds contempt. Public schools are so sexual. I went to a Catholic school; they sweep sex under the rug and behind the altar and into the confessional where the priests can get their cookies off.

Rupert says, "Sometimes, the beat is more important than the rhythm."

Rupert also says,
She told me that she loved me in the morning
So I raised my head from down between her legs
I smiled at her and said, you are delicious
Today I think I'm going to skip my eggs.

Chorus:
'Cause love is wonderful for breakfast
It's the best way that I know to start the day
Yes, love is wonderful for breakfast
Burn the toast and substitute foreplay.
I used to wake up early and have waffles
Two, three cups of coffee with a smoke
I'd scratch myself and read the morning paper
I celebrate the day my toaster broke.

Chorus:
'Cause love is wonderful for breakfast
It's the best way that I know to start the day
Yes, love is wonderful for breakfast
Burn the toast and substitute foreplay.
A morning shower's always done me justice
It's always helped to raise me from the dead
I take more time and I get clean and squeaky
When I've got someone giving me some head.
All together now:
Yes, love is wonderful for breakfast
It's the best way that I know to start the day
Yes, love is wonderful for breakfast
Burn the toast and substitute foreplay

Rupert likes to rhyme.

Sweet Ermonie, I've seen you once too often in the morning to let you go without a song. Rupert says, "Attitude is a very important part of the ACT."

* * *

The past few days it's been too wet to walk through the woods. My pacing has been wearing ruts in the ground and floor. The muddy road from Santa's cabin has become my obvious outlet. I've ventured up the asphalt road to the top of the hill where I can see for miles.

It's all rather strange to me because I'm so nearsighted. On each walk two or three cars have driven past. I always wave and smile; there is no return, not even a stare. I'm fit to be stared at with the country garb I'm costumed in. My beard and hair have grown wild and free. My white painters pants are baggy and soiled and my torn straw hat keeps blowing from my head. I have been carrying a hand-carved ebony walking stick to keep the pace.

Tripod always tags along, carrying a small plastic baseball bat in her mouth. The walking stick is rather interesting. It once belonged to a friend who committed suicide. A black serpent with ivory eyes is wrapped around the stick, paying homage to a very contented-looking big-lipped African native with etchings on his face. He looks very high and happy. He must not be from South Africa. I've also been wearing a prison-issue, badly torn and worn Levi jacket. I'd think someone would at least call the authorities. I look like I've escaped from an institution. I don't know why I think anyone should care.

Myron said, "Nobody gives a shit." Myron was right.

I hadn't seen Myron in two years. I saw him on my journey. It was Wednesday, the day before I became God. I was in San Francisco in the company of Ramona Pearl. She and I had previously enjoyed the pleasure of one another's company for a little over a 24-hour period, a connection of and for the road. We spoke by phone the night before; she agreed to meet me at the ferry on Wednesday morning. I had spent the previous night in Mill Valley and hopped the 7:30 ferry from Marin Peninsula across the bay to San Francisco.

I arrived at the dock a half hour early and was lucky enough to get a window seat; it was much too foggy to see anything besides the courageous man who stood on deck and braved the morning chill and dampness. He stood with his chin to the wind, looking like Spencer Tracy watching for whales.

It was a relaxing ride. I sat with my duffel bag squeezed between my legs and my feet on top of my typewriter. I didn't wish to take up more room than my ticket allowed. All of the seats were taken, except the one next to me. I was certainly the only tourist. Everyone else looked as though they had a purpose.

No one spoke. They all looked straight ahead, either reading the morning paper or examining the scalp in front for bugs. What ever happened to, "If you're going to San Francisco, be sure to wear some flowers in your hair." I wasn't wearing a suit. My clothes were clean, honest, and I had bathed the night before.

Sometimes I forget, someone has to speak first; if you wave and smile enough and speak first enough, someone will eventually wave or smile or even speak back, or shoot back. Fuck this shit. What the hell am I doing here in the middle of nowhere, freezing my ass off, almost out of candles and booze with only a three-legged dog to talk to. Shitting in a bucket on top of it all.

I still don't know what to do with the bucket when it's full. I've been here for nearly five full days without accomplishing anything. I still have a limited vocabulary and nothing makes sense. Where's Rupert? Where's Damien? "Rumsford has a better idea." Sweet Ermonie will never speak to me again. The sleazy marine was drummed out of the service on a mental discharge—mental my ass—he set it up; he knows what he's doing. And it ain't no doubt in my mind where he's headed with Oscar dead. Andrew LaVay is no dummy. He's on his way to play in Ermonie's Valley for a while. And why shouldn't he—she loves him; he says he loves her. They'll be happy together. Isn't that the way it should be? I was the bodyguard and they'll never find the body. Shouldn't I be happy for them, isn't that what true love is? Wanting the person you love to be happy regardless of self? Bullshit, it comes from the eye.

Rupert says, "Who are you?" I don't fucking know. Who gives a damn? "Easy now."

"Sometimes the lights all shinin' on me. Other times I can barely see. Lately it occurs to me, what a long strange trip it's been,"

Ramona sang as we walked through the streets of San Francisco and then took the Muni to the mission or thereabouts.

I'm afraid I've achieved some sort of tunnel vision—to think I've been God twice. Could it be that my head is so far up my own ass my own shit has become comfortable to me? It's not a matter of the gun anymore. I believe I'll hang myself. I haven't enough drugs for an overdose. I'd slash my wrist, my friend Paul did that. I have his walking stick. They found it before he died and took him to the hospital. Johns Hopkins released him after treatment, a few stitches. The next morning he was found with a knife sticking out of his chest. He never seemed that determined to me.

I'll never forget the look of terror in Paul's eyes and face when I identified the body. It must have taken a lot of effort and conviction to pull the knife in. I won't do that—I didn't like the look on his face. It didn't seem to be his solution—too much work. My gun has a hair trigger once it's cocked. It's easy. Maybe I'll shoot the Marine. That won't accomplish anything; Ermonie would really be pissed.

* * *

Rupert says,
I love the way they gossip--I love the way they lie
If you want something pleasant said
You only have to die.
You gotta watch your P's and Q's and R's
Along the way--But then it doesn't matter
Cause they'll make up things to say.
Expose yourself for all the world to see;
If you've got the nerve and if you think you're free.
They'll preach at you from pulpits
They'll get down on your case
Just look and smile back pleasantly
And say, this is my space. The next thing
That they'll do to you is probably crucify,
So spread your arms out royally--They'll love
To watch you die. You stand up for your rights
You throw back all their words

But all the pain that you go through Is really
For the birds. Somewhere in this story
There's a message to be read.
You better watch your P's and Q's
Cause Jesus Christ was murdered.

Rupert says, "I am only a player in the band but please allow me my solos." Rupert likes to rhyme.

* * *

My night on Monastery Beach the Indian spoke of Richard Brautigan. There's one of Brautigan's lines I'll never forget though I'm probably misquoting it. It was in a book called Sombrero Fallout. It goes something like, "A lightning bolt of despair suddenly fried his brain into a thousand pieces of dancing bacon." I love that line. That line describes my friend Paul's face on the mortician's table. Perhaps tomorrow, I'll begin my fast. If I'm going to kill myself, I may as well save the food I have for someone else.

* * *

Such a glorious and exhilarating day it was in San Francisco. Ramona took me to the apartment of her friend. I had a Hefty trashcan liner full of fishy clothes stashed in my duffel bag—I didn't smell anything—and was given access to a washing machine and plenty of detergent and fabric softener. I had spent the week on board a funky old scow, fishing for salmon; my fish clothes had been sealed tightly in plastic for four days. They had to be washed twice.

Ramona and I had freshly ground coffee and homemade bread with apple butter and havarti cheese while the washing machine nearly died from exhaustion. I reached my friend Myron by phone and arranged a meeting for later in the day. There was no dryer; Ramona and I split a hit of blotter acid and trekked off to the Laundromat to use the tumble dryer.

* * *

It's time to call it a night. I was having such a good time in the depths of despair when Tripod began barking. Tripod very seldom barks; she went wild. I was visited by a neighbor. It was the man who lives in the house at the top of the muddy road. He keeps his property well. His name is Clyde. His curiosity must have been aroused by my walks. We sat and talked for a while. He is retired and cuts firewood for extra money. His wife is a seamstress.

I tried to explain that my gun is sitting on the table fully loaded because I'm writing a story on handgun control. He mentioned he had noticed it, but figured it was for shooting game. I assured him I don't believe in shooting defenseless animals. I wasn't about to tell him I meant to shoot myself; he'd think I was crazy. He sure is a nice man. He invited me to Easter dinner. I asked if I could use his bathtub and gave him a jar of mayonnaise and a five pound bag of Domino sugar. Tomorrow is another day.

DAY 6

Tomorrow never comes and today is here again. I've just copped a hell of a buzz from the type cleaner fluid. I am beginning to realize I have much more will and determination than ability.

"How do you get to Carnegie Hall?"

"Practice, my boy, practice."

And so,

ON. . .

"Hey, mate, what would you care for today?" Ramona asked as the LSD began to take effect in the Laundromat. She had a wonderful Australian accent and a faint blonde mustache of which she was very proud. It gave her character. She was also proud of her sideburns which ran to the tips of her cute little earlobes. She wore no earrings; I had two in my left ear, so we were amply decorative.

Ramona was a very pretty lady with a touch of the bizarre. She always carried her ukulele, either strumming it for effect to a song or a walk or over either shoulder. It seemed to be very much a part of her body, like an arm or a leg or her mustache.

Ramona was my hostess. The acid was my eyes. We had learned enough of one another's lives while thumbing and bathing together two days previously; there was total comfort in our mutual company without expectation. The acid we shared drew us tighter together into the same wavelength we were already sharing, but on another plane, soaring. Ramona had lived in San Francisco for a while and knew her way around quite well. She continued.

I was there enjoying the freedom of being, knowing that nothing else mattered. The laundry dried and Ramona taught me a new way to fold jeans by buttoning and zipping them first and pulling the crotch forward and the outer belt loops back and then rolling them up for travel. We eavesdropped on a man who was searching for a runaway girl and had lost his wallet and money and credit cards. He bitched at the bank over the pay phone in the laundry about all he had been through.

Ramona and I giggled to ourselves, thinking the hunt was now equal. We returned to the apartment in the Mission; it was a second-floor walkup, large and spacious and clean. We dressed for the day. It was all there in milliseconds, though time was standing still.

"Oh dear, oh dear, what should we wear?"

"A dress, oh a dress, yes, by all means, wear a dress. Our caps, we must wear our caps."

"I like your blue shirt with the four pockets. May I iron it?"

"Please, please iron my shirt. We must look fit for the public eye. Ten cent tours for only a dime."

"Will you wear your Nikes or your thongs?"

"I believe my thongs. I simply adore the noise they make, flip-flop, flip-flop."

"A red bandana, dearie, you must wear a red bandana about your neck."

"Yes, yes, I must wear a red bandana about my neck. Your uke, you will take your uke, won't you?"

"By all means, mate, I must have my uke. Go for it."

"Go for it? It's on your shoulder."

"No, no, go for it."

"Go for what?"

"Go for it all, mate, go for it all. Sometimes your cards ain't worth a dime if you don't lay 'em down."

We walked and counted the church steeples to Market Street from the Mission. We continued on down Market to Castro and watched the fags holding hands, but not before stopping in a store loaded with cacti and sand on the floor. Ramona sang to me and we danced.

We stopped in a store on Castro Street where I picked out a three-dimensional picture postcard to send to the twins for their birthday and we played in the underground train station. I bought a Snoopy notepad to take notes, but was too stoned to write much more than an occasional "YEAHHH!"

The entire universe was laid out plain and simple and all the problems of the world were solved, but I couldn't take notes. We stood on top of a hill and watched the clouds roll by. I confessed my murder and Ramona confessed the murders of an aunt who had performed mercy killings in the '20s. We agreed how necessary it all was to confront the negative and accentuate the positive.

Ramona led me to the Haight, where we found Myron's address and were welcomed to the kitchen table. I wasn't able to do much more than nod and say, "I'm tripping."

Myron sent out for a six-pack of Schlitz and a pint of Southern Comfort. Ramona strummed on her ukulele and we sat in a circle with two other fags besides Myron and a blonde bisexual female mud wrestler. Damien would have hired her, she was beautiful.

We had been sitting there for three and a half years when a young freckle-faced red-headed boy with a runny nose stuck his head in the kitchen and the room grew silent. He disappeared and we were told the story of how he appeared the night before looking for a place to crash. They let him in. In the middle of the night he stood up from a dead sleep and pissed on their living room floor. He was still there. I didn't understand any of it. I still don't.

The party grew tired and I still had to mail the birthday card to Star. Myron was very drunk; he joined us anyway. We walked to the Post Office along the crowded afternoon street and accomplished my mission and then to the Question Mark Bar. Ramona watched a dark-skinned hussy in black leather pants shooting pool, while Myron and I stood at the bar drinking Pabst Blue Ribbon and shots of Jack Daniels, speaking of old times.

"Sullivan, how have you been?" he asked, slurring his words.

"I've been writing a book and realizing my guilt," I said in my enlightened state.

"Nobody gives a shit," he said.

We were sitting next to a woman who was trying to look like a man. She was selling Thai Sticks for five dollars. "Nobody gives a shit," she said.

I was so high from the acid I felt the booze leveled me off, but Myron tried to sit on a barstool and fell to the floor. Ramona and I looked at each other and decided it was time to go. We carried Myron back to the entrance of his apartment where he kissed me on the mouth and Ramona cheered at the sight. I think she was rather kinky.

"I'm try-sexual," she claimed. "I'll try anything."

We left the Haight and found ourselves at Zimms, where I had coffee and Ramona had tea and we shared a plate of french fries. We left Zimms and turned a corner where flags appeared before us, echoing in red with gold lettering across our path. "PICASSO, PICASSO, PICASSO, PICASSO, PICASSO," they whispered.

Ramona answered, "Go for it." We entered the Volpar Gallery and were greeted with a smile as we strolled by the receptionist and into the realm of history. We lingered for years, not understanding but witnessing and experiencing all that was offered. The works of several other artists were present. I can only remember one by M.C. Escher. I became totally involved in "DEVELOPMENT" and all that remains to be seen, quite pleased with my present. We lingered until it was obvious the gallery was closed; no one asked us to leave.

We left on our own because it was time. We ventured to the Greyhound bus station where Ramona was to pick up a backpack that she had sent ahead from Seattle. I ventured to the men's room.

I was approached by a man who had been beaten badly and was bleeding from the nose and over his left eye. He had been approaching everyone, asking for a cigarette. He drew stares but no cigarette. I gave him a cigarette. I noticed his mouth was also battered and his lip split. He couldn't hold the cigarette I gave him in his mouth. He only wanted a cigarette.

"You better find a cop," someone said.

"Cig'rette," he slurred and he had one in his hand.

I met Ramona outside of the men's room and we retrieved her backpack. We left the station to find a man lying on the sidewalk in front of the door with a knife sticking out of his side. A policeman ran by blowing his whistle and a crowd gathered to watch the man bleed. I understand Picasso with no need to explain. I still don't know what's real. We walked and there were only shadows in ethnic neighborhoods where here now is all that mattered because nobody else gave a shit.

We stopped in a Spanish produce market; Ramona gathered our dinner and paid. I expressed a wish to see the Golden Gate bridge at night. After a dinner of broccoli and mushrooms and homemade bread and white wine, there was only a hot bath and music and sleep. The bridge became only a distant representation between worlds I had seen in pictures. I presented Ramona with a rhyme and she presented me with a button with the picture of the devil saying, "Trust me."

> Rupert says,
> Death came to me in a dream
> I was floating in the cosmos--At One
> With the Universe. I was very mellow.
> My appearance was everything
> Which had appealed to me through my material
> Eyes. I understood everything that had confused
> Me in my limited mind.I was alone but not lonely
> For others had passed before me. We were all
> One with the Universe.

Rupert likes to rhyme.

* * *

Ermonie, Ethel, Jennifer and Star and Catherine and Heather began their cross-country journey on a Sunday morning. Damien Rumsford had come to the Valley to help me ease into the isolation of the summer. I was afraid of being alone in the Valley with a river and trees and chickens and cows and dogs and sheep and a goat and a cat and me.

There's a warm breeze today, singing and slowly dancing with the clouds. Tripod lies in the wet grass, entertaining the fleas.

* * *

Ermonie was still in the hospital when I arrived in Vernal, Utah by Greyhound. Once more I had a purpose. Once more my chance to play the role of hero galloping across the plains on my white horse with its harness decorated with birds and butterflies.

I had arrived in Salt Lake by plane and then taxi at two o'clock that morning. After purchasing my ticket for the 7:30 bus and stashing my gear in a locker, I treated myself to a Spanish omelet with cinnamon toast and sausage and coffee at Howard Johnson's. Finishing breakfast, I returned to the bus station to wait, finding its doors were locked until 5:30.

I walked around Temple Square, impressed by the well-lit, golden, Disney-like structure proclaiming the glory of whatever it is Mormons believe in besides having a bunch of wives. I was confused by the towering wall and the locked iron gate with a sign proclaiming KEEP OUT. I continued walking down the clean deserted streets. I began to wonder what I would do for the next four and a half hours; I was very tired.

I picked up a Wall Street Journal from a coin-operated machine to check on the daily stock quotations. I needed something at least a little familiar to hold onto. I chose a bench across from the bus station and Temple Square, where I relaxed and merely turned the pages of the Wall Street Journal; my thoughts were elsewhere.

Thoughts of Ermonie and what lay ahead bombarded my brain as well as the pleasant memories of my flight out. I was uncomfortable where I was. It was all so unfamiliar. I was alone. A few hours earlier on the first leg of my flight, which took me from

Baltimore to Atlanta, I had been in the company of Elizabeth.

She was wearing an Oriole baseball cap and shared her seat with a tennis racket and fishing rod. Elizabeth was 13 and her dream was to become a famous tennis player at Wimbledon. She had been visiting with one of her five sets of grandparents in Baltimore and was returning to her home near Disney World. We shared private thoughts and played Connect-the-Dots on a scrap of paper that she autographed and gave to me. I won by one point.

I switched planes in Atlanta and found myself sitting next to Kathy, who aroused my sexual curiosity to the point of motivated fantasy. She was 16 and played the tuba in her high school band. I pictured her lips around my penis at 30,000 feet. I attempted to be very casual as I broke the ice before the plane got off the ground. I offered her a tangerine Lifesaver. Her honey-blonde hair and plump Liv Ullman lips turned me on all the more when she said, "No, thank you," with a Southern accent.

I asked her if she wanted to play Connect-the-Dots and showed her the scrap of paper Elizabeth had signed for me. She pulled a portable cassette tape player from her satchel; I was soon being entertained by a recording of her singing gospel music in her church choir. Kathy was on her way to Denver to visit with friends. When we landed she gave me a cherry Lifesaver.

From Denver to Salt Lake I sat alone and thought only of Ermonie. Now I was sitting on a bench across from Temple Square, playing with a Wall Street Journal a familiar brand. Now is what I couldn't handle. Now I was lost in dreams and illusions which seemed real in their time, overlooking the Journal and the peace which surrounded me because I wasn't being entertained. An angel recognized my plight; she finished her business and came to me.

I'm very nearsighted and sensed death as the cloaked figure appeared and seemed out of place a block away on the lifeless streets. I turned pages in the paper and watched the figure from the corner of my right eye. Long, flowing red hair came into focus.

"It's a woman," I thought. It seemed rather odd. I hadn't seen another person since I left Howard Johnson's. When she drew near enough, I turned my head and looked and smiled. She smiled back.

"Hi there," I said. "I'm Sullivan Duda from Baltimore. I'm waiting for a bus. Where is everyone? I thought you were a cop. Are you?"

"No," she said softly, "Have you seen any?"

"I ain't seen a soul, babe. What it is."

"I don't know. I'm on my way for a cup of coffee."

"My bus doesn't leave until 7:30. Would you mind if I joined you?"

"You have a long wait. Why not?"

I was very impressed with this fast-talking fast-walking beauty. It didn't matter who she was, what mattered is, she was there. I folded the paper under my arm and followed briefly to see how her jeans fit. She was wearing sandals. With the pace she kept, my flip-flops flip-flopped loudly and sounded like a snare drum in a marching band. I believe she was on amphetamines. She spoke sounding like an electric mixer working a thick batter; she ran down our choices of where to have coffee. We were the only sound; she did all the talking. We walked a city block when I was overcome by a tremendous need to speak. "Are you a working girl?" I managed to squeeze in.

"Yes," she answered.

"Are you working now?" I asked.

"Yes," she said, and then continued rambling on about where we should have coffee.

"How much?" I interrupted.

"BJ twenty, straight missionary forty, back door fifty and seventy-five for a double cum," she said, then immediately kept speaking of coffee as we turned a corner and kept on trucking. I thought for a moment about the way things were. I thought about Ermonie in the hospital and how horny I was. I thought about the 16 year old gospel singer who had aroused my carnal desires for the evening, but I listened to her sing instead.

I looked once more at the woman I was walking with and her long red hair and tight-fitting jeans and then I attempted to fondle the Wall Street Journal.

* * *

It's raining again. There's also thunder and lightning. It began raining so hard I had to shut the door, the floor was being washed clean. This isn't the time for cleaning floors. It's only two in the afternoon and already I've broken my fast with sardines in mustard sauce and whole wheat pita bread washed down with Thunderchicken. The rain has eased and the door is open. The air smells fresh and sweet. Mustard sauce is fouling my keys. The sardines were delicious. Tripod rests at my feet and my t keeps sticking. The wind is causing the trees to sway and the air is becoming chilled.

This is tobe a graphic suicide. Ermonie will be screwing the Marine tonight. Why did Oscar have to die in that plane crash? He would have killed Andrew. Now I'll be sleeping with the dog. It's so bright in here. Maybe I should turn out one of the lights? But I like sex with the lights on.

Rupert says,
There are times when I'm sad and I'm lonely
There are times that are hazy and blue
But the times when I'm with you only
Are the times when I'm thinking of you.
Things that I do make me crazy
Things that I don't, make me mad
My vision's so fogged and I'm lazy
My time is so short and I'm sad.
So come sit here right down beside me
And rest your sweet butt in a chair
I'll need all your body to hide me
I'll need all your lovin' to care.

Rupert likes to rhyme.

* * *

"I'm on a limited budget but I think I can afford twenty bucks," I said.

She didn't answer directly but said, "Sambo's is open. Let's have coffee."

I really wanted a blow job, it didn't matter where. The pressures of being a hero are overwhelming. We continued towards Sambo's and as we crossed the street a drunken spaced-out Indian was crossing the same street towards us. He was red and round and greasy; he ambled like an undercooked-overfilled jelly donut.

"Hey, time," he slurred. I wasn't wearing a watch; my companion was.

"Yeah, three-forty-five," she spit out like she was dislodging phlegm. "That's the biggest problem here," she commented. "They leave the reservation and come to the city; they can't find work and become a nuisance."

"Maybe they should become Mormons," I said.

We entered Sambo's and sat in a booth. Soon we were approached by the most beautiful girl in the world. She was an Indian. She asked for our order. I ordered coffee and my companion ordered a half-glass of milk. A tremendous urge swelled in my pants as I watched the waitress walk away; I looked at my companion.

"What about the blow job?" I asked.

"The cops in this town are heavy on drugs and Indians and vagrants. Most of the vagrants are Indians. I had a good night tonight; I really don't want to go home to my parent's house. Suppose we split the cost of a room," she said.

The waitress returned with my coffee and my companion's half-filled glass of milk.

"I'm waiting for a bus," I said. She reached in her satchel and produced a half-pint of cream and a short bottle of Kahlua. She meticulously mixed some of each with her milk.

"Would you care for some?" she asked, holding up the bottle of Kahlua. "Don't worry about the cops. Like I said, they're more worried about drugs and Indians," she added.

I began counting the freckles on her face and was drawn to her eyes. Her reality caused me to ignore the waitress. "Are you good?" I asked.

"Look, honey, I give the best head in Salt Lake," she said.

It's important to me that a person believe in what they're doing. I emptied a packet of sugar and two little containers of half and half into my coffee, passing on the Kahlua for fear it was a set-up. "The room sounds good," I said.

"I have a little reefer; we can cop a buzz in the room, too," she said. She left her bottle of Kahlua on the table. Though there were only a few other people in the restaurant besides us, I felt everyone was watching us. She took a long gulp from her glass and added more Kahlua and cream. She ran her mouth constantly with the exception of when she was drinking. Whenever I wished to speak, I had to interrupt or wait until she was drinking. She had strong jaws and good teeth. I inspected the merchandise without becoming obvious.

"Hey, honey, you're kinda cute," she said.

"Thanks, you're beautiful. What about the room?"

* * *

I need a maid and a sweater; it's getting cold. I'm so confused. I'm down to my last cup of wine.

* * *

"Honey, you don't mind if I call you honey, do ya?" she asked.

"Not at all, sweetheart," I said.

"Honey, suppose you give me money for your half of the room and I'll check in as a single. You can hide in the bushes or around the corner or something; after I get the key, I'll come and get you."

"Sweetheart," I said, "Come on now. An apple this big," I said, holding my arms outstretched and hands up in the air.

"But it would be cheaper."

"If you wanta call it off, makes no mind to me," I said, lying through my teeth, because I sensed a game in the making, like I'd be in the bushes forever or something with her taking off with the cash. I would've done anything for a blowjob.

She gulped down what was left of her drink and returned the bottle to her satchel. She stood up and said, "Let's go."

I flagged down our beautiful waitress and grabbed the check. She touched my hand by accident and I didn't want to leave. My blowjob was already walking out the door; I left twice the amount of the check and followed. We walked a block up and two blocks over holding hands. We came to the Travelodge.

My companion rang the night bell one time; within seconds, a gray-robed, gray-haired man opened and dragged himself through a side door into the office. He walked around the desk and unlocked the glass door without looking. He returned to behind the desk and switched on a light and pushed a stack of registration slips to the front of the desk in one feeble motion. I allowed the lady to enter first. Before I was in the room I heard, "I have one double room left for thirty-two dollars plus tax." I believe it was a recording. I didn't see his lips move; his eyes were closed.

"Thirty-two dollars!" my companion screamed.

His eyes exploded open as if he heard the word "FIRE" while standing in front of a firing squad. His eyes were gray. He gained his composure and once more shut his eyes.

"I'm sorry, I don't think you'll find anything else this time of night," he grumped.

"Sir," I said, "I'm Sullivan Duda from Baltimore. I've been on a plane most of the night; it's after four, and I'm leaving on a bus at seven-thirty. Hey, man, can't you cut us some slack?"

Once more he opened his eyes. "I'm not supposed to," he said. "Since you're only staying for a few hours, the best I can do is twenty-five." He didn't wish to be disturbed without collecting some money.

We agreed to the price. After tax and a deposit for the key, it still came to over thirty-two dollars. I nonetheless felt victorious. My companion forked over the full amount and signed in as Jane Fonda. It didn't matter, the man didn't look.

I've always wanted to fuck Jane Fonda. My companion did bear a strong resemblance to Jane Fonda. She gathered in the key the way one would pick a petunia, and we both snubbed our noses and turned to each other with my companion taking my arm. I once more allowed her to pass through the door before me, holding it as we took our leave. The gray-robed, gray-haired, closed-eyed man shuffled behind and locked the door.

* * *

I've just been on the most exhilarating walk since I've been in Santa's cabin. I was cooking some rice with pineapple and peanuts and evaporated milk when the rain suddenly stopped; the sun broke through the clouds and the wind disappeared. Large thunderclouds began dispersing in all directions. Tripod, her bat, my stick and I walked quickly up the muddy road to the asphalt and then to the top of the hill overlooking the kingdom. I was looking for a rainbow. I didn't see any. I wasn't disappointed; the clouds provided ample entertainment. They depicted the charge of the light brigade in 16-millimeter black and white.

I took in as much as I needed and began walking back with my stick under my arm instead of maintaining its beat. Two cars passed and the occupants smiled and waved back. One person sort of guffawed; they were alive. My neighbor, Clyde, called out and invited me to use his bathtub this evening. I told him I was out searching for a rainbow. He said, "You don't have to search for rainbows. They happen wherever you're at. Open your eyes."

"Down there in the trees?" I questioned.

"It don't matter," he said, "wherever."

You know something, he's absolutely right. Sometimes I forget.

* * *

My companion became very quiet after I asserted myself in the office. I don't wish to analyze everything, but looking back, I believe my assertion was very necessary to bring her to the point where she could suck my dick with respect. Who wants to blow a wimp besides another wimp? We walked past a row of numbered doors and the motel ice machine until we came to room 28. I took the key from her hand and unlocked the door, once more allowing her passage first.

She switched on the lights; I closed the vinyl drapes while she found music on the TV. I returned to the ice machine with the ice bucket, the ice was free. Ice water in the night pleases me. I was still unsure of how the ritual was to progress.

There was only one double bed in the room so half of my problem was solved. On my return with the ice, my companion helped herself, mixing a drink in one of the plastic cups provided. I had ice water. Music from Zorba the Greek filled the room; I slipped a twenty from my pocket and left it on the vanity.

"I must shower," I said. I felt I was in a John Waters movie but had to shower anyway. I washed my private parts extra special because I didn't want to leave the girl with a bad taste in her mouth. I kept my belongings with me because I didn't want to be ripped off. I also locked the bathroom door.

Rupert says, "Nothing makes sense but there's a reason for everything; it's a matter of perspective." I didn't bother to put my clothes back on after my shower. I had half a hard on and felt very sure of myself as I carried my belongings to the dresser nearest the door. My companion had chosen the dresser with the vanity to stash her satchel. She had more money than I and was also wary of my intent. We were still strangers.

My script told me to lie down in bed. Without a word, I did. My penis had a mind of its own and called out to my companion who began to remove her clothes. I looked at her seductively, watching her perform, noticing freckles. She looked like the end of a very complete sentence, many sentences. . .Ahhh. . .

She didn't end, but began as she approached me in the bed with her long red hair caressing my thighs in a ritual snake dance. My cock snapped at her earlobes. This is so obscene. "Your dick is beautiful," she said, contemplating it. And then she took me in her mouth.

"Before you go any further, there's something I got to tell you," I said. I don't know why, but that's what I said.

"Don't tell me you got the clap?" she said, looking up with her concentration snapped like Social Security sooner or later.

"Hey, babe, hold on, I'm clean," I said. "It's just that there's nothing I enjoy more than watching a beautiful woman suck me off."

"I don't mind," she interrupted.

"I know, I know," I said. "The thing is, I don't think I'll be able to cum and I like to cum. Nothin' against you. I got this thing, you know."

"You queer?" she asked.

"Naw, babe," I thought I was relating. "It takes a lot."

"What's the problem?" she asked, still stroking my penis with her hand checking for textures.

"I don't know. It's just—it's just that I've only been able to get off by straight mouth one other time in my life. The only other time I've been with a hooker. But she was black and she stuck her finger up my ass," I said. This is embarrassing—not really.

"Relax, honey," she said with a smile of extreme self-assurance, "I'm a Professional."

I presented her with a challenge. She confidently emerged into character. I tried to relax; with Zorba it was hard. She licked my thighs as her hand left my penis and stroked my balls as if they were crystal and she was a gypsy manipulating the future. She pulled her hair back with her left hand and homed in on my dodging dancing penis with her mouth. I do wish there were some way to avoid this pornography. No I don't, it's too much fun. She ohmed. She sucked up and ohmed down.

At first, I stifled a laugh. There is extreme pleasure in laughing. But this pleasure was different. She got down. She reminded me of a trombone player with the noise et al. It was nice.

"Ohmssshhohmsshohmssshohmsshohmssshohmssshohmss," she said. I watched her for as long as I could. This beautiful woman was making love to my dick and enjoying it. I felt like a soufflé in the hands of a master chef, and then Kathy's tuba. My head was thrown back into my pillow.

"Ohm, OHMOHMOHMOHMOHMOHOMOMOMOMOMOM OMOMOMOMOMOMOMOM," I heard. My mind and my body experienced nothing but extreme pleasure. I was being sucked by Ermonie and Ethel and Elizabeth the thirteen year old tennis player. My dick was in the mouth of Rhoda and Cleopatra and Helen of

Troy and Jane Fonda and the Dallas Cowboy cheerleaders and the waitress at Sambo's and every man and woman I have ever known or desired. She was the entire perfection of everything.

"OMOMOMOMOMOMOMOMOMOMOMOMOMOMOMOMOM OMOMOMOMOMOMOMOMOMOMOMOMOMOMOMMMM."

I screamed with ecstasy, passion and pain so the whole world could hear when I came.

She sucked from me my frustration and my strength and my paranoia and my sperm and my hate and all my love. She took it upon herself and swallowed me whole. She ate me alive, all for twenty bucks. Actually it was purely physical.

* * *

I've just now come back from having my first bath in a week. I've been conditioned to shower every day, using lots of camouflage to hide my natural body odor. I've never enjoyed soaking in a tub more. Clyde and Betty Beggs sure are nice folks. After my bath we sat around and looked at photographs of the family; Clyde showed me some old furniture he refinished.

I drank a cup of tea with lemon and honey, and they threw Tripod an old bone to gnaw on. I thought about confessing my murder to them, since they're the only humans I've spoken to in a while; they didn't give me a chance to say much. They seem quite happy in their environment, having accomplished most of the goals they set for themselves. Their children are all grown and married. They feel successful. I think I'm the first renegade they ever met.

Today I stood on the hill and saw for miles; tonight, walking back to the cabin I looked up and saw forever. I feel clean. Clyde and Betty Beggs sure are nice people.

Rupert says, "Life is many steps. Climb your ladder and look around; there's always a little bit farther to go."

* * *

The nice thing about Jane Fonda was after she sucked me off, she didn't gargle. The black hooker ran into the bathroom, brushed her teeth and gargled twice. What a bummer. Intimates don't gargle.

The best blow job in Salt Lake smiled and licked her chops and crawled into the bed beside me. I tasted myself when we kissed for the first time.

"Do you like to cuddle?" she asked.

The business over, a bond was formed between two people for a moment. "There's No Business Like Show Business" played over the television and we held each other close.

"How did you become a hooker?" I asked.

"I used to be a private secretary. My boss said put out or get fired. I did. I charged him and I quit. Been doin' it ever since."

"Wow."

"The money's better and I pick my customers."

"You do good work."

Rupert says, "Stroking is a very important part of life."

DAY 7

I didn't intend to say anything, but I'm fed up. It's not so bad that my t keeps sticking, or that Tripod keeps hogging the heater. It isn't earth-shattering that I'm out of wine and down to my last three ounces of brandy. Hemorrhoids, now I've got to deal with fucking hemorrhoids.

This is my seventh day in the woods, and my vocabulary certainly isn't improving. I have discovered thirteen different uses for the word fuck. I still haven't shot myself yet. I'm going to shoot the fucking t on this typewriter in a moment.

* * *

Our cuddle became a shackled embrace as we drifted off to sleep. Neither of us wanted to lose our possessions; we were entwined like a hunk of string cheese, rest assured, exhausted after the banquet. It seemed logical to fornicate, but herpes is always a threat. I had learned from Rhoda Apple, the anarchist who works for the CIA, that there is a cure, but it's being withheld to reverse the sexual promiscuity of the seventies and to strengthen the family unit. As if that's the real problem.

I thought of throwing caution to the wind, thinking that the cure could only be suppressed for so long. I really wanted to indulge in Jane Fonda. And then there was the strong possibility that she was herpless or at least in remission. Maybe not. The power of inflicted fear is immeasurable and the manipulation continues. I reasoned my way out of it by conveniently remembering I couldn't afford another forty dollars for my pleasure. Ermonie needed me.

* * *

There was no moon, the evening of the afternoon we arrived in Cherry Grove, Oregon. Camp had already started and the women were anxious to plunge right in. Ermonie had undergone abdominal surgery only ten days before, so understandably her duties in the art program remained light. She was in charge and the staff of young, bright-eyed, perky-eared counselors was eager to fulfill her needs— for arts and crafts.

Ethel was in her glory. At last she was in an environment of freedom to work with children who wanted and needed help. It was also a great experience and adventure for Jennifer and Star and Heather and Catherine to be exposed to children who were different, not in mental capacities, but simple speech.

The raffish Duda not only became a dangling conversation, he was greatly intimidated. I once had the role of Billy Bigelow in a CYO production of Carousel—no big deal. I sang "If I Loved You" and "My Boy Bill" and "When You Walk Through A Storm;" I couldn't say my lines without stuttering. I was dropped from the role. I should have understood the plight of children after all the years of being frustrated, trying to get any message across verbally, being mocked by some, laughed at by others, and pitied for the most part as I stood, knowing what I wanted to say, but jumping and spitting and belching out half-syllables and burp-gun consonants.

These inexorable stutterers and frenetic stammering children needed understanding above all else. Understanding and environment they were getting from the counselors and the camp. I was intimidated by mere children who were going through what I had already gone through. It was camp, not the every day drudgery of education and socialization. I had no role.

* * *

My eyes popped open; I was still wrapped up with Jane Fonda. I felt secure that my possessions were still intact. Hers popped open a second later. She must have had radar; I hadn't moved a muscle.

"Sweetheart," I said, "I gots to go."

She looked at her watch and tightened her hold around my leg. "Honey, it's only six," she said.

Thoughts of her wanting to pry another 40 bucks from me attacked my venal mind. I couldn't afford it. As much as I've always had some need to eventually copulate with Bree Daniel the morning light reminded me of my purpose. Ermonie and Ethel and Jennifer and Star and Heather and Catherine were in Vernal and they needed me. This was only Barbarella.

"I gots to go," I repeated.

She let loose her leg lock and I rolled from the bed with a thud onto the carpeted floor of Room 28. I scurried about, remembering my mission and forgetting my companion.

"Hey, honey," she said, rolling out of bed and walking to the vanity where her possessions were stored in various different compartments. My pants were on and I was butting my shirt when she approached me and handed me four one-dollar bills. "Your half of the room was only $16," she said.

I kissed her hand, accepting the money and exchanging smiles. I promised her I would see *The China Syndrome* the first chance I got.

"I've liked all of your movies," I said.

"I've liked all of yours," she answered. The Shrimp Boats Are A-Comin' played over the television.

I pulled her naked, freckled body close to mine; we exchanged foul tasting spittle. There was a drum roll and the "Star Spangled Banner" filled the room. I flashed a peace sign and took my leave.

"No nukes, honey," she said as I walked out the door.

"Jane, you are the river," I said.

I marched past the ice machine, up the walk and past the motel office, back to the streets of Salt Lake. Sex was eased from my brain. I must admit, sometimes my brain is in my penis. I mentally prepared myself for the four-hour bus ride to Vernal. "It's only a bus, it's only a bus," I thought. It'll always be a prison on wheels.

I walked past a colorful corner glistening in the morning sun. Rainbow Gas, it said. I thought of Ermonie. I saw Salt Lake in a whole new light with the morning sun. The gates to Temple Square were unlocked and opened; I wandered through the still vacant paths and gardens, looking for the choir. I had coffee and cinnamon toast in a restaurant next to the bus station, where I sat alone in a booth, killing time and wishing I was in bed with Jane Fonda.

After breakfast, I once more walked the streets around Temple Square, amazed at how much money there is in GOD. I thought of the first time when I was God; it didn't make me any richer.

Rupert says, "Whenever in my life I have been a judge, I've always learned a short time later, I've also been an idiot."

* * *

In case you haven't noticed, I've found a book in Santa's cabin entitled, *21 days to a Bigger and Better Vocabulary*. Kicky. I can play if I want. It's my book.

* * *

Nine days earlier I was in the Valley with Damien Rumsford. "Rumsford has a better idea." I was preparing to spend the entire summer alone; I was totally freaked out by the absence of Ermonie and her children. Damien was helping me ease into the situation. He was used to the fast lane of the city and could well afford it with his lucrative drug business.

He enjoyed the mellow solitude of the country, but could only handle it in small doses. He was constantly studying and searching to broaden his horizons. Damien immensely enjoyed the social scene of the city but was always confused, momentarily, whenever someone would ask what he was. Of course, he always answered "regional sales manager," but if the matter was pursued he began speaking of women's rights, unions or indoor soccer. He couldn't very well tell a mayor or a judge that he was the regional distributor for the best drug on the market even though it's completely legal. The Feds don't know MDMA. Yet. He moved in many circles and some very high places. So he dabbled, whenever he could, in anything he felt gave him depth, for Damien always attempted to observe decorum in any situation.

Damien and Dominic Rodriguez Sepulvida, the manufacturer of Easy Now, had once planned to turn the entire country on to Easy Now. I thought it was a marvelous idea. When Dominic became successful as a ladies' lingerie distributor, he decided to keep it very low key. "Why take a risk of being rejected, by giving something in which I believe, but perhaps some wouldn't understand, when I can be safe and successful in ladies' lingerie?" he said. At least that's what Damien told me. And then he sang, "They call me mellow yellow."

There we stood, Damien and I, on the porch of the old farmhouse in the Valley, waving goodbye to Ermonie and Ethel and Jennifer and Star and Heather and Catherine, who were departing from the Valley near Friendsville, on their cross-country jaunt to Cherry Grove, Oregon leaving a trail of dust, rainbows and dirty sox.

Ermonie was a terrible housekeeper.

Damien looked slightly out of place as he stood on the porch of the old green farmhouse with an alligator on his shirt and cows mooing in the background. He did have his shoes off. Damien was a walking contradiction. If Buddha ever came back as a preppie, he'd be Damien Rumsford because "Rumsford has a better idea."

It was good to have that pudgy little body and that handle-bar mustache and those burnt-out eyes smiling and saying Easy Now, while my life was being sucked from me as the old Dodge station wagon disappeared up the drive and over the mountain. Everywhere I turned there were reminders of Ermonie and her children, dirty dishes and broken toys. I nearly cried when I noticed Ermonie had forgotten her vibrator. Such moments we had shared with that little musical hum playing along in accompaniment like Yehudi Menuhin on the violin.

Damien walked with me to the river, but the river wasn't the same. We had a lot to talk about, but the magic of Ermonie was gone from the Valley. So was the last of the supply of Easy Now, so I couldn't even create an illusion of magic. The absence of sex was also playing a role in my depression.

Ermonie Hunter certainly hadn't been easy, I was. And then I couldn't get enough. YEAH. All of a sudden I was left there with Damien and the animals; it wasn't quite the same. He was my friend. Though bisexuality seemed perfectly logical and acceptable to both of us, the thought of him and me becoming lovers was like a junkie being handed a joint after weeks of wallowing in the mud, the finest. I wasn't very adventuresome at the time. I was going through withdrawal. It wouldn't have worked. Besides, that sexual chemistry just wasn't there between Damien and me. Our entire friendship was based on calf brains and drugs. It was all very cerebral.

I began speaking to the sheep. After three days in the Valley, Damien began taking walks with one black sheep in particular. On his return from one such walk, his glowing eyes seemed strained and his usually relaxed brow was tightened severely.

"Sullivan," he said, breathing heavily, "I can't stand it. I've got to get away from here."

"Damien, what's the matter?" I yelled, grabbing his shoulders, totally taken aback, for he is always calm and smiling and mellow.

"It's Constance," he said.

"Constance!" I shouted, "the black sheep, is she hurt? What's wrong?" I feared the worst, for Constance was Ermonie's favorite.

"I want to fuck her," he said.

"Why not? You're in the country. Haven't you heard all the stories?" I smiled.

Damien immediately called Dominic Rodriguez Sepulvida on the west coast and discovered it was time to fly out to LA and prepare another batch of Easy Now. Since Damien always needed another reason to take the trip because of a slight case of insecurity about his role and a need to broaden his horizons, Dominic informed him of a business venture he might wish to dabble in. After his phone conversation, he was very excited and immediately began to pack.

"Damien, where are you going?" I inquired.

"To LA," he answered.

"You're going to leave me alone here with the sheep, are you?" I asked.

"But Sullivan, this is my big chance," he said.

"Why sure, go ahead," I said, "What?"

"Female mud wrestling," he said.

"But Damien, I mean, isn't that a little sexist? I mean, I thought you were a supporter of women's rights."

"Yeah," he said. "They got as much right to wrestle in the mud as anybody else."

I wasn't particularly enthusiastic at the prospect of being alone with the animals, but Damien's mental health had become important to me. I understood his need to broaden his horizons and perhaps one day find a legitimate label he could speak of at political gatherings. Certainly female mud wrestling was a possibility. I knew he was torn in his role as a drug dealer. He knew Easy Now promoted gentleness and made one feel closer to his immediate environment and God; he also had a need to conform like his partner.

It had been my choice to spend the summer in the Valley to look after things; he was helping me to adjust. The sheep and I waved and smiled and said, "Easy Now," as Damien drove off in his 1958 Austin Healey 106.

* * *

What a marvelous lunch I just finished. It consisted of succotash mixed with coconut and peanuts and peas over rice, seasoned with one jalapeno and teriyaki sauce. I hope my hemorrhoids don't complain.

* * *

Alone we were, Constance and I and the other animals. Ermonie called every evening to inform me of their progress on the trip. The gap that was left each time she hung up the phone intensified my need to seek more with her. *At the time* I had no idea she was carrying my baby—it was still merely an idea taking shape, but with enough substance to cause an impact on others.

I attempted to work on my novel about the Hope Springs Eternal Hotel, but only managed to write long unsendable letters to Ermonie. I picked wild flowers and wandered aimlessly about the plush pastures, striking up pointless conversations with Constance and the others. I knew much could be learned from the river; my thoughts kept taking me elsewhere.

Rupert says, "A cluttered closet needs much attention, before it can hold anything else."

The week passed like an aggravated assault as I drank constantly, bludgeoning myself with self-pity and a realization of my purposelessness. Constance and the other animals could have very well taken care of themselves, and I believe because of my resistance to their seductive manner, a plot was under way to have me ostracized as the master in residence.

Sunday morning came around, and it was just like the rest of the week since Damien's departure. I drank two shots of Jim Beam and toiled over a bowl of Raisin Bran. I let the sheep in the meadow and the cows in the corn, and wandered through the barn, picking up an egg here and an egg there. The chickens were very indiscriminate layers.

I walked to the river with Constance and chucked a couple of stones, returning to the house for another shot and to stare at my typewriter until the words of another indiscriminate layer gushed from my fingers, crying how I wished to mend my ways for the love of a beautiful woman. I was also very pornographic, the reason the letters were unsendable. My handwriting really sucks.

I received a call from Ermonie in the early afternoon, which was a shock in itself, for she had been calling in the evenings.

"Not to worry," she said. I was immediately upset.

"What happened?"

"I was having stomach pains and passed out in a state park. I'm in the hospital," she said. Even under the circumstances her voice was very seductive; I was confused by her manner, with what she said.

"Say what?"

"They're running some routine tests on me, but everything is fine."

"I'm on my way," I said. "Where are you?"

"Steamboat Springs," she said, "in Colorado. Oh, Sullivan, I didn't call to upset you. I just wanted to talk with you. Everything is fine, really."

"You're in a hospital, Ermonie, I'm coming."

"I promise you, if anything is wrong, you'll be the first to know."

I was very confused by my isolation and immediately began to pack for my excursion to Colorado. It made much more sense to be pacing in a waiting room as opposed to a farmhouse, the noises are much different. I still wasn't sure what I would be waiting for. The Raisin Bran greatly distorted my vision. I neglected to feed the chickens that beautiful Sunday afternoon. They began hurling themselves against the windows to bring the fact to my attention, and my curiosity was aroused. I feared the revolution was under way. The phone rang.

"Did you feed the chickens?" came Ermonie's voice over that obscene piece of plastic with pock marks.

"Ermonie?"

"Did you feed the chickens?"

"Are you all right?"

"They're keeping me overnight for observation, but I'm fine. Did you feed the chickens?"

"Maybe that's what's wrong. What do you mean, they're keeping you for observation?"

"If you forget to feed the chickens, they hurl themselves against the windows. Oscar was always replacing windows when I was away."

"Why are they keeping you, Ermonie?" I asked, very concerned with her levity.

"Oh, it's no big thing, they're running some routine tests to make sure I'm okay for travel."

"I think I should be there."

"OH, Sullivan, they'll release me in the morning."

We spoke for several minutes about chickens and Constance and space travel for the common man. Ermonie convinced me to wait for her call in the morning before I made any drastic moves. I immediately began packing and making arrangements to have someone look after the animals. I fed the chickens and they discontinued their assault on the house, allowing me to remain at my vigil by the phone in pieces.

Monday morning Ermonie called to say everything was fine and she was being released. Her stomach pain was tossed off as gas and her fainting as anxiety. I was like a little wooden airplane with a plastic propeller turned by a rubber band. My rubber band was as tight as could be, and I was placed on the side unattended. I was relieved and glad that everything seemed to be fine; I had a need to communicate with other human beings eye to eye.

While I was exploding in a burst of frustrated energy, wanting to be with Ermonie for whatever reason I could find (I would have flown out to change a flat or what have you), Ermonie and Ethel and Jennifer and Star and Heather and Catherine were driving into Utah. I felt the conditions had become extreme and made use of Ethel's VW to drive into Baltimore for release and distraction so I could once more face the animals and myself for what I thought would be the remainder of the summer in the Valley.

Once in Baltimore, I popped in on several friends and screamed, "REALITY CHECK—REALITY CHECK!" and left, no time for discussion. I was home without stepping on any bases; there was no game.

Very late that Monday evening I received word from my mother to call Ethel in Vernal, Utah. Ermonie was in the hospital undergoing an operation; I didn't know what it was for because Ethel attempted to keep things at a level that everything was under control. I had to see for myself; there were no chickens to distract me and Ermonie was being cut.

"I'm coming out," I said.

"I don't know," Ethel said.

I returned to the Valley for my gear, wondering—thinking things out—and then back to Baltimore I raced where I was on a plane by Tuesday evening.

* * *

I thought I was just going to have to shoot Tripod. She looked as if she were foaming at the mouth, poor bitch. I grabbed my gun, cocked it and took aim. She stood there on her three legs, wagging her tail and smiling. It was then I noticed she had been drinking water from a pot with the remnants of today's rice. I don't think she realized how close to the edge I am, with a loaded gun yet. I've been listening to a public radio station out of Pittsburgh during my hours of drought. The complexity yet completeness of a symphony is such a turn-on; simple fragments all brought together by gentle—but sometimes drastic and violent—movements.

* * *

I arrived in beautiful downtown Vernal, Utah, by bus at high noon on the first Wednesday of July. The bus passed the motel where Ethel and the children were staying. Then a few blocks farther along at the station it came to a stop. My typewriter and briefcase were with me, and even the few moments I had to wait for my overstuffed strawberry red suitcase to be retrieved form the belly of the bus were dickering with my attitude.

I dragged my gear—along the dry sun-bleached sidewalks—to the motel where I sighted Jennifer and Star playing hide-and-seek between parked cars in the parking lot. I called to them and they ran the other way into the room. I fooled them; I saw the room into which they ran. Uh-huh, I did—I did—and I followed them, lugging everything through the open door where dear Ethel was chattering away on the telephone, holding the receiver with her right hand, conducting a symphony with her left.

"He's here," I heard her say in a tone describing syphilis.

I kissed her on the cheek and left my things by the door, confident by the ambiance that Ermonie was fine. I found Jennifer hiding in the bathtub and Star under the bed. Heather and Catherine were playing gin.

"Did you bring money?" Catherine inquired.

The illusion of my galloping across the plains on my white horse to save the day was shattered. I still had a small stack of bills so I reached in my pocket and held it up for all to see. It was a very small stack.

* * *

Tripod and I have been walking; we directed ourselves to the top of the hill. There's a graveyard under what seems to be a good hanging tree off in the distance on another hill. There is one large pointed marble stone which reminds me of the Washington Monument surrounded by several smaller monuments to death. Perhaps I can see further than I thought.

I've cleaned up some on the knoll today. I'm watching a beautiful fire fueled by the rubbish as I type in the cluttered closet on the cluttered table. It's a fine wooden table—large enough to hold: two empty wine bottles, Swisher Sweets with tips, Prince Albert in a can (perhaps I'll give him some air), my coffee cup with the figure of an orange-and-black striped cat with faraway eyes hanging out on its side, type cleaner, splattered wax from candles, a Sweetheart cold cup, honey oil, a ceramic dish of peaches, the top of my portable typewriting holding unclean pot and seeds (maybe I'll plant some), a box of semi-jacketed hollow points minus seven (one semi-jacketed hollow point sits staring at me.

Five semi-jacketed copper-coated hollow points are loaded into the cylinder of my 38 which is also on the table—I lost one somewhere), my high intensity lamp. The mirror is on the table next to me. I don't know what happened to the missing hollow point; maybe I'll find it later.

The table is in front of the open door; the fire sizzles against a large multi-colored rock under a not-yet-blooming maple tree. Fire needs fuel to burn, but if you overload it before its time, it goes out. Revelations and simplicity in the weeds.

* * *

Ethel hung up the phone and immediately looked drained from the strain. Her long flowery dress was limp and damp hanging from her tired sloping shoulders. A look of "what's next?" was pasted all over her like a billboard selling space. Dear Ethel gave the impression of a former virgin who had just been had by 59 drunken sailors waiting for the captain and the first mate.

"Ermonie's fine," she said.

"What happened?"

"She almost died."

"What happened?"

"She almost died."

"What happened?"

"She's fine now. Why are you here now?"

"How are you?"

"I'm fine. Where are you going to stay?"

The girls came out of hiding, laughing and playing and making faces; Ethel was struck by the light of responsibility.

"It's time for lunch!" she shouted as the flowers on her dress bloomed again. "Girls--To your places. Sullivan, you will stay for lunch, won't you?"

ENTER THE GLADIATORS boomed from the heavens as Heather grabbed a loaf of whole wheat bread and Catherine carried a pile of blue tin plates and cups to the sidewalk in front of the door to the room.

"What can I do?"

"The juice is in the cooler."

Ethel dug in a picnic basket and came up with a jar of jelly and a large plastic container of peanut butter. I found apple juice and followed the procession to the veranda where Jennifer and Star appeared in the circle while Ethel barraged the bread with brown and purple gook while conducting her band.

"Where's the salad?"

"What can I do?"

"The salad is in the cooler."

I returned once more to the cooler to find cole slaw and potato salad swimming on the bottom. Luncheon was served. Ethel was in complete control of the world; she wanted me to know it. I was overcome by jet lag and the feeling of not being needed; Ethel was fighting off feelings of not being able to handle the situation alone. The children were making the best of each moment, enjoying themselves. A clash of egos was imminent.

Ethel said, "Now that you're here, I guess we're all in this together; we may as well make the best of it." And she meant it.

That woman missed her calling; she should be president. I can see her now standing on the White House lawn, amongst the hordes of Vietnam vets and nuke protesters, unemployed, farmers, boat people and drunken spaced-out Indians, unwed mothers, teenage pregnant girls, and whatever in her long flowery dress with her hands on her large hips saying, "Now that you're here, I guess we're all in this together. We may as well make the best of it."

The little tribe became so involved in the moment, eating on the ground at that motel, it reminded me of all of the other dinners I had shared with the group in the little farmhouse in the valley. It was just another time without Ermonie while she was out with her other lover. Only now she was in the hospital and I had no momentary delusions of sexual rewards.

After lunch, I was given the keys to the car and immediately drove to a flower shop, then to the hospital. I entered the semi-private room which at the time was occupied by Ermonie alone, and was stopped momentarily by the vision of a woman I would be willing to die for. She was gazing dreamily at a magazine, simply turning the pages, lost in her own thoughts which I knew she was quite capable of having. She sensed my presence and looked me to her bedside.

"Hiee," she sang, and smiled as if I were her date coming to take her to dinner. "How was your trip?"

That's the only thing I didn't want her to say feeling a bit like a cad with only sex on the brain. "You almost died?" I asked.

"Something about internal bleeding and a low blood count," she tossed off like a peach pit.

"Ermonie, what happened?"

"I was pregnant. It was an ectopic pregnancy. The little devil was hanging on the outside of my tubes."

"Holy shit."

"No, it was a baby."

* * *

The moon tonight is like an over-indulgent flugelhorn buying space in a coliseum. My fire is down to embers and it glows and sparkles like fool's gold against my large multi-colored rock which has become invisible. The night air is becoming cold and damp while my last candle burns and protrudes from the wax-covered wine bottle as my penis burns and extends from my being. The candle will melt and my penis will shrivel.

I think I'll take a walk to the top of my hill and smoke a joint. I can't dance and it's been a long day. Tripod will walk with me tonight as she always walks with me. Everything looks different by the light of the moon when the moon isn't competing with neon.

When I was driving a taxi, before I came to Santa's cabin, I drove from six in the evening until six in the morning. I watched the sun set and then rise again, with everything in between. There was neon; still I watched the moon. It was something I had to do. It's the same moon, but there's a difference. It's a question of balance. Shitting has always been a pleasure, but with hemorrhoids there's a difference. It's the same shit, but still there's a difference. It's a question of balance. Hemorrhoids remind me of neon. If it's there, you've got to deal with it. Sometimes there is simply no choice.

Rupert says, "What do you do with an artichoke?"

DAY 8

Brushing my hair, looking in the mirror while my scalp and beard are massaged, I notice the same conviction in my eyes as when I stick the gun in my mouth and pull the trigger. I'm also going bald. I do enjoy looking in the mirror.

This is the beginning of my eighth day in the woods. The water in the pot outside the door froze last night; so did I.

Today is the Thursday before Easter. If I remember it correctly as a Catholic, we called it Holy Thursday, the day of Christ's last supper. It's merely a coincidence that I became God on a Thursday evening after having supper with another group of derelicts who enjoyed their wine.

The way my t keeps sticking, I may never get to it. "Praise the Lord and pass the ammunition." The last of my brandy is gone.

* * *

Rupert says,

> Visions are before us
> Don't take it lightly
> Leave it for the painters
> They interpret what they see.
> I can only listen and oft not well enough;
> What I hear are visions, my eyes read only signs.
> My ears have closed from wax build-up
> Folly is my game.
> Distractions are all around me.
> So leave it for the painters.

* * *

The proprietors of the Lamplighter Motel in Vernal understood our plight of limited funds. They graciously refunded Ethel the money for the room that Wednesday evening; we went out in search of a campground. The women and children had been sleeping in a tent on their entire journey—until Vernal where the situation demanded a room with a phone.

Now that the crisis had passed, frugality was once more in order, especially since I had little money to contribute. I gave Ethel a hundred dollars towards expenses, leaving myself with fifty for mad money.

In my suitcase were two bottles of cheap scotch and one of Irish whiskey in case of snake bite. The booze would also come in handy for that brief period of adjustment in the changing realms of life. Okay, so once in a while I like a good stiff drink.

With Ermonie still in the hospital, Ethel and I located the Dina campgrounds on the outskirts of Vernal. The facilities seemed adequate, though I had nothing to compare them with. There were coin-operated showers and cold-pop machines. The grass was cut and the grounds were patrolled regularly for trash. They allowed pets and Frisbee throwing if kept under control.

The idea of sleeping in a tent had always appeared to me to be some sort of masochistic tendency to revert back to the earth without really trying, especially in a campground among trailers and campers and battery-operated televisions. I had always thought that a Coleman was the one who kept the train running.

We pitched our tent in a special area for tents—away from the bourgeois trailers. It was the middle of the week and we had our choice of spots in the tent area. There was access to a picnic table and the shade of a tree. Ethel prepared our dinner of macaroni and cheese with orange slices on the side, while I played with the girls in the playground on the swings.

Jennifer and Star and Heather and Catherine retired shortly after dinner to the six-man tent that had been borrowed from Damien Rumsford. The tent had been left over from Damien's six-month excursion into the realm of "Scoutmaster-at-Large." He had mentioned his fondness for young boys but remembering how Damien always observed the proper decorum in any situation, I knew there was no connection.

Rupert says, "It ain't what you think, it's what you do about it. The shadow knows. Free thinking opens the door to creativity."

With the children fast asleep in the safety of the tent, Ethel and I sat at the picnic table on the wooden benches and shared a good portion of a bottle of King George IV Scotch. With the aid of the lubricant, we each reconstructed our stories of the trip. Their trip had been longer and more eventful than mine, but I guess I did most of the talking. I got the feeling Dear Ethel didn't know what to make of my presence. After all, she and Ermonie were on some type of vague crusade—that they could make it on their own without the help of men, including me. That was okay by me, but I was there and I didn't know what kind of help I would be anyway. They had had some car problems; I ain't no fucking mechanic. Ethel was still slightly intimidated by my presence, though the strong friendship which was our foundation began to seep through the barrier of sex.

She soon left me alone in the company of King George IV, giving me time to figure out where I was. I realized that some things are better left a mystery. I soon found myself in the northeast corner of the tent, alone, in an extra sleeping bag.

Breakfast was an event. We bickered and squawked and laughed and ate generic raisin bran and corn flakes and drank generic reconstituted orange juice.

I was granted the privilege of washing the breakfast and previous evening's dinner dishes in a red vinyl pan under an open spigot. The cold water was refreshing. Ethel crocheted and Jennifer and Star amused themselves with the universe and the seesaw. Heather and Catherine played gin. I found myself walking in circles when the dishes were through; Ethel came to my rescue. She suggested a late-morning swim in the pool of the Lamplighter, where we were invited back and welcomed to enjoy the facilities for a little recreation.

I cannot honestly say that I will always regard driving in a hot car, through a desert to a tent, in a wet bathing suit, as recreation. At the time it was fun. Yeah. My clouded brain does not completely permit me to disclose the extreme pleasure I endured. I did, however, feel I was an almond-stuffed olive in a perfect martini— with limitations. The olive gets eaten; I was in the family way without sex. The limitations confused me. My limited experience confined me. My ego consumed me.

On Thursday evening we gathered our family—minus Ermonie—and went to a drive-in. *The China Syndrome* was playing.

My obligation to Jane Fonda was fulfilled. The girls slept while Ethel and I enjoyed hot buttered popcorn. I loved the movie; I kept thinking of neon. It ain't going to go away but there's a place for it and there must be a way.

Rupert says, "What's in a message: What's in a hollow point?" Myron says, "Nobody gives a shit." Dominic Rodriguez Sepulvida says, "Money is love." Fat Grew says, "Some do, some don't, some never will, Fat Grew always does." "QUESTION AUTHORITY."

I'm sure it's just a temporary break,
Such things take nothing but time.
Break, hell
The die is cast
There's no one else around.
Leave it for the painters.
I have no more to give
And if I did,
Why should I give it to you?
You wallow in the pond.
Because I'm one of the good guys.
I've carried my burden enough.
Because I dream of the way it should be,
I think—I do
That's where my road lies.
But you wallow in the pond.
Leave it for the painters!

Friday was the Fourth of July. We ventured into the desert to see what beauty surrounded us. Ethel and I took turns pointing out where the MX Missiles would hide. We followed signs and eventually ended up in Rainbow Park. There were signs commanding us not to pick the rocks or vegetation; rafters waved back as they sailed past on the Green River. I became a mushroom in an omelet when I was sucked in up to my knees by the mud on the bank of the river. The girls looked on, and the interest soared at the spectacle in this age of computers at the river bank.

We lunched with a beautiful Park Service Ranger—figs and

baloney were the bill of fare, along with ice water from the ranger's jugs. I had forgotten to pack anything to drink besides a bottle of King George IV. He refused to be mixed with baloney and cheese. The ranger suggested we drive to Dinosaur National Monument. We listened to her directions very carefully, three times.

I sat in the rear compartment of the station wagon with Star while Ethel drove and Jennifer was the co-pilot. Heather and Catherine played gin in the back seat. We could see perfectly well where we were going; the dust from our wake made it impossible to see where we had been.

There was no other traffic that afternoon in our little circle of the Utah Desert, not that the road could have handled more than one car at a time. Ethel was in complete control as we passed what looked like the Eiffel Tower burrowing for oil—the only sign of civilization. Our gypsy wagon continued slowly as I became very excited at seeing my first oil well close up. I pointed and shouted and drew stares from the girls. I turned and strained my eyes, looking through the dust cloud, being just as amazed by the monument sucking earth as I was by the ones in Temple Square sucking heaven. Actually Jane Fonda did more for me than either of them. The car came to a stop. I thought Ethel was granting me a longer look.

"Oh, shit," she said (strange words for one who was granting me a pleasure, I thought).

"We must have taken the wrong turn," she said, with an attitude of desert dust and distemper.

I diverted my attention from the shrouded oil well to the road ahead, as our wake overtook us like a forgotten memory uncovered by inactivity.

* * *

Such a day! I've washed my 27 handkerchiefs in the brook. Like so many different national flags mingled with truce flags, they flutter in the soft spring breeze. The day is so clear. I drove the four miles in my gas-guzzling Ford station wagon, to the store, and restocked with tobacco and cigars, Swisher Sweets with tips. I counted out $22 in change, tips from driving a cab. It wasn't all for tobacco.

I purchased two Hershey Almond Bars, a box of Cocoa Wheats, $5 worth of gasoline, a jug of California Moselle, a six-pack of Schmidt's and 750 milliliters of Kamchatka Vodka. I mustn't forget to mention the jar of hot mixed cauliflower and pickles and peppers and onions and pimentos. My rice is cooking; such a glorious day it is. I also bought a local newspaper: "ARMED STRIKERS RETURN TO MINE."

I'm having a good time.

* * *

"NO TRESPASSING," "KEEP OUT," "CAVEAT EMPTOR," "AN APPLE THIS BIG," "YOU ARE RESPONSIBLE FOR YOUR OWN WAKE," shouted silently through the dust cloud from signs hanging from the rotting wooden rail fence and archway at the end of the road. Confused by the material haze, there wasn't time to speak or investigate when Ethel shifted into reverse and began to back down the narrow dirt road, avoiding certain death at the hands of the signs.

Ethel strained her neck stretching to see the entire length of the wagon; I couldn't help but wonder why she didn't drive through the open archway to turn around.

"We're stuck," she said.

"Naw," I said.

* * *

I've added jalapenos, tomatoes and tamales to the rice. My hemorrhoids are going to scream tonight. I've been cooking in a wok. This is such a contrast from the city, like taking a Wok on the wild side.

My concoction needed a touch of Moselle and a can of Jack Mackerel. I'm cooking enough for 12. Holy Thursday. It's mackerel. Peanuts give it crunch. It needs pineapple; I have no pineapple. I think I'll have a drink.

* * *

Ethel shifted and rocked and it soon became clear that we were stuck. The right rear tire of the station wagon danced in the soft shoulder of the dusty road with an attitude of mellow contentment.

"Whirrr," said the tire.

"What are we going to do?" said Ethel.

"Everything will be fine," I said.

King George IV was hiding under the front seat.

"Shift into low," I said.

The tire sang as we remained in our position of immobility. It was then I volunteered to try my magic touch at the wheel. Getting out of the car on the passenger side, I noticed how close we were to a three-foot ditch with bright orange water running along its bottom. The earth crumbled beneath my feet and splashed into the undrinkable Tang. I felt very silly.

At my suggestion, Ethel and the girls climbed from the car and backed away. I climbed in, shifted into gear and dug us in a little deeper. "WHIRRR," the tire sang, the earth crumbled, Ethel cried comforted by Heather and Catherine, and Jennifer and Star were amused by the orange water as they stood waiting in the motionless afternoon air, heated by the fire of the sun.

"What is it?" said Jennifer, staring down.

"It's a ditch," said Ethel in her schoolteacher diction.

Jennifer and Star began to giggle and chase each other, squealing "Stitch! Stitch!"

I climbed out and jogged in the direction of the Eiffel Tower. "Have no Fear," I exclaimed, hoping to find the International Red Cross to come to our aid. Instead, I came upon a bill-capped man driving a red pickup. The man was the color of a ripened beefsteak tomato and was unconcerned until I pointed out Ethel and the children. I saw myself in the reflection of his General MacArthur sunglasses.

I was a Neanderthal man describing an apple this big.

"You gotta chain?" he asked.

"I've gotta bottle of King George IV," I said.

"An apple this big," he said.

I jogged behind as he drove to the Eiffel Tower. Cherry tomatoes in billed caps walked about; the beefsteak tomato in General MacArthur sunglasses disappeared into a trailer. I stood in awe as I watched the earth being sucked by robots. A cherry tomato passed. "An apple this big," he said.

"An apple this big," I answered.

The beefsteak tomato returned and tossed a heavy chain into the rear of his pickup and drove off. I jogged behind, barefoot and blistered.

> But I will drown
>
> So? People drown every day.
>
> Do you shed a tear?
>
> Who are you, who thinks he is a God?
>
> Leave it for the painters,
>
> Or a man with a hammer and nails.
>
> What can you do that could be worth a damn?

* * *

On our return to the wagon, Jennifer and Star were climbing a small mountain while Ethel wept in the sagebrush. Heather and Catherine continued their game of gin on the embankment.

"Green eggs and ham," Jennifer called out.

"An apple this big," I answered.

General MacArthur and I hitched the chain between vehicles; we struggled with the dust while the right rear tire of the wagon whirred with both rear tires of the truck joining in.

"WHIRRRRR!"

The truck stalled and the general climbed from the cab swatting dust, looking for apples.

"Nope," he said.

He drove off leaving the chain; I jogged off toward the rail fence and archway in search of an apple this big, or a tractor. I ignored the foreboding signs with reckless abandon. The silence of the deserted shacks informed me I would find no apples there. I rushed to Ethel to tell her of a wonderful shade tree I came upon.

"Green eggs and ham," she said.

"An apple this big," I answered.

I needed time alone to speak with the car about what we should do. Ethel and the Girls walked off in search of the shade. I discussed matters openly with the King present; he went right to my head with the help of the sun. Not being able to come up with a logical solution, I began to walk in the direction of the homestead. I was passed by a silver van. It seemed to be searching for apples. It stopped by the shade of the tree; I ran in pursuit of an apple this big. I approached; he passed going the other way, back toward the wagon.

"Green eggs and ham," I shouted to Ethel.

"An Apple this big," she answered.

I turned on my heel, racing back to the wagon and the silver van. A bill-capped cherry tomato was hitching the chain in between the vehicles, back to back.

I sat in the driver's seat as tires sang and the front wheel of the wagon was dragged into the soft shoulder. The cherry tomato turned his van and once more attached the chain between vehicles, back to front. There was no singing when the wagon became tired of waiting for an apple this big and slid into the ditch. I climbed from the partially submerged station wagon, quite confused.

"An Apple this big," I screamed.

"Green eggs and ham; I'm really sorry," said the frightened cherry tomato. He unhitched the chain and drove off.

Ahh, my friend, is it really that important, To do much more than live and allow your mind To conquer other worlds?

> But you wallow in the pond
> And your body's made of bones

And they'll crumble when you die
And you've nary left a mark.
But my spirit will linger on.
When in Rome eat pasta
And you wallow in the pond,
So leave it for the painters.
But I've nary left a mark and painters paint
But pictures--Canvas crumbles like my bones.
I wish to seek new worlds
And tell all where I've been.

* * *

Emmett had a bucket to shit in on board the Mary Patt. I didn't shit when I was on board the Mary Patt. I did what I had to do over the side—I wouldn't shit in the bucket. I held it until we docked.

Here I am in the woods. If I must shit, it's either the bucket or the woods. First of all, the squat would kill me. Secondly, I plan on walking in the woods often; I still don't know what to do when the bucket is full.

Hemorrhoids make it real. If I shoot myself in the ass and make another hole, perhaps the shit will come out there and it won't hurt as much. Perhaps not. I wish I had a toilet.

* * *

Rupert says, "One asshole is enough."
You wallow in the pond,
And your ears are filled with wax.
You'll never tell--Lest first you clean your ears.
So leave it for the painters
And the carpenters who build,
Besides, what can you say
That's not been said before?

* * *

I walked dejectedly back to the homestead with all hopes of finding apples drowned in Tang. Ethel came to me and touched me with compassion.

"An apple this big," she said.

I fell into her arms and cried. Heather began jumping up and down. "An apple this big! An apple this big!" she shouted, pointing in the direction of our dilemma.

I saw the reflection of General MacArthur's sunglasses and several cherry tomatoes and a Sherman tank. I ran with hope and bloody feet back to our lopsided wagon. The tank dragged us from the ditch; the salad cheered. I presented General MacArthur with King George IV and miraculously drove to the homestead, sloshing Tang and smelling burning rubber.

"What's that horrible smell," Ethel said.

"Green eggs and ham," answered Jennifer.

Star looked up into the wheel well of the right rear tire. "An apple this big," she said.

She was right. It was wedged between the tire and the body. I jacked up the car and removed it so we could be on our way. We saved the apple. Against our wishes, we also saved the stench from the orange liquid in the ditch.

"Green eggs and ham," said Jennifer.

"Stitch," said Star, holding her nose.

We returned to Vernal and our campsite before we visited with Ermonie in the hospital. Fireworks appeared after dark.

Rupert says, "Sometimes life's a stitch, but there's always an apple around."

> It's all been said before; I wish to say it all again.
> I have seen more, than one painting of a tree.
> But you wallow in the pond,
> And you will surely drown.
> Rupert likes to rhyme.

No, my friend, I'm merely cleaning my ears.

DAY 9

It's Good Friday. My high-intensity light has just burned out. I've replaced it with a bulb like a penis. I have no lamp shade for it; the light from the electric penis is glaring.

This is my ninth day; it's 9:30 in the morning. I'm eating what is left of yesterday's lunch, with olives added. It's raining—not a heavy rain. It's the kind when you can't see any drops. I walked in it and was immediately drenched from the ground up.

Both my stomach and my asshole are conspiring to shoot me in my sleep if I don't ease up on the spicy food.

Tripod is such a good dog. She only shits in private. I've never seen her shit. Tripod has only three legs. She never squats. It must drop out the side. I still don't know where she leaves it. She eats enough. Thank God she doesn't like booze. Maybe she can tell me what to do when the bucket is full.

This is the day of Passion, the day they nailed Christ to the cross and put him on display. Someone's been collecting admission ever since, tax free.

My knoll is looking better every day. Perhaps I'll never leave.

* * *

Saturday began with our daily visit with Ermonie, who was recovering nicely. She was one strong woman. The station wagon was also recovering nicely from its dip in the ditch. It was a little noisier than Ermonie--No, a lot noisier. She just sort of took things in stride. She sighed quite a bit but laughed even when it hurt.

The gypsy wagon made noise like an orange-stuccoed ceiling; couldn't get away from it. The pipes were a little bent but we were still mobile. The stench from the ditch, or, "stitch," bore a strange resemblance to old rusty bacon. That old Dodge gypsy wagon had 115,000 miles on its original engine and holes were rusting through the body. Ermonie had purchased it for $200 two weeks before the trip, long enough for it to become part of her magical family, and it kept on trucking, even with its occasional reminder that it was only a car.

Ethel once more took the lead by suggesting we venture westward for our afternoon and early evening activity. We attended an Indian powwow near Roosevelt. Indians from different tribes and areas gathered, wearing feathers and bells and paint. Tourists stood in a circle while the Indians danced and chanted and sold leather and turquoise.

Our tailpipe fell off; we saved it with hopes of repair. The pressures of the road and the absence of Ermonie began to take their toll on Star. She reacted by throwing fits and food, causing us to return to camp before the Indians finished singing and dancing. Jennifer's outlet came in the form of concern for her twin. Heather and Catherine played gin rummy. Ethel and I tapped into the Irish whiskey.

Sunday passed while we relaxed in an atmosphere that had become our temporary home. We cooled ourselves with an afternoon water battle at our comfortable campsite. Ermonie was up and around, still confined to a room but growing stronger for travel because she wanted to continue. She felt she had to continue. Maybe after months and months of pressure from Oscar, the physical pain she was enduring seemed more bearable than the mental anguish and fear still attacking her in the shadows of her home. She needed distance and time.

There was a picture—Ermonie waved from behind an uncurtained window to her children in the parking lot, needing her. Ermonie was a level higher, above it all, but with such a connection; Ethel and I became spiritual lovers with the responsibility for our children. I needed to be touched.

* * *

At Monastery Beach, the Indian told me of a game he played as a child. The game was taught him by his grandfather. The object was to sneak up behind a deer, tapping its tail. The deer would run off. The Indian claimed to have learned the game well. Red and Woody had gone for more wine. Crazy Tom prepared the fire and prepared the stew.

Slim sat in the dark, playing his flute and giving the impression of a charcoal streak across a still life in oil on canvas. The sparks from the fire hovered at his command. The Indian told me of the game.

* * *

On the road, I waited near Elmira, Oregon, where the Country Fair had been. It was a Monday morning. I was mellowed out from my weekend. My destination was Winchester Bay, where I was told I would find work on a fishing boat. I stood next to a blackberry bush. The blackberries were ripe and sweet and worth the price of a few scratches from the thorns.

* * *

Rupert says, "There's always a price."

* * *

A slow strutting cowboy, carrying a brown paper sack with a loaf of bread sticking out the top approached from the west, the direction I was headed. He wore a Stetson hat and an Easy Now smile.

"Howdy," he said.

"What it is," I said.

"You hungry?" he asked.

"No. Care for a blackberry?"

"No, thank ya. Better chance a getting' a ride a half mile down the road, the other entrance to the fair."

"I'll wait."

"Easy Now," he answered, not missing a stride, strutting on by, heading east. He disappeared.

A Volkswagen station wagon stopped, driven by a young man with a beard and long hair. He had been an exhibitor at the fair. His exhibit was a pyramidal meditation hut. He dropped me at the west entrance of the fair.

A man named Dave picked me up, headed for Coos Bay. He wore a short-sleeved, powder blue Van Heusen shirt. His striped tie hung loosely around his neck and his summer gray suit coat was draped across the front seat. He placed it in the back to make room for me and my typewriter. My army surplus duffel bag, with my briefcase stuffed inside, was also stored in the rear.

Dave had been an active participant in land use hearing in Portland the previous week. He said he picked me up because he assumed I was a hippie. He worked for a large lumber company in public relations. Public relations between his company and what he termed hippies had been poor, he said.

I always thought his company made toilets, honest.

"We're one of the largest producers of building materials in the world," he said.

Dave gave the appearance of a very nice used-car salesman. His fingernails were manicured as was his manner and speech. He explained his purpose at the land use hearings as "HERBICIDES." He worked for Georgia Pacific; I really had thought they made toilets. I even mentioned it to him. We drove westward in the direction of the coast, with Dave pointing out mountains his company had clear cut and reclaimed. He told me of a game his company played.

"We quadron off sections on a map and periodically send in groups in vehicles for a controlled deer kill. The deer eat vulnerable saplings before they have a chance to grow; it hurts our production of lumber."

He was friendly and gentle. I sensed guilt as only another guilty man can sense.

"The deer kill is necessary for productivity and the growth of the company and the country. There are too many deer in some areas."

I told him I appreciated his involvement in his job; I even said I was sure he did good work.

"I'm a moral man. I have a wife and kids. I wouldn't argue for anything I thought would be harmful. We scout the colleges and universities in search of the best foresters in the country and they're all moral people."

"We deal in scientific fact. The environmentalists play on emotions. They bring in pregnant women, crying, saying they're afraid of what the runoff into drinking water from the use of herbicides will do to their unborn babies. My company has conducted costly studies, proving the runoff would be so minute there would be no harm to anyone or anything. The Douglas fir needs light to grow. When we clear cut a mountain we need herbicides to protect our crop of trees. Don't they understand? Lumber is the major industry of the area. We need production. We create jobs. The marijuana industry is our chief opposition. The marijuana growers are afraid of what the herbicides will do to their crop, not to babies or animals. Marijuana growers don't pay taxes on their crop, we do."

"The government interferes too much in our lives," he said. "There are too many controls. I believe in freedom. We should be allowed to do what we want with our property. They bring these people in to testify and they want the same things that we do, unrestricted land use. They fight us, yet they fight themselves."

"Fat Grew believes that prohibition caused the great depression because of all the tax money lost. Shouldn't they legalize drugs to help the economy? And maybe use the proceeds for treatment programs so people can find out who they really are?" I said.

"Now that's just silly."

We reached the coast and headed south. I explained I had been told to stop in Winchester Bay if I wanted to fish. Dave said there were more fishing boats in Coos Bay; my chances of signing on board one would be better.

"Scientists hoping to make a name for themselves conduct experiments on rats and scare the public half to death with their findings. Even the DDT scare was blown way out of proportion. I've seen a scientist drink a water glass full of DDT and live to tell about it."

I told him I was a writer; he told me much more. He dropped me in Winchester Bay and I wrote down all I could remember. Dave was a very nice man.

* * *

Rupert says, "Progress is our most important product."

* * *

The first thing Monday morning, I located a garage; they repaired our tailpipe for 30 dollars. They couldn't pitch the stitch. Ermonie was released from the hospital and felt sunlight for the first time in a week. She carried herself bravely, her left arm across her stomach. It was time to move on. She was reunited with her daughters at the campground.

Ermonie's abdominal surgery had sucked much of the vitality and playfulness from her, and she still experienced a great deal of pain and discomfort. I found even her grimace quite sexual, but lust must be kept in its place.

We broke camp and headed west toward Salt Lake City, not yet sure where we would spend the night. We played a hospital game, always looking for signs of one, not quite sure if it was a game or not. I confessed my encounter with Jane Fonda (leaving out a few details of course) as we drove into Salt Lake, because I thought it was funny. We parked near Temple Square and joined other tourists, listening to tour guides proclaim, "An Apple this big," in many languages. There were no bill-caps. After an hour of walking it was time to find a place to camp for the night. Ethel suggested Antelope Island.

Antelope Island is situated across a seven-mile bridge in the Great Salt Lake. Great storm clouds danced across the sky, shooting forth tremendous streaks of lightning for our visual pleasure, as we made our way across the bridge to what looked like a desolate turd waiting to be flushed.

The women with their strong pioneer spirit chose the barest of the campgrounds to spend the night. Even after spending a week in the hospital and with all the pain she was obviously experiencing Ermonie was game for roughing it. I didn't question anything; it was their trip. I just wanted to be there with them. I was doing the driving, but I didn't take command.

* * *

Rupert says, "What it is."

***

Rupert says,

I'd like to know which way to run,

I wanta find that path to the sun.

If I could fly I'd find the way

And when I'd get there I'd wish to stay.

But I'd return in just a while.

The sun shines bright here with your smile.

Well, La Dee Daa. Come on, Rupe, you can do better. Well, a little better anyway, maybe.

Rupert says, "Take time to smell."

* * *

We pitched our tent next to a large rock within sight and smell of the lake. There was a smell like a heap of dirty gym socks. The camping area was equipped with a double outhouse and a water tank in a tower labeled "SHOWER." The storm we watched on our entrance gave us nothing but wind and a beautiful rainbow while the sun was setting. Ermonie began preparing dinner of a fresh green salad and Chinese vegetables. Ethel, the children and I raced to the top of a ridge, dodging sagebrush and thorns, the only vegetation on the island.

The ridge was higher and steeper than it looked. I ran ahead, wishing to reach the top before the sun went down. The children followed with Ethel, in her long flowery dress and sneakers, taking up the rear carrying her strapless camera. I caught sight of a female antelope catching sight of me. We made eye contact. I called to my troop but they were nowhere to be seen. I happened upon a family of ducks who startled me as they scattered. Gosh, they were beautiful.

The sun quickly began to sink into the water when I finally attained what I thought was the top. I spent a few moments walking in circles, deciding it best to start down. Ethel and the children were there, right with me, watching the sun go down. We had one more brief moment as a family, sharing not blood but experience. Together we descended the mountain; twilight was upon us in all its grayness when we reached the campsite and Ermonie's first home cooked meal since her brush with death.

I desired to be with her and hold her close for a moment, forever, while she sloshed gobs of bamboo shoots and water chestnuts and bean sprouts and slithered slivered almonds from the pot onto my tin plate. Her eyes flashed the flame of the Coleman stove back at me from a distance that time can't tell. The communication was confused; there was too much going on. Things became lost. We were on an island, not in her Valley. I wanted her but she had been cut and a child gutted from her, my child, I knew this; there was no peace in my arms.

The dishes waited until morning with Ermonie and her children, in need of time together, retiring early. Ethel and I sat up by the light of the stove, finishing what remained of the Irish whiskey. We were joined by three young boys from an adjoining campsite. The eldest was 20. They brought along some beer and we furnished potato chips. They were from Massachusetts. We were swapping vague stories by the Coleman and Ethel remarked, aside, that the eldest looked like a Greek god. I told her she should have him if she wanted him. She soon disappeared with the Greek god while I entertained the youngsters with my stories of wanton waste and luxury in the drug-dealing business. I was clean, so I felt safe.

Rupert says, "We all see things differently. That doesn't make what you see any less than what I see, or otherwise."

* * *

> Still I must go and drift away,
> I have to find what's in another day.
> Please believe the words you hear;
> There's nothing more than when you're near
> But to be complete I have to find
> What it is that muddles my mind.

Oh, well, Rupert likes to smell.

* * *

Having been dropped by Dave in Winchester Bay, I stood on the side of the road, lost in space. "What the fuck am I doing here?" I thought. "Easy now, you're going fishing. Oh, yeah, why not?"

It was a beautiful sunny Monday afternoon. I had made good

time; it was a little after one p.m. I had plenty of time before dark to sign on board a boat. I just had to put myself out there and allow someone to find me.

I walked down the hill from 101, carrying my typewriter and duffel bag towards the basin of Winchester Bay. Like so many fingers playing a gentle rhapsody on the piano, the boats moved in time, but separately, each seemingly knowing what the other was doing. There was also the involvement of an orchestra and its audience in the air. All were there for pleasure; some did it for a living. I was there because I had never been there before and to find out what to do when the bucket is full.

"Easy Now," was my first impression of Winchester Bay, though there seemed to be much activity. I walked along the main road at the top of the basin; I stopped a young man and asked where I could find work. He directed me to a cluster of one-story wooden buildings at the north end of the basin. I stopped in a small restaurant and enjoyed a cup of chowder and good coffee. On my inquiry, I was directed to a fish-packing building.

It seemed like a mortuary for contaminated cunts, with the odor and everyone walking around in white gowns and rubber gloves. I approached a man wearing a billed cap. He was the boss. Sometimes it seems like this country is in the hands of people in billed caps. Whether it's the birds or the military remains to be seen.

Rupert says, "Sometimes life stinks. But you still gotta breathe the air."

* * *

We broke camp as the noon hour approached. Everyone pitched in. Ethel and I took down the tent, while Ermonie cleared the dishes and Jennifer stacked the shells we had gathered. Star kept watch for Indians. And of course, Heather and Catherine played gin.

With the wagon loaded, we drove the length of our deserted campground, looking for a place to turn around. Ethel was finished with doing any driving since her encounter with the soft shoulder; she didn't even wish to sit in the front seat. Our organizational abilities were faltering quickly with hundreds of miles still to be covered until our destination. The women were determined for their journey to remain a pleasant adventure as opposed to a race against time. The car stalled in front of the water tower. I shifted into park and switched the ignition. The car was dead.

I gazed at my companion in the front seat, smiling, wishing only to take her in my arms as if stranded on a desert isle where (I hoped) we would never be found. I'd hunt for food and fish and learn how to prepare sagebrush stew. We'd find peace once more in each nother's arms. "The car won't start," I said.

"Hmmm," Ermonie responded, not particularly surprised.

"Oh, shit," Ethel said, reminding me that others were present and I was there to see them to their destination. I continued turning the key, not knowing what was wrong but fearing I had caused it in some way.

"Do you think we're out of gas?" Ermonie asked calmly. I became slightly upset and worried, knowing somebody had to do it; even Ethel's "Oh, shit" wasn't out of surprise.

"Fire," Heather shouted as smoke began seeping from under the hood.

"Hmmm," Ermonie said, looking and sounding calm but tightening her arm across her stomach. I panicked, yelling for everyone to jump from the car, and racing myself to see what possibly could be wrong. I lifted the hood while the women and girls looked on, watching flames hop between wires in a sizzling display of Murphy's Law. I violently pounded the flames with a damp rag, wondering what I had done to make that happen. The car wouldn't start. It was all too obvious that no one wished to be stranded on a dessert isle. We were miles from any other life. Ethel and Catherine began walking down the dusty road in search of someone who knew what he was doing. Ermonie asked if I could fix it, and all I could do was laugh, but I looked at it anyway. I found two wires that had burned completely through, so I twisted them together. The car started. I couldn't believe it. I had done something mechanical.

Heather gave my self-esteem a shot in the arm when she called me a magician and said I was wonderful. Even Ethel was surprised when we pulled up behind her slumping down the road looking for a tow truck. "Gosh, I'm fulfilling my purpose," I thought.

Once more, we were on the road. The beautiful Utah countryside with great rocks and mountains, off in the distance growing from miles and miles of sand, soon made way for Idaho where we continued along 84 and passed on the outskirts of Rupert. At Ethel's urging, we sought out and found Bruneau Dunes State Park, where the wind was so strong we were forced to dine in the car. The wind did subside long enough for Heather, Catherine and me to climb partially up the walking sand of the largest lorn dune. We decided not to camp that night; the women were becoming eager for their destination.

We returned to 84, where we caught sight of the Snake River as the sun went down. I continued driving into Oregon, seeing signs of Lewis and Clark and much darkness. I was there with my family, loving them, wishing for them to be safe and reach their destination.

They felt safe with me, too, and they slept. I drowned my body with coffee and insulted my stomach with caffeine pills, stopping whenever I felt the need for relief or caution. I had no particular fear of driving all night or falling asleep at the wheel; my own history told me I could cope. I wouldn't put them in jeopardy. I loved them. I knew who they were.

In the wee hours of the morning, Ermonie, who had been sleeping across the front seat, awoke to relieve me. She hadn't been out of the hospital for two full days yet. She drove while my mind vanished into oblivion.

Rupert says, "Build your towers from within."

I was shocked by daylight and some feeling of the car slowing down. Ermonie brought us to a stop along the banks of the Columbia River near Arlington, after taking us as far as she could continue with her pain. I was still in no shape to drive and the sun felt warm so I stretched out on the hood wishing the front seat were a double bed, only to be close.

Gaining strength from the sun, I resumed driving to where the John Day River meets the Columbia, where we stopped to freshen up for breakfast. We spent a little time and I took a swim in the River, feeling clean while my family used the public facilities and many campers in the surrounding campsites still slept.

We continued to The Dalles, where we enjoyed buckwheat cakes in a restaurant next to a bowling alley. Then it was on to Portland, where we arrived in the early afternoon. There was a fabulous fabric shop where we played and I skipped on the streets with Jennifer and Star, thinking how special I was. God, it felt so good, so right.

We stopped at a corner store for juice and fresh fruit and I was approached by a man asking for a handout. We were parked in front of a fireplug while Ethel shopped. I was broke. I couldn't give. He began crying and explained he had six children in North Carolina. "Save the children," he said, looking at Jennifer and Star as he walked off. He was crying.

We escaped from Portland as rush hour approached, getting tied up in heavy traffic and urban sprawl for miles. The traffic and neon soon disappeared; I pulled to the side of an old country road where we had our final picnic as a family. With me and my purpose exhausted, I climbed into the rear compartment of the wagon as we set off in search of the camp. The women and girls grew excited and I grew afraid as we neared our destination. It was Wednesday and the camp had been underway since Monday.

We pulled into camp and stopped next to an enormous barn. All were relieved that we had finally made it—everybody but me, penniless and pointless.

* * *

I sit alone but desire to be foaming at the mouth, to have someone find me. I haven't the courage to pull the trigger myself. I would gladly hand them the gun, hoping that they would at least shoot the t which continues to stick. It drives my ambition to drink and drown in its confused state of being. I have more time than I care to admit.

Only pushed to the edge can I pursue my choice of continuing; the edge is so sharp and cuts so deep. I'm sure if I survive there will always be scars. Scars are a sign of survival, I'm told. I enjoy brushing my hair and looking in the mirror, smoking cigars. I want more. I'm afraid of the sacrifice and the sharp edge which can cut so deeply if one is too careful. I'm controlled by my penis, but protected by my mirror, which tells me I'm right for me now. Reflections are confusing but honest. It is what it is.

Sweet Ermonie, I need you. I long to taste your groin again—and again. Yet, I know the truth is in the mirror. I love to brush my hair. My electric penis on its marble base is rigid and the glare hurts my eyes. My last candle flickers as it melts into its next realm of design. There is so much work yet ahead; the edge hangs so close to my jugular, hoping to melt me into my next realm—a design of which I have no control. What it is. The glare hurts my eyes.

Rupert says, "There ain't nothing wrong with jerkin' off, just don't cum in the cornbread."

DAY 10

It's the day before Easter; I sit on my keester. There was a heavy thunderstorm in the middle of the night. Tripod jumped into bed with me; I tried to screw her. She jumped back out and spent the rest of the night cowering in the corner. I was even being gentle. It must be time for another bath. She didn't smell none too sweet neither.

The sun has warmed a bit today. I just got back from sticking my head in the brook at the base of the knoll. Everything is beautiful.

Rupert says, "A dip in the brook is much more refreshing than a dick in the dog."

Such a thing I found here in Santa's cabin. It's an old beveled glass mirror. It's very rough and foggy, even after cleaning. It has a wooden frame, attached to what seems to be a miniature false vanity with two wooden knobbed drawers. It's perfect for my table, directly in front of my typewriter. The glass has several nicks and imperfections.

If I position my head in a certain a way, I can create a hole directly between my eyes—kicky. At the same time, it also gives me the appearance of a severe case of acne. Now I'll *never* quit brushing my hair.

My journey. I mustn't forget my journey. Memories can only last so long in a burnt-out brain, like history can continue for just so long in a burnt-out world. And my teeth are really rotting.

* * *

There we were at Camp Let's Playhouse. Ermonie and the girls were shown to their cabin; Ethel was led through the meadow, down a maze of paths through the woods and into a clearing next to a stream where her teepee was situated. I was led into the volcanic ash-covered forest and shown a spot I could clear to pitch the tent.

The camp accepted 20 campers a week. Including Ethel and Ermonie there were 10 counselors. I got the immediate impression they didn't need 11.

We had been at the camp for two hours when I finally got up my nerve to approach Ethel. "What am I going to do?" I asked.

"You'll figure something out," she said with a smile. "Before you leave, will you please check the wires on the car again?" She strutted to her teepee.

I returned to my section of the ash-infested forest to work out my frustrations on dead trees and the tent while I contemplated my immediate future. It was also a temporary relief from my sense of inadequacy in the presence of children who reminded me so much of my own youth, when I feared I would never complete a sentence without squirming and spitting for as long as I lived. That first week at Camp Let's Playhouse was exclusively for stutterers.

Having pitched the tent, I was invited to spend the night in the company of Ermonie and her children. I was enjoying just being with them and wanted to stay, but at the same time becoming fully aware—within myself—that I just didn't fit into the situation anymore. Above anything else, everyone needed to be comfortable and my own hang-ups were stirring the stew that only needed to simmer. I was bruising the vegetables with my extension.

Waking up, Thursday morning, two weeks before I became God, I remembered: Damien Rumsford was in LA. And Rumsford always has a better idea.

* * *

Rupert says, "Buy American."

* * *

I reached Damien in Beverly Hills where he was staying with his partner, Dominic Rodriguez Sepulvida. Easy Now and ladies' lingerie had been good to Dominic. He was the manufacturer of Easy Now. I explained my circumstances to Damien.

"You get down here and we'll get you home," he said. "Why travel west and not see it?"

I had never been to LA. The idea appealed to me. A former lover also lived in LA. Her name was Carla Smersh until she changed it and became a semi-famous movie star. I'll always know her as Carla Smersh. Such a love we had. Up until Ermonie Hunter, Carla Smersh had been the big love of my life—even more so than the lesbian.

Carla knew me when I was God for the first time—my ultimate moment of inflicting complete destruction of another's material—issuing him passage into the next realm of dimension I created for him at that moment with the extreme of hate (a hollow point) and premeditation because I carried a gun. And he was real close and pissed off because it was His territory. And life and death changed me forever. I really could feel no love for one who was trying to kill me. Does God kill what he loves? They try to tell us he does. Is his fodder food for his ego? Is God pure ego? Is God pure idea?

Rupert says, "God is a function of society and order. They created him for us. We are they."

* * *

I contacted Carla. We hadn't seen each other in years. She invited me to her hideaway in Venice Beach; she also gave me the number of her friend in Mill Valley, thus providing me with a half-way point. I was looking forward to seeing Carla in person again, especially since I had seen her in a few soft-core porn movies. As I recalled, she didn't have to act, not Carla. She really did like the taste of mustard regardless of what it was on.

The only problem was that I had no money. Ermonie agreed to front me $25 from her dwindling funds. Ethel agreed to do likewise, after I performed the obligatory begging and blackmail routine. I told her she'd be stuck with a whimpering Duda if she didn't come across. Jennifer and Star contributed 50 cents each.

My grubstake and destination set, I was told I could stay as long as I liked and needed. My plan was to leave the following Monday, giving me time to mentally prepare myself for my journey. I hadn't hitchhiked in 10 years.

Everyone was quite relieved by my imminent departure, including me, though I was very shaky at the prospect of traveling 1100 miles on 51 bucks. Now I could play and appreciate the immediate environment, knowing (almost) what was and was not expected of me.

The operators of the camp were very much into the environmentalism and conservation and recycling. There were containers for aluminum and paper, miscellaneous garbage and compost, and even a separate place for chicken bones and plastic. I didn't know I wasn't supposed to pick even a handful of wildflowers.

There were thousands and thousands of wildflowers decorating the meadow at the base of the hill from the barn. If I didn't have them in my hand, no one would have missed them. I was off walking with the girls and picked some flowers for Ermonie. I was scolded like a child. I recognized no endangered species. Environmentalist shit, do your homework, damn it; I clear cut no mountain. If you want to take a shot, use real ammunition, because some shoot back, even if your targets are illusions.

Rupert says, "My eyes may deceive me, but the belly doesn't lie."

* * *

There was a picnic by the lake on Thursday afternoon. The campers stuttered and stammered and laughed; there was no pressure to do otherwise. There was fishing and swimming and canoeing. There was even a competition between groups for the best theatrical skit. I was ferociously intimidated, watching those imperfect little monsters in their various stages of redundant maunder, in an environment that gave them the opportunity to be so without fear of being labeled as freaks. They knew they were different, but no less. Above all, there was no pity. The frenetic but sanguine Ethel, who was in her glory, saw to that. I couldn't bear my reflection in the children, so I helped Ermonie cook chicken dogs and prepare salad and slice watermelon. A good time was had by all, including Jennifer and Star and Heather and Catherine, who joined in everything, not the least bit self-conscious, for all that they were latecomers and a bit different from the rest.

Once more, on Thursday evening, my pleasure was the company of Ermonie and her children and a bedtime story. I bunked with Star, but it was fine; my love was beyond a pure sexual experience. Could I be in love with Ermonie and not be in love with her daughters? I didn't fully understand any of it then and I still don't, all of those different kinds of love, but I felt that the feelings were pure and honest. And yet, I was still the outsider. Ermonie had her duties in arts and crafts and Ethel was busy communicating with everyone.

Friday morning, my mounting inner pressure was apparent to everyone. The parents of the first week's campers came for them in the afternoon. Wishing to rescue Ermonie from me, Ethel invited me out for a farewell dinner.

We drove back to the neon, where I dropped her to shop while I attempted to purge the wagon of the lingering omen of the orange water which had become as much a part of it as the polished smell is to a new car. I washed it inside and out—no soap.

Ethel treated to fish-and-chips and purchased a bottle of cream sherry to take back to the camp. On our return, she even invited me to spend the night with her in the teepee. I guess one of the biggest fascinations I have had with mine and Ethel's relationship is our mutual suspicion of one another. But there was still no getting away from the love that always seemed to seep through any thoughts of ulterior motive.

We walked through the meadow, down a maze of paths, through the woods and into a clearing next to a stream, where the teepee lay waiting in the twilight of the evening. I gathered wood for a fire; the night air chilled, moistening the skin of the teepee like a bottle of champagne in a bucket of ice. The sky became speckled with even more stars than I had witnessed from Ermonie's Valley.

The teepee glowed like an inverted ice cream cone filled with fluorescent banana ice cream. The rest of the world had disappeared. We rolled back the smoke flaps of the teepee and the banana ice cream shot for the sky.

Ethel changed from her long flowering dress to a long flowery nightgown and came leisurely to rest on the comfortable mat floor of the teepee. The bed consisted of several thick quilts and Afghans over softened earth and straw and mulch. We sipped sherry while I attempted to spark a fire in the pit at the foot of the bed.

Sparks from the kindling became stars as they reached for the opening above, which soon disappeared behind the smoke. We sipped more sherry. The smoke crowded in the teepee, slowing any movement to a crawl and then stillness. The cloud hovered just above our noses as we lay motionless, speaking of apples. Ethel looked beautiful lying there—next to me.

* * *

It's something magical when a tree begins to blossom. It's like remembering something very painful, and then realizing you have lived through it and are free to continue. Every tree has a different blossom when the time comes; there are always some that don't survive the winter.

Many trees surround my knoll. There is one that stands out from the rest. It's arched like a colorless rainbow reaching back to the earth from which it came. It has no fewer buds than the others. It seems to be remembering where it came from, yet it continues to grow. It stands out from the rest.

The moon is full tonight. I'm smoking like a fiend. My lips are numb, my teeth are black and my ashtray is overflowing. I believe I've begun my fast.

* * *

The bill-capped man in the fish-packing house suggested I walk from boat to boat if I wanted to fish for salmon. "Somebody might need a last-minute puller; the silver season starts tomorrow," he said.

I didn't know what the fuck he was talking about, but I didn't want him to know I was a rookie, so I didn't ask. I figured if I went from boat to boat, I'd find out soon enough.

I sauntered lazily carrying my burden past the cluster of one-story wooden buildings. Along the main street at the top of the basin, past a recently built restaurant that sold pizzas and sandwiches and beer, I walked around to a peninsula parking lot with rows of boats docked on either side; they played to their silent music in the wind. I chose the west side—the side closest to the ocean—first.

The afternoon sun was burning my brow as my flip-flops echoed in my brain. I walked down stairs leading from the peninsula to a pier where many large fiberglass boats were docked. The first boat I came to contained three men, leisurely sitting, sipping cold beer. One was tying knots. They watched me as I approached.

"Y'all wouldn't know of anyone needin' an extra hand, would ya?" I asked.

"No."

"Oh, thank you."

I decided I had better work on my approach. I left my bag and typewriter on the end of the dock and continued on down the pier. I spotted two men speaking across the gap between two docked boats. I walked between them. They noticed me and ceased their conversation.

"Good afternoon. I'm Sullivan Duda from Baltimore. I'm lookin' for work on board a boat. I was told the best way to go about it is to go from boat to boat and ask. That's what I'm doing."

"That's the best way. I don't know of anyone lookin' for a puller right off hand."

"What's a puller?"

"He's the one who pulls in the fish and tends the lines. What kind of work are you lookin' for?"

"That sounds good. I don't have any experience; I'm willing to work cheap."

A man with a silver perm working on the next boat overheard us. "Where did you say you were from?" he called out.

"Oh, ah, I'm," I hesitated, "I'm from Baltimore."

"Back east, huh? I'm originally from Altoona, Pennsylvania."

"Well son of a gun. It's a small world."

I thanked the gentleman I had been speaking with for telling me what a puller was and walked around to where the silver permed friend's boat was tied. His beautiful fiberglass boat, a fifty footer, was called *Do It Again*. He was called Brad. Brad had been busy attempting to attach two 500-gallon tanks to the rear deck to make a 1500 gallon fuel capacity for longer trips. His 17-year-old son was sleeping below. He saw me as a possible helper. I saw him as a contact.

"Have you ever been fishing before?"

"Yeah, pleasure fishing on charter boats back in the Chesapeake Bay. It's always been a dream or nightmare maybe to fish commercial. I was told to come to Winchester Bay by a man who ran the chicken stand at the Country Fair near Elmira."

He seemed to be struggling with the tanks, so I volunteered to assist. I retrieved my gear and was soon aboard the *Do It Again*. The boat was equipped with all the modern conveniences, including a refrigerator, radar, an electric range and a television set.

We worked on the tanks and in between sipped on cold cans of beer; I explained I was in the process of learning and seeking a life's work of writing. I told him I was always open to new and exciting experiences; commercial fishing was included in that category. I wasn't looking for fistfuls of money. I just wanted to do it and be part of it. If I could pick up a few bucks along the way, all the better and If I found myself in such a position again, I'd know what a puller was.

Brad was on a three-week vacation, with his son, from a factory job in Portland. He was divorced; he looked at my earrings curiously. He said his older son would be joining them in a few days' time, so he didn't need an extra hand. I worked extra hard in moving the tanks into position, thinking a show of physical strength might compensate (along the grapevine) for my lack of experience in my quest for a boat in the small fishing port. I hurt my back, but covered it with a smile.

* * *

Rupert says,

See you on the next reel

Me too on the next reel.

The movies we all live are ever changing.

The feelings we all give keep rearranging.

But still it's all a show as we come and go

Yet we all look the same until we speak our name

Connections are all real, no need to pursue them.

You're as anxious as you feel,

If you misconstrue them. And yet the records show,

We don't know when to let it go

We grasp at things and hold too tight

And learn a little slow.

See you on the next reel.

Me too on the next reel.

Rupert likes to rhyme.

DAY 11

Ah, sweet preparation. It's Easter Sunday, my 11th day in Santa's cabin. I've been invited to have Easter lunch with the Beggses, the good Christian people up the road.

I've just had the most wonderful stand-up bath on this overcast and very chilly morning. First, I hauled several pots of water and started them heating on the electric stove. Then I ran back to the brook with the aluminum wash basin and filled it half way. The teapot started screaming; the other pots of various sizes began cooking at various temperatures because of bulk. I just had the most wonderful stand-up bath on this cold Sunday morning. Rupert says, "Whatever gets you through the morning. There is no one way."

Rupert says,

I get high on Sunday morning there ain't nothin' else
To do. I get high on Sunday morning
But I think I'd rather screw.

Rupert likes to rhyme.

* * *

Besides apples, Ethel and I spoke of many things while sipping sherry in the smoke-filled teepee. She thanked me for flying out to Vernal and (finally) admitted that it was good that I was there. She informed me I should back away from Ermonie, who had enough off-the-wall men in her life already. There was Oscar, her husband, who kept trying to control her through fear tactics and strangulation. And Andrew, the marine, who kept passing through and with whom Ermonie was truly in love—she said—but he was still very young and had yet to find himself in a world that's victimized him since childhood. Ethel put it to me straight.

"Sullivan," she said, "look at your life—running bars, women and drugs. You even kill people."

I didn't understand what she meant by running women. I had run after them and from them. I didn't see myself as a pimp.

"But I love her more than anything and I know she loves me."

"You're the bodyguard," she said.

"It's much more than that. I *was* the bodyguard. Things change, don't they?" I said.

"Oh, yeah, that's all Ermonie needs—another Perpetual Peter Pan who doesn't know anything about living in the real world."

"What do you mean? My life has been as real as anyone's and maybe more so than many; I've had a good exciting life. I'm ready to continue. I'm in love with Ermonie and Jennifer and Star and Heather and Catherine. I'm prepared to do whatever is necessary for a chance of making a life with them. I know I can rise to any occasion."

"Do you know how many people you just mentioned? Sullivan, you were going to shoot her husband and their father. Is that part of whatever's necessary? Would you shoot Andrew, too?"

"I don't know. If he went off like I think he's capable of doing—if he finds himself losing the control he has over Ermonie—like Oscar did—if it was a life or death situation concerning the lives of people I love—it wouldn't be their death if there was anything I could do about it."

"You are still the bodyguard. You set yourself up as a judge."

"So do you."

"Andrew says he loves her, and she's very much in love with him, and it's none of your business anymore. He's just a little mixed up; it's out of your hands. Sullivan, I think it's time for you to go."

"Maybe it is. Can I still wait until Monday?"

Ethel turned very soft. The fire flickered in her eyes like a young woman trying to understand an unborn child. "Of course you can wait until Monday. You know, it really was good of you to come out when you did."

"Damn it, Ethel, enough of this talk. We all have a long way to go. My journey lies before me and your camp lies before you."

"Sullivan, you're beginning to act strange."

"Ethel, my dear, I'm overcome by the sherry and the campfire and the power of the teepee and you. I'm incredibly young dumb and horny and getting old—I'm almost 31. I intend to marry Ermonie; I know the love I feel is more powerful and meaningful than words could begin to describe. It's beyond explanation. I know I'm ready to change my life and focus it on a family. But it's a crazy world and 1100 miles is a long way. I feel I must be open to the adventure of it. This journey may be my last chance to fulfill some boyish fantasies."

"What are you getting at, Sullivan? Do you want to do IT, now?"

"The thought has crossed my mind, my dear sweet Ethel. But, no, we can't. I've just proclaimed my love for Ermonie, and I see a future with her. This wouldn't be the right time for us."

"Well, then, what?"

"What's the best way to go about giving a blow job?" Though Jane Fonda was the best, as she'd told me herself, I felt I needed another perspective in an instructional sense. I had no intentions of becoming a professional. I wasn't sure what my intentions were. A bomb had dropped on me and I was covering up.

"You're serious, aren't you?"

She seemed game. "I think so, it may be the sherry."

Frank Sinatra stood outside the teepee singing "Strangers in the Night." The smoke cleared and the fire crackled and the bottle of sherry was drained. First with her tongue, and then with her entire mouth, Ethel became intensely involved while demonstrating her technique on the empty wine bottle. We laughed it all off, as the fire slowly died and the air became chilled; we warmed each other with a mutual embrace as we drifted off into a deep conjugal sleep.

Rupert says, "Process is our most important product."

* * *

It's really strange. I haven't felt the urge to commit suicide for a couple of days now. It feels like something's missing: the initiative seems different. When I added the false vanity with the foggy mirror, I also added a few knick-knacks.

There's a corncob pipe and a button, rose-colored. A figure of a llama sits on top of a little handmade, orange green and black clay pot. The pot looks like my shit bucket with lips in miniature. That's it. The llama looks like he's taking a shit. I can tell by his facial expression that he doesn't have hemorrhoids.

On my miniature false vanity there are also a little coke mirror and a razor blade in case I decide to slash my wrist. There's a small blue and yellow clay pot containing roaches. Finally, standing on half a Hershey bar, leaning against the foggy mirror, is the figure of a tiny mermaid playing the ukulele. She reminds me of Ramona Pearl. Ramona, my tour guide in San Francisco—the wonderful lady with the downy blonde mustache and sideburns. What a wonderful trip we had. I must be careful. Too many cooks at once spoil the stew.

Rupert says, "Well then, take a break, before you overcook the coffee."

It's almost time for lunch at the Beggses; they have some beautiful wood. They promised I would be the only guest. I assured Clyde I'm confused enough with all these different people making noise in my head. They're all talking at once. The mirror on the vanity is so foggy; the one on the table next to me is pretty clear though. The hollow point won't get back in the box and the electric penis glares in my eyes. I must replace the bulb in my high intensity lamp.

It's Easter. I don't even have an egg; I do have my two hand painted clay pots. Eureka! I have an Easter Egg. Now Easter seems like so much more, clay on clay make more. Now I remember God. The llama has no place to shit.

Rupert says, "Whatever it takes, to get you through the night."

* * *

Baked country ham, lima beans, corn, mashed potatoes, homemade bread, fresh butter, homemade strawberry jam, hot brown gravy, deviled eggs, celery sticks, peaches and whipped cream and homemade zucchini bread washed down with fresh cold spring water. Tripod got the ham bone. Fuck the fast and pass the mashed potatoes. I ain't even Irish.

Easter lunch with Clyde and Betty Beggs has resurrected my hope for the continuation of the human race. I was beginning to believe my only life was on paper in a one-dimensional world of cartoon characters and magnified memories drawn in a state of distorted bliss.

"Easy now," Betty said as we sat around the kitchen table, exchanging thoughts from different worlds, enjoying and sharing a simple home-cooked country meal.

Rupert says, "Now is the moment you may remember forever. It is always now. Visions are before us."

* * *

Here I am, back in the woods alone. There are no visions, only reflections and other worlds which are very real, passed into other dimensions, exposing themselves occasionally to feed the mind and nourish or reprimand the soul. Everything is so far away.

* * *

Early Saturday morning there was a salvo of howitzers. No one heard it but me. My eyes exploded open like a flash cube staying lit.

"I'm leaving today," I heard, still on my back, hearing through my ears.

I was in a dark funnel being sucked up towards the blueness of the sky. I felt the presence of someone lying next to me. It was Ethel. She was sleeping. She hadn't said anything. It occurred to me I was in a teepee and the smoke flaps were rolled back. I repeated the words, "I'm leaving today." I recognized the voice. I felt a tremendous surge of power as if Ethel had died and her being had detoured into my left ear with all the savoir faire of an egg being thrown against a car on Halloween.

I nudged her; she growled. She was alive. The air was chilled and Ethel had swiped all the covers. A few charred pieces of cold wood slumped in the pit at our feet. I sat up and listened hard for those words once again. "It's time to go," I said. Surrounded in a circle with a patch of blue above, I knew I must take it all with me, yet leave it all behind.

I crawled from the teepee without further announcement, taking my dark circle with me before I changed my mind. I fervidly found my way through the woods and up the maze of paths and through the meadow, past the barn and to Ermonie's cabin. Looking peaceful in a pink satin gown, she was busy preparing breakfast for her children.

"Good morning, Sullivan, would you care for some breakfast?" She spoke softly with eggs crackling over hot butter. Willis Alan Ramsey sang "Angel Eyes" from the inside of a radio positioned behind a pitcher of cream. Jennifer and Star were having a pillow fight in the loft of the cabin—they laughed and shouted. Heather and Catherine were playing gin. I froze in my tracks—stranded in the open doorway.

I wished to be tied by the long braid of black hair that ran down her back—it touched my heart. I couldn't think of food, but only the blush in her cheeks—her lovemaking blush. I desired never to move again, but only to watch her stand there—turning an egg—breaking the yolk—with a golden stain splattered above her left breast, with one droplet, like a tear. I was mesmerized by her beauty with shared moments braiding my thoughts. I wanted more and sucked everything I could from each precious second I could still grasp—being there. Suddenly, it hit me, like a renegade pillow—reminding me of a journey that must be taken, for a book that must be written.

"I'm leaving today," I said as gently as I could. I wanted to hear, "Please don't go."

"Oh," she said. "I thought you weren't leaving until Monday."

"I know, but something is telling me it's time."

"Did something happen last night with Ethel?"

"I had a wonderful evening. Everything is fine," I said. "It's something I know I have to do; I'm as ready as I'll ever be." I said. "I'm pushed and pulled at the same time, away. You seem to be recovering well."

"Hmmm," she said. "Oh, Sullivan, I've been acting terribly lately. I'm feeling something from you, but you know I'm in love with Andrew—you've always known that. I want to apologize, and to thank you for coming when we needed you."

"You almost died. I'm your friend, first and foremost. Never ever forget that."

I showered and gathered my belongings I learned of a ride from the camp with a woman and her children heading south to Eugene. I traded my suitcase for a duffel bag and packed with time to spare before my departure. I risked the revenge of nature and the wrath of nature lovers by stealing a bouquet of flowers from the meadow while walking with Jennifer and Star. I presented them to Ermonie and she pressed a note in my hand when it was time to leave. I saw Ethel. She asked me if I was leaving so soon because of something she said.

Goodbyes are such a trauma.

I dressed for the road in my tweed slouch cap and 89 cent flip-flops. My jeans were clean, my shirt had four pockets and I wrapped a red bandanna around my neck. I left with a woman and her two children; one cried and the other stuttered. When the camp and Ermonie were no longer in sight, I read the note.

"Sullivan,

> "You live in myth. You drink the wine
> You eat everything. I am peaches.
> You are cream. I am drawn to you.
> Together we have desert and cover the table.
> You are the apple. I am the sauce.
> It is hard to forget you. When I think of you I burp
> Being close to you, I must sniff you.
> You are a piece of fruit. I am a piece of cake."
> Ermonie."

The words became embedded in my brain and heart and gut, and made me hungry. I wanted my cake, and to eat it too. I ate the note, moistening it with my own tears.

* * *

Now there is no Ermonie. I feel empty. My reflections give me strength, especially when I brush my hair. With two mirrors at different angles the glare of the phallic light bulb is much more intense and blinding, without focus.

Rupert says, "Communication is a very important part of life."

The confusion, the constant confusion, lies in my sitting here, torn, with violin music playing in the background. Maybe I should turn off the radio and eat something.

My knoll seems peaceful today. A fire smolders against my rock. I've gathered up five bags of old cans and bottles that were littered about. There is no end to the litter in my mind. Luckily only a portion finds my fingers, or I would really be exhausted. It's beginning to rain.

* * *

And so my journey began, the second Saturday in July, from Cherry Grove, Oregon to LA. Lalalala lalala. I didn't have my gun.

This time I had come out to help—not defend. I decided during the ride to Eugene to head in the direction of the coast, to go fishing.

The woman and her two children dropped me on a corner without a name in Eugene. Lost in a maze of traffic and construction sites, I sought out a gas station, where I purchased a road map for a dollar and used the facilities for a dime. The gas-station attendant pointed me in the direction of 11th Street, which would take me out of town to Route 126 headed for the coast.

I walked along the edge of the downtown section, carrying my bag and typewriter, ignoring the sights, with all of the attention focused on my self-pity. I stopped a moment to switch shoulders with my bag.

A plainclothes police officer approached me. He appeared to be about 16 years old.

"Are you headed for the Country Fair?" he asked.

"I'm on my way to LALA land, but I think I'm going fishing first."

"I need a favor," he said.

"Sure."

"If I give you the money and an extra $5, would you pick me up a fifth of Jack Daniels? The store's right there," he said, pointing.

I was barraged by feelings of insecurity and a set-up.

"I think not. I'm a stranger here with no place to go, and I really can't take the chance," I said.

"If you need a place to crash, I live in a group house near the college. You're welcome to stay."

"I want to make it to the coast before dark. Thanks anyway. I wish you luck with the booze. I just can't do it."

"No problem. Easy now."

Rupert says, "Sometimes man is willing to pay any price to satisfy his needs; sometimes his priorities are confused. It's a matter of priorities and a question of balance."

I continued walking in the direction of 11th Street. Once I arrived, I took my position on the corner in front of the Catholic

Church. There I stood, with traffic passing and sweat pouring down from under my cap and arms. With my thumb sticking out, I felt I presented a colorful image to be reckoned with—though no one seemed to look. Negative thoughts crept into my brain—of being stranded forever—on that corner—with my thumb sticking out. I had yet to learn the importance of patience and waiting for the right ride, which always comes along.

Rupert says, "Waiting for the right ride is a very important part of life."

I cursed the passing traffic silently behind my constant smile, and tipped my hat to all the ladies. Occasionally someone would look in my direction and hold his hand up with the thumb and forefinger shaped to form a horizontal U. I didn't get it, but thought they were being obscene. At least it was a reaction.

Time passes slowly waiting for a ride, especially when you carry a self-inflicted attitude. A tricolor jeep—orange-green and black—with a roll-bar passed. It was driven by a shirtless man wearing jogging shorts and a thin sinister black beard. He looked at me. I smiled and tipped my hat. He held up his hand in the sign of the horizontal U and continued on. A few moments passed and he appeared once again, coming from around the block. He looked like Bluto from the Popeye cartoons.

"I ain't going far, but you'll never get a ride here," he said as he came to a stop and offered me a ride. "You going to the Country Fair?"

"I'm headed for the coast and then to LA. Lalalala lalala," I said. "What's the country fair?"

"It's the summer's big event," he said. "Everyone in Eugene is there. If you have the time you shouldn't miss it."

"I haven't got a lot of cash. It's a long trip to LA. I'm hoping to find work on board a fishing boat. If I can't find work, I don't have a lot of time."

"It's a beautiful trip; my jeep and I have taken it many times," he said in an almost boastful tone. "If you're in a hurry, you're doing it wrong. Take your time and be easy now. You'll enjoy yourself."

We drove westward along 11th. A tape of the Beach Boys played loudly over a makeshift stereo system patched in unobtrusive spots of the caricature on wheels.

"Where I leave you, might I suggest, if you have 50 or 60 cents for the bus, catch it. You'll have a much better chance of getting a lift farther out of town."

"Does the jeep have a name?"

"It's the 'Animal,'" he said with a belly laugh. "And you might need exact change."

I was dropped next to a Pizza Hut, where I decided on the bus and found I needed change. A beat-up old pickup was parked in the lot with a half of a pizza still in the box on the hood. A peaceful looking fellow wearing a ragged leather hat leaned against the bed making sounds between nibbles with a guitar.

I entered the restaurant and bought my change. The country troubadour smiled when I passed on my way to the bus stop across the street. I could hear him singing.

> "City lights leapin' and falling through the night
> The back seat of a taxi is the only way to go
> Through the London Snow.
> And the taxi man says,
> Come on take a ride
> See the sparkling diamonds fall outside
> Come on take a ride
> "Westminster Abbey is right outside your window
> Rushing sighs, rainbow rings around your eyes
> Ticking meter keeping time
> So many sights to see
> But you're running out of money
> Come on take a ride
> See the sparkling diamonds fall outside
> Come on take a ride
> "Picadilly Circus is right outside your window
> You've gone as far as you can go

You've only got a quid or so
The taxi man looks in your eyes
Says he can dig your high
And tells you it's for free
What a place to be
Cause the taxi man says
Come on take a ride."

Rupert says, "There's always a price."

My fire still burns, still fueled by the air as the water replenishes the earth. The water continues to fall from the sky. The fire will surely die. A moth is swimming in my coffee, so all is not lost.

Rupert says, "Is there any fire that can continue to burn when there is so much water around? Quench my thirst; don't drown me, for the fire in me is fun."

****

RAINBOWS

DAY 12

And so it is Monday morning, the 12th day of the events leading up to my suicide. I have come here for the easy way out. Yet my conscience will not permit me to come to my conclusion until I come to my conclusion. As long as I have spare change for alcohol and tobacco, I am able to continue. My destination is clear—it is my path that is uncertain.

Rupert says, "There is no easy way."

* * *

A bus headed west soon approached. I carried my burden aboard. The bus driver was humming and had an easy now smile.

"I understand this bus will take me a ways out of town."

"Eventually," he said between hums. "We twist around a bit. If you have the time, we'll get you back out to 11th. It's a nice pleasant ride."

"I have nothing but time," I said, depositing sixty cents.

I immediately headed for the back of the bus. There were many empty seats; the ones that were occupied wore masks. The driver wore glasses but no mask. I returned to the front and sat in the seat directly across from him. I placed my typewriter under my feet and my bag in the empty seat next to me. I noticed the driver had been humming Camptown Races. "Oh du da day," he sang, then stopping, but still driving, he looked over at me with his constant easy now smile.

"I guess you're going to the Country Fair," he said.

"No," I said, "but that's all I've been hearing since I arrived in Eugene."

"No wonder. It's a wonderful gathering of thousands of people."

I was curious about this man in space. I looked around to see if the bus was still there.

"Who are you?" I asked.

"I am Milborne," he said as we turned from 11th and headed south. "Don't be alarmed; this is where we detour. Who are you? You're from the east, aren't you?"

"I'm from the east. I'm Sullivan Duda."

"Oh du da day." He chuckled. "What do you think of Eugene?"

"It seems clean and peaceful. I expected more activity."

"Ah, the fair, you've forgotten already."

"Yes, the fair. I'm headed for LA. Lalalala lalala, or perhaps to the coast to fish. I want to reach the coast before night."

"I thought there was no hurry."

"Oh, that's right. Sometimes I forget."

"You'll pass the fair on your way to the coast. You may change your mind. Beneath your feet, is that a typewriter?"

"Why yes, it is."

"Are you a writer?"

"Yes, I'm unpublished, but I'm a writer. I've been working on my first novel."

"That's good. With all I've seen and heard, one day I may write a book. I live in a cabin with my son, back in the hills. If I should break my leg so I can't hunt or fish or get around, I may write a book."

We turned again and again and drove down clean streets with beautiful manicured lawns. Milborne smiled and waved and tooted his horn at occasional faces.

"Yeah, Eugene is a nice mellow town. I was passing through on my way to Hawaii fifteen years ago. I decided to stay."

One corner we passed was a fenced-in parking lot for recreational vehicles. "That's what this town's all about," he said, "recreation. We get a lot of rain, but it doesn't matter. We also get a lot of rainbows."

"This looks like the end of the line. The road ahead will take you to the coast. Sullivan, easy now," he said.

I gathered my things. I heard him singing as I climbed downward from the bus.

"Row, row, row your boat, gently down the stream. Merrily, merrily, merrily, merrily, life is but a dream."

* * *

Fuck, break a leg, he said. If that's all it takes I'm going to break my leg. I've got to threaten myself with suicide; I still don't know if I'm doing it right. It's got to be right. Rupert says, "There is no one way. How does it feel?"

I'm beginning to wish Rupert would leave me alone and let me die in peace. Et cum spirit tu tuo. Rupert says, "Straighten out your priorities and get down to business." Fuck you, Rupert.

* * *

I crossed from the bus to the side of the road, once more headed west. I began to feel relaxed, that everything would work out fine. I waved to Milborne as he turned the corner in his big bus, headed back to town. He tooted the horn.

I stood on the side of the road at the edge of an old vacant used car lot and waited. Traffic continued on by; I constantly reminded myself—there is no hurry. The intersection where I was standing was in the shape of a T. The traffic signal permitted me to check out each new wave of traffic before it came to me. It also gave them time to check me out, whoever they were. I waited. Time passed. I smiled. Occasionally I was greeted by the sign of the horizontal U.

Finally a green Firebird passed heading west. Someone yelled something from the moving car.

"To the coast!" I answered and waved.

I watched the car continue up the road; the brake lights came on and the car turned around and headed back. The car had two occupants. It pulled into a bank parking lot across from where I was standing. I gathered my load and dodged traffic, running across the street to where they stopped. I kicked off my flip-flops and carried them from the middle of the road. Their noise became confusing at a gallop.

Confident of a ride, but breathing heavily, I approached the green Firebird with its two frizzy-haired occupants.

The driver said with an attitude of "I've got wheels," "You gotta joint?"

"No, man, I'm trying to make it to the coast. I'm clean," I said.

"Good luck, chump," he answered and smiled as they squealed wheels and headed west.

I wished I had my gun.

* * *

I have it with me now.

Rupert says, "Welcome to my knoll, on the outskirts of my nightmare."

What purpose does any of this have? Why am I here? Who the fuck am I?

Rupert says, "I am but a dream, passing through time, enveloped in the splendor of the moment, tasting the grapes as well as the brine."

* * *

I crossed back over to the side headed west and managed to gather a smile as I cursed. Why should I inflict my anger and new-found negative attitude on others when only a Firebird shit on my shoulder, I thought. Like a grief-stricken widow attending the wake, I stood smiling, as if to say, "He was a good man," all the while thinking of what he's done to me by dying. A gray Volkswagen pulled into the driveway of the vacant lot I was in front of. He tooted his horn. "Glory be," I exclaimed, running to the car which was driven by the first black man I'd seen in Eugene.

He checked me out in his mirror and popped open the trunk from the inside. I hustled to the front of the car and stashed my bag. I noticed he had freckles when I hopped in the front seat with my typewriter. We immediately pulled off, headed west.

"What's happenin'?" he said.

"What it is, man. I thought I would never get a ride."

"You going to the Fair?"

"I'm beginning to think I ought to. I've been studying my map. I've been thinking in the line of Coos Bay. I want to see if I can sign on board a fishing boat."

"Do you know someone there?"

"No."

"Have you ever commercial fished before?"

"No. It's something I've always wanted to do."

"If you don't know anyone and you don't have any experience, you'll be better off trying your luck in Winchester Bay. It's a nice friendly fishing village. Who are you?"

"Sullivan Duda, from Baltimore."

"Back east, huh? I'm originally from Maine. I'm from a long line of Portuguese whalers. I'm Filmore."

Filmore seemed to be enjoying himself just cruising along the highway, speaking of fishing and what a nice town Eugene was.

"Is that your axe, man?" he asked, nodding at the black box beneath my feet.

"It's my typewriter."

"That's your axe, man."

"Okay."

"If you're not in any great hurry, you really should check out the Country Fair. It's just a real nice gathering of thousands of people. There's music and food and displays and entertainment and beautiful women thirsting for love."

"It sounds electric."

"It is. Plug in, man. It's a scene worth scripting, and it's possible to get lost there until Monday."

"Yeah, there must be a price."

"I believe it's five or six dollars or something along that line. The price is cheap for what's offered. There are no topless laws in Oregon."

"Sounds like a dream, but right now five or six dollars would put a hell of a dent in my boogie fund."

"There's an outdoor sauna and showers and many more women than men. Life is but a dream."

"I take it that's where you're headed."

"I sure am."

"I could probably get lost until Monday, huh?"

"Without a doubt."

"Maybe I can afford to go. Why not?"

I explained to Filmore how I arrived on the West Coast and my destination of Lala land to send me back east.

"I tell you what," he said. "I've got a booth at the Fair. It's called Fowl Filmore's. I'm selling chicken. I had to run home for supplies. Maybe I can get you in for free."

"Yeah? Just show me the building I have to burn down."

"You don't have to burn any buildings. It's my pleasure."

"Wow."

We drove on towards Elmira and the Country Fair. I wondered what the price might be.

Rupert says, "There's always a price, but it's also a question of balance."

* * *

The injury in my back was no more than a nuisance. I was thoroughly enjoying Brad's company with his head full of silver linguini on board the *Do It Again*.

We soon had the two fuel tanks attached. With the major job completed, Theodore, Brad's 17-year-old son, who had been napping below in an air conditioned cabin, made his first appearance.

Brad was in his early forties and maybe because he was recently divorced gave the appearance of disco fever. Theodore, on the other hand, reminded me of nondescript cheap wood paneling. It's there, it just doesn't do much of anything. I began to think, the DO IT AGAIN may be the boat I was to end up on. It looked as if Brad would need all the help he could get.

We sat for a while, sipping beer. Theodore's eyes felt like a severe case of the hives. He examined my bag and my typewriter and my earrings. Brad had to scold him continuously to leave things alone. I was the stranger, being checked out. My role was simple enough: act natural, be helpful, but not pushy.

"Look, Sullivan, I wish we could take you out with us tomorrow; I do my own pullin'. Theodore runs the boat fairly straight. He hasn't run into anything yet. Besides, I have another son we're to meet up with in a few days up the coast. It would be a little crowded."

"Brad, I understand. Do you know of anyone who may need a hand?"

"You picked a good day. The silver salmon season starts tomorrow if the weather holds. Most of the fishermen already have their pullers. I wouldn't give up though. You may still find a boat."

"Do you have any suggestions?"

"The pub is a good spot to check. It's sort of a meeting place. Or maybe the bait houses."

I was invited to ride with Brad to the end of the peninsula, where one of the bait houses was located. I took along my gear. Brad, Theodore and I squeezed into their overstuffed VW. At the bait house a young looking blonde-haired girl wearing tight shorts and a tee shirt was the only one around. Brad placed an order for two dozen herring; we watched her as she dipped her net in the fish boxes.

"I haven't tasted her yet, but I understand she's real sweet meat, Sullivan," Brad said aside. "She's just a young girl. I know she won't know if anyone needs any help."

We drove to a tackle shop on the mainland. Once inside, Brad introduced me to the woman who ran the shop. "She's a hot number," he said, "you may wanta stop back and check her out later."

We learned the price for silver salmon would be $1.25 a pound. The price was down a dollar from the previous year. I was along for the ride—it didn't matter to me. I wanted to fish and taste the salt air and have the spray in my face. It didn't matter that those whose life it was would be getting a dollar less a pound in a year when prices had only gone up.

We ventured over to the pub, the most recent addition to Winchester Bay on the main street at the top of the basin. I had walked past it earlier in the day on my way to look for a boat.

Rupert says, "Things aren't always where they seem to belong."

We entered a large room with wooden beams and tables. Brad pointed out the bulletin board for me to check for work. There was a bicycle for sale and a babysitting service available. We poured our own coffee at a stainless steel counter and sat at a table in the middle of the room. There were many little groups of men who looked as if fishing was their money more so than simple pleasure. "Your pleasure is my business," echoed throughout the room, separating the tourists from the salt. Brad didn't depend on fishing for his livelihood, but he had been involved enough not to be considered a tourist.

There was a constant hum of shop talk and low-keyed resentment toward prices and new rules and regulations. Brad thanked me for helping with his tanks by buying my lunch of a fish sandwich and fries. Men in rubber boots and billed caps and work shoes and some even in flannel came and went at a steady, easy pace. Brad pointed out the women who were good prospects. Theodore glared at everything.

* * *

I haven't walked to the top of my hill today. I feel like dying. Sometimes the days are so long and the work seems so senseless.

Rupert says, "Nothing makes sense; there's a reason for everything."

Even as I speak of my journey, a journey where love and the natural flow of life overshadowed every ounce of bitterness or negative thought I ever had, I feel like a lost soul, grasping at straws and missing my own point. Far away in desperation and from faraway I write. Everything is so far away, including my work which eludes me. I'm reaching for everything; I barely sense the air I come up with in my sweaty palms. I look in the mirror and who I am confuses me. I wish to run away, far away, but I'm already there. I'm lost without purpose, without point. I can find no humor, yet everything is so funny.

I'm not nearly finished. I'm not even sure what I'm doing. Does every day and every chapter need an ultimatum to continue? If I'm only here to take my own life, or in simple terms, die, why should I continue?

> Rupert says,
> Kick the bucket, watch them run
> Even though they're having fun
> You think I'm crazy, no, I'm just lazy
> I'd rather walk in the noonday sun.

Rupert likes to rhyme.

DAY 13

This is the thirteenth day. I have climbed the steps to the gallows. How unsure I am of things. I race around like a madman consumed, eaten away by indifference, possessed with a need to love. I am driven by an obsession to prove myself, knowing—all things take time. I must clean the cabin. I've never seen an unclean coffin.

> Rupert says,
> Should I ever be so humblet to deny myself
> Moments of godlinessor moments
> That don't really care. And God I can be
> It's what life gives to me as well as the depths
> Of despair. How simple everything is.

Rupert likes to rhyme.

DAY 14

This is the fourteenth day. FUCK IT.

Rupert says,
I like to grab some sun on the beach
Suckin' on a big juicy peach
Watchin' all the girls walkin' by, I'm just a happy guy.
I like to stick my pole in the water
Catchin' fish is something made to order
Cruisin' on a lazy day, sorta like to fade away.
I've got nothin' to do—nothin' to say
Ain't got no money comin' my way.
Guess I'll wake up tomorrow and go look for work
I might get a job as a government clerk.
I'll make all kinds of money; I'll be so fulfilled.
I'll work thirty years and still be unskilled.
I'll get sick pay, vacation, and time left to spare.
I'll sleep on the toilet and learn not to care.
I'll preach and I'll gossip and lie through my nose.
I'll be true to my wife and I'll wear panty hose.
I'll buy me a house and a bureaucratic shield.
I'll misspell some names with the power—I yield.
I'm gonna grab me some sun on a beach
Suckin' on a big juicy peach, watchin'
All the girls walkin' by. I'm just a happy guy.
Rupert likes to rhyme.

DAY 15

I repositioned tons of rat shit in the process of cleaning the cabin. I was also out wallowing in the pond, being entertained—with the help of a $50 repaid debt. I'm delirious with wealth. I was this morning, anyway. I have $5 left. I've replenished my booze.My electric penis has burned out; I thought it would last forever. I've purchased and replaced a high-intensity bulb in my lamp. I've also acquired a decorative bulb for the marble-based lamp that kept my

penis erect. It's all very electric. Lighting is very important in suicide. Alas, if I am to shoot myself, it must be tonight—I think I found a buyer for my gun.

> Rupert says,
> Insanity is such a silly game to me
> If I weren't crazy don't know who I'd get to be
> I'm hung up on such foolishness as making me a buck,
> But I ain't made a penny since my mind it ran amok.

Rupert likes to rhyme.

But I ain't got the time to go messing with his silly ass any more. I wish he'd leave me alone. You don't know what it's like, his silly ass rhymes. It's worse than hearing chimes. What I need is a $20 whore. My fucking t, this damned journey, my vision's all distorted. My windshield needs a wipe. I'll let it go and watch the show and just sit here and gripe. See—see what I mean? He won't leave me alone. There's nothing more obscene than a burnt-out, penis-shaped light bulb.

* * *

There was an ocean of parked autos when we finally left Route 126, pulled by a flow of traffic. We wove our way down dusty roads, past people holding unlit flashlights. Filmore was sure of where we were headed; each time someone tried to direct him, he waved and smiled and continued his course. The mellow black man with freckles piloted the VW as if it were a magic carpet through hordes of people with Easy Now smiles. Nothing mattered but the weather. It was sunny and hot. There were no expectations. There was no guilt. More than anything else, there were no rhymes. Absolution was in the air. Come as you are—we don't care.

We came to a stop near the people entrance where no cars were allowed any further. I unloaded my bag and axe while Filmore unloaded his supplies. We were immediately approached by Regina. She was thin and unassuming in her manner. She came pushing a shopping cart over uneven terrain. She wore a white toga and a wreath of orchids on her head.

* * *

What a need there is to confess. First to one, and then to another and another. Now to anyone who has a moment. Smile at me and I'll confess to you. Wave at me and I'll bare my soul. It comes from the "I." "We're all in this together. We may as well make the best of it." Especially the burden of it all. Cop out.

How far can I run? I don't wish to die by my own hand. I want someone to do it for me. Then I can haunt them, and I will. Et cum spirit tu tuo.

* * *

We sat in the Pub sipping coffee, feeling the enthusiasm for the opening day of silver salmon season.

"It don't start till tomorrow."

"Yeah? The commission pushed it back two weeks already. I'll be surprised if it starts tomorrow."

"At a buck and a quarter a pound, I don't know if it matters."

"I blame it on the new fish hatcheries up the coast, the ones that Weyerhaeuser opened. I thought they grew trees."

"Maybe the other guy does make toilets."

"Huh?"

"Yeah."

"They're tryin' to put the little guy out of business, that's what."

The sounds of anticipation with the excitement of the hunt filled the room. Brad introduced me around as the writer from Baltimore.

"He doesn't want a lot of money," Brad said. "He wants to taste the Pacific salt and get windburn to turn on the women. He thrives from experience."

"So you're a writer," said one fisherman. "We get a lot of them around here. I had one writer ask me 10 different ways the same question, he did. Tryin' to get me to say I'd lose my ass and my boat if we had another season like last year. Fuckin' writers."

"Sounds like a journalist," I said.

"He was still a fuckin' writer."

"I read a beautiful article about the Oregon coast in the National Geographic. I just wanted to see it firsthand."

"I read that same article. He didn't talk to us, the ordinary men. He picked people who were different," said the fisherman.

DAY 16

I've been contaminated. This is my 16th day in the woods. I've been living in peaceful coexistence with suicide: Happy—to brush my hair and look in the mirror, to stick the gun in my mouth and pull the trigger. I've been overjoyed with my words and walks to the top of my hill with Tripod. What kind of a world is this, where a man can't die in peace? I worked today. I earned $25 auditioning for the role of a grunt—waxing fiberglass boats for a marina on Deep Creek Lake—Maryland's "Best Kept Secret." I also sold my gun for $100.

What am I living for? I love guilt. I was raised a Catholic. How can I feel guilty if I can't look my own murder weapon in the muzzle. Besides my one act of violence, I've been good. So I've sold a few drugs—but only to those who wanted them and needed them to cope in a peaceful coexistence with grunting. Easy Now is more than a drug. It shows the way. This is a society of preachers. Easy Now doesn't preach—it smiles. My lungs are black from cigarettes; they rot my teeth and give me bad breath and make my clothes smell.

If I didn't kill myself, I was preparing to be a Trappist monk. Now, I have a job. How can I be an idealistic suicidal maniac if I'm distracted by grunting? How can I live in the past if I'm too busy in the present? I know what I need. I need to be reminded of the vile act I committed, and how indifferent I felt. But this is the story of my journey, and it's all related.

* * *

I waited with Regina holding onto the shopping cart, keeping in touch with reality, while Filmore parked the car. Regina had long wavy blonde hair, highlighted by the wreath of lavender orchids. Tiny erect breasts showed through her thin white toga which was wrapped at the waist with a rainbow of twine. She wore no shoes; the gravel she was standing upon didn't seem to affect her.

"Welcome to the Country Fair," she oozed. Her skin was creamy, and her occasional words poured softness into the air. She was fit to be a human sacrifice.

Filmore returned; the shopping cart was stacked with his supplies. My bag was balanced on the top. Regina led the way with Filmore pushing, and me walking alongside the cart, holding my bag on the top in its unstable position, carrying my axe. We made our way through the gate uninterrupted. The crowds parted like a zipper on a pair of tight Levi's. I was too preoccupied with my bag and the cart, Regina and the crowds, to visually notice much more. I was overcome by the feeling of Easy Now.

We arrived at Fowl Filmore's. His stand was positioned where circles joined. The promenade of the Country Fair was a figure 8, I was told. The cart was unloaded. Filmore approached me with the tender breast of a barbecued chicken in his hand. I accepted the gift. I ate and I drank.

I finished my feast and approached Filmore. He was busy working behind the stand, cooking chicken. There were several helpers. Everyone was keeping busy in a mellow sort of way.

"Filmore," I said, "thank you. What can I do? May I cook some chicken or build something or carry trash? What can I do to earn?"

"Enjoy yourself," he said, with his greasy hand on my shoulder.

I didn't mind. I was approached by Regina. She seemed to be walking on air. "May I show you around," she said with a smile. Braces on her teeth cautioned my sexual inclination—while on the other hand, I was lured by her simpleness and fascinated by the naked body exposing itself through gauze. I allowed myself to be led—by curiosity.

The booths and many stands seemed to grow from the ground as if from seeds. Mellow rock and roll was performed on a stage with the layout of the fair permitting volume, while each change of scene still maintained its own sound without being drowned out by the last or the next. Wandering minstrels swayed on their own time. There were teepees and a pyramid meditation hut and international foods, tofu and tempe and yogurt.

We watched a mime troupe perform miracles and walked past displays of organic gardening and cosmic disassociation. I was overcome by a euphoric state of attitude, atmosphere and mood. I felt myself glowing, as if I had been injected with fluorescent banana ice cream, melting towards the sky. The sight of the vestal virgin, whom I was being led by, kept my feet on the ground and my mind in the gutter. We circled and circled—the figure 8—and arrived back at Fowl Filmore's. Regina seemed fascinated by the fact that I traveled with my typewriter so I gave her a short story I had written and walked off in search of a cup of coffee.

FOR AMUSEMENT ONLY

The room is empty, except for the body lying comfortably in the corner, in a pool of its life's blood, and except for the witnesses, whose form the body has taken. Now, the former person is lifeless, more so than the refrigerator with its motor running, fulfilling its purpose, keeping cold things necessary for life, such as food and kosher pickles and beer and wine, the blood of the grape. The body is losing all of its blood to the tiled floor and to the molding, against the base of the nondescript paneled wall, and the foot of the bar, and later to an old rag mop and rusty bucket, and finally to a storm drain, or, more than likely, a toilet flushed into a sewer, diluted, losing all identity. The outer shell of the body has been pierced. It has no more use besides research or compost. Its ghost has departed.

A witness, the pinball machine, provides pleasure. The swinging door hit him in the rump when he stumbled through it at its entrance, keeping a journal. Looking in and out and in and out and in. The body will only provide grief. The machine has been pierced and will still make noise and flash lights. The body is dead. Only the living machines make noise and flash lights—some too much, some not enough.

The room, with its barred windows, seems a typical back room, drab and confused. Otherwise, it would probably be more than a back room with a bar and swinging doors of the type that would hit a Keystone Kop in in the rump--Seeing all, revealing little, only to keep company with some pinball games, for amusement only, the kind with flippers and bikini-clad women hiding in the open, and a refrigerator humming and an ice machine spitting ice.

The bar top is black and sticky and littered and abused and as high as Elmer's navel before he became grief. Elmer, poor Elmer—he was a big man in structure. He made too much noise, and now the lights of the pinball machine flash at his feet and the voice of the refrigerator hums at his head, and he couldn't reach the top of the bar if he tried.

There is a front room, the main room--Loud and confused. Where no less than a dozen witnesses with ghosts intact, flashed and made noise, showing how much they care by dwindling to three. A tragedy has happened— the wake is moving.

Gabe sits at the bar in the front room which seems distorted as the parade of picture takers and ambulance drivers and technicians and Keystone Kops and detectives and finally the medical examiner file by, using, but ignoring, the wooden swinging doors that look in and out and in and out and in. The back room is confused, but no longer drab—it is honored by death. The army of light-flashing, noise-making, self-important picture takers and answer seekers take pictures and seek answers from the pinball machine and the refrigerator and the ice machine and the bar top and the blood-soaked knife at the head of the grief and the foot of the refrigerator and the gun, smiling with afterglow, resting on the bar top.

Distortion is a judgmental opinion and a movie is a blur while it's being made and no one knows how it will turn out until the reviews are in. Reviews are merely opinions.

Gabe was the producer. He owned the set. Now he sits like a back room—acting—drab and confused. He's very much a part of the movie. (You see) he just killed Elmer, shot him--Blew his mind out with a hollow point.

The inevitable happens; there are no more questions to ask or pictures left to take of the refrigerator and the pinball machine and the ice machine. It's a shame all they could do was hum, flash and spit. That's certainly more than Gabe intends to do, at least until the director arrives.

Besides, an army of distortion has conducted interviews and taken pictures. Gabe has his role, and everyone else plays their own role, doing their job.

There is no grief; that would come later—with the wake. After all, a man has died, and very violently at that. The strange feeling of no soundtrack or newscasters to highlight etchings in the fog gives life to the machines. And the swinging doors are only pushed through, out and then in and out and in and out--things.

The grief—no—the piece of meat covered neatly with white deli paper is moved from the loud and confused back room, through the ignored but much used swinging doors as an item in a journal—to become—grief in the morning as it is prepped and dressed and boxed and put on display.

Finally, enter the lawyer, that high-priced director responsible for the rest of the movie—editing and adding and directing—except for the grief.

And grief there is, for a while anyway—tears and threats. But time always passes. And Gabe gets a glass and fills it with ice and then with wine while he waits for his turn on the machine.

* * *

But then. . .

"Coffee with cream and honey," I said. I was standing at a booth on the outer edge of one of the circles. The centrifugal force of my ego had pushed me there while Regina, my little groupie, was being amused. It was also necessary to feed my coffee addiction. I felt a headache coming on.

"Decaf or regular?" the girl behind the counter asked.

"I've been conditioned. I need the caffeine."

She prepared my coffee and accepted my quarter; I lingered for a moment. I could make out the stage from where I stood. I thought I saw and heard John Lennon singing Imagine. I began to wonder what I would be doing for the evening. I didn't wish to impose on Fowl Filmore more than I felt I already had. I expected Regina to disappear after she read the story. She was a sweetheart, but jailbait just the same. I looked around at all the smiling faces and suddenly it didn't matter what I would be doing.

I sipped my coffee and relaxed.

"Coffee black, please," I heard from a voice with an accent a few feet away.

DAY 17

LALALALA LALALA!

DAY 18

LALALALA LALALA!

DAY 19

This is my 19th day at the home. I was given my freedom for the weekend. I haven't written a word in two days. I've been wallowing in the pond. Hey—I needed a break.

I had the opportunity to speak with the man who tried to convict me of murder so long ago. I mentioned I was writing a book on handgun control. He said that would be very wrong in this day and age. "If you didn't own a gun, you'd be dead now," he said.

I mentioned how I was in favor of rehabilitation by capital punishment. "Some people shouldn't be allowed on the streets," I said. That's how I justified the execution I carried out. The victim was a menace and only understood a hollow point. "Peace, Brother" doesn't always work.

Rupert says, "The illusion of justification is a necessary tool for survival."

I went to the man myself to remind myself of my guilt. He had lost his case and it was over as far as he was concerned. I told him I had finally sold my gun. He said I shouldn't have done that, and attempted to convince me I should have another gun to protect myself against the lawless.

Rupert believes in capital punishment. He says they should have hung me. Then he laughs. Rupert says, "The only second chance anyone should get is through reincarnation." Rupert claims to have been a cockroach in a past life where he met up with *Archie and Mehitabel.* With everyone bearing arms to defend themselves, something's got to give, he says. When the world is destroyed by nuclear holocaust, he believes he'll return as a cockroach and be king because he's been through it once and knows how it's done. And I thought he only wanted to live on an island and write sayings for greeting cards. Watch out for the revolution, Rupe.

Rupert says, "The revolution is as constant as evolution. How does it feel?"

Without my gun I feel lost. Perhaps I could soak myself with gasoline and light a match. That would make a statement. But it would only go up in smoke.

* * *

Honeysuckle pierced my ears; I turned slowly to see who belonged to the voice ordering coffee black so sweetly. Hair the color of the noonday sun and eyes the color of the southern ocean greeted my glance. She carried her large breasts like a cocktail waitress carries a full tray of drinks in a crowded bar. It worked.

Our eyes met. I knew we'd be spending the night together. The rest of the Fair ceased to exist as we exchanged smiles.

"Another coffee addict, I see," I said.

"Only on Saturdays," she said.

"You're not from around here either, are you?" I asked.

"No one who lives here is from here. I'm from Savannah originally."

"Who are you?"

"Melody Lingers."

And she did. I walked with her to a patch of vacant grass in front of the stage as the music ended. Everyone else around became strands of whole-wheat in a peaceful meadow singing ballades in the wind. There were shadows of palm fronds dancing around us though the forest was filled with Douglas firs. We exploded into deep conceptual conversation, bypassing the first several layers and steps of interrogation and analyzing. We spoke of apples.

The idea of everything being prewritten along some creative design began to creep into my brain. The eerie feeling of being chosen by this woman caused me to follow a script.

"So, you live in Eugene?"

"Yes."

"And you work in Eugene?"

"Yes."

"What do you do?"

"I'm a court reporter."

"Can you afford to keep me for the weekend?"

"Why not?"

I left her for a moment to retrieve my belongings at Fowl Filmore's. I thought perhaps she would be gone on my return; then I remembered, the connection was too easy. She must surely be working undercover for some organization trying to locate the source of Easy Now.

Regina was nowhere to be seen around Fowl Filmore's. Filmore approached me with my short story.

"Hey man, Regina said to make sure you get this back. You having a good time?"

"I'm being kidnapped by a beautiful woman. I appreciate your kindness. Perhaps one day I can return the favor."

"Or maybe to someone else," he said.

We shook hands and I once more crossed, carrying my bag and my axe, to where Melody lingered.

* * *

I just now came back from a walk to the top of my hill. Seems like it's been years. It's still there, but it changes constantly as spring emerges. The winters are long and hard where I am—in the western panhandle of Maryland. It takes a little longer for new growth where the winters are long and hard. I am constantly finding pieces of broken glass with sharp jagged edges on my knoll. Rupert says, "It takes a long time to patrol the knoll when you like to stroll."

* * *

Rupert says,
Love me forever--These are the words
They would tell. So listen, my darling,
My thoughts, they may send me to hell.
I want you to love me, just for a moment
Maybe an hour or two. Don't love me forever
I don't mean never, I couldn't do that to you.
Hold me my darling, Let's enjoy love for a while
You know that we both like to screw
Let's start making love now

Tomorrow you'll know how
You know I could do that to you.

Rupert likes to rhyme.

DAY 20

What kind of a country is this? A confessed killer is given work release. For only 20 days I've been in prison. Already I'm allowed out on the streets with the masses.

I knew it would come to this, full-time grunt work for the Marina on the Lake—rubbin' boats—one stroke at a time. I think I'm into the Zen of waxing. Minimum wage, menial labor is what makes this country keep ticking. Tied to the chain and I'm feeling no pain. Work all day and you stay insane. GRUNT.

* * *

On my return to Melody, I was soon introduced to her precocious seven-year-old son, Horatio Edward Lionel Lingers. Melody confided that he was so named because she and her ex-husband were still determined to raise a little H.E.L.L. at the time of the birthing. The marriage lasted for two years. Melody gained custody on holidays and birthdays. It turned out the kid would be eight the next day. I offered to do the cooking.

"I should have mentioned Horatio before. I'm sorry."

"No need. I love kids."

Watching Horatio running in circles with other children all paranoia left me. There was no fear at the Fair. The attitudes were positive. Easy now is contagious. Things became so clear. There was no need for heavy thought—I was being led.

Melody soon gathered her son. He carried my typewriter as we followed the flow to the exit. A great number of people were staying for the weekend; I didn't have a sleeping bag, so I would have a bed to sleep in. Back to Eugene—lalalala lalala. Little did I know that I would become God in less than two weeks. The fair lit my fuse. A simple connection with a beautiful woman was taking my mind on a course where it believed there is no wrong in the world. There is only right. The world was right there. Not since my time in the Valley with Ermonie and Jennifer and Star and Heather and Catherine had I felt its rightness. I had been wrapped up in Paradise from which evil was expelled. Now I was cast out into the world and was finding a preferred illusion.

Rupert says, "Those who are impatient must learn to be happy with crumbs."

We stopped for bottled beer and bottled water in an organic store in the wonderful world of TREND. I read the bulletin board while Melody shopped. There was advertisement for Lesbian Love, Concerts and Lectures on Organic Living. Everyone coming out of the small grocery store had that Easy Now smile. They all seemed very heavily drugged. The only two people I had had actual contact with in Eugene that didn't have that Easy Now smile were the two turkeys in the Firebird; they were looking for a joint. If only Dave, the PR man from the lumber company, realized what he was doing by wishing to use herbicides, and quite possibly wiping out the marijuana crop. Keep everyone drugged and sedated and they could clear cut every mountain in Oregon and nobody would notice. This is the land of the burnout. Thank God for the redneck.

You're welcome.

Rupert says, "Everything has its purpose."

* * *

What am I doing?
I don't know, what are you doing?
I thought I was searching for my role.
Your roll?
My role.
You're a hot dog in search of your roll. Haha.
Cut the crap.
You can't even cut the mustard.
I wish to write, I wish to relate.
It's all related.
I'm no fucking relative of yours.
If you so choose.

* * *

Having finished shopping, we drove to Melody's comfortable cottage. She prepared tacos for dinner; I was given washing machine privileges. Horatio immediately retired to his occasional room which was cluttered with space-age toys and stretch dolls and one-kid games and an electric train and race cars. It was his occasional kingdom; I was allowed to look briefly.

At my request Melody played recordings of Phoebe Snow over her expensive stereo. Her spacious combination living room-dining room provided ample room for me to pace the floor and work things out with my body in its attempt to ease into the environment. Horatio was his own little space-ship. He flew from room to room connected to various tools of distraction. For a minute I thought I should have tried to entertain the kid, but he didn't want any help. The way I was pacing it sure would have helped me. Seeing I was having a tough time adapting, Melody handed me a Rorer 714 Quaalude (a chemical adapter). I washed it down with Michelob beer and began pacing at a slower speed. My mind was eased; it was my body that was racing.

I stashed my gear in a spare room and showered for the second time that day. Melody led me to her room where I stretched my naked drugged body across her brass bed. With Phoebe Snow and the echoes of spaceships in the background, Melody soon joined me.

She took me in her mouth and reminded me of Ethel sucking on the wine bottle. Passion swelled in my groin and my body wished only to pace. I pulled her next to me and was soon on top attempting to dot the I. My desires and her large breasts clenched against my chest made molehills out of mountains. I wrapped my tired hands with her soft white hair. I was enveloped in the splendor of the moment. The door drifted open.

"Mommy," I heard through my ears.

"Mommy?" I repeated. It wasn't the same voice. My body continued on its journey. Melody's eyes popped open. I thought I was doing something right.

"Horatio?" she said.

"No. Sullivan," I answered.

"Mommy, are you busy?" came the voice.

My dreamlike state caused me to continue fucking.

"Yes, Horatio, mommy is busy. Go to your room."

While making love, I love to be spoken to. Her southern accent enhanced my pleasure.

"Mommy."

"Yes, Horatio."

"Are you making love?"

"Yes, Horatio, mommy's making love."

I felt encouraged by her affirmative answer and secure in my pursuit. I continued fucking.

"Why are you making love?"

"Mommy likes to make love."

"Oh. Does it feel good?"

"It feels very good. Mommy would like some privacy while she makes love."

"Oh, okay."

My ego soared like a helium-filled balloon.

"What program are we watching?" I asked. Heavy breathing and the Mormon Tabernacle Choir filled the room.

"Mommy."

"Yes, Horatio," she sang in scat.

"Why does making love feel good?"

"I've conquered my guilt. You'll find out when you're older," she said.

"Oh, okay. Are we going to MacDonald's in the morning?"

"Yes, Horatio," she moaned.

"Is he hurting you?"

"No, Horatio. Goodnight."

"Goodnight."

The door drifted shut. The sound of the spaceship soon diminished to the shutting of a door. I came like a neutron bomb, conquering all life, leaving the building still standing. I couldn't go on. Melody rolled me onto my back and became the aggressor.

Suck me, fuck me, treat me like an object. Just smile and say you enjoyed it. So it was in the land of trend as I drifted on a brass framed magic carpet to a place where nothing else mattered but the pleasant dreams of another realm that can only be entered through sleep or silence.

Rupert says,

>I'm tired, oh, so very tired
>I just can't stay awake.
>I'm tired, my time's almost expired
>How much can I take?
>The time is late, my eyes won't wait
>I can't take the time
>To roll off of my date.
>Shave and a haircut, two bits—I'm tired.

Rupert likes to rhyme.

DAY 21

This is the beginning of my 21st day in Santa's cabin. It's 7:00 a.m. All night I had wonderful dreams about what I wanted to say and how I wanted to say it. Now that I'm awake it's time to go stroke and grunt. GRUNT.

I don't want to do that kind of work. I want to be a suicidal maniac. I want to hang out and get stoned. I coulda been a contender. It's all such a grand illusion. None of this can be real. I've sold out my only chunk of reality—the gun—for a hundred bucks.

Tripod hates me. I leave her alone all day long, and what for? My quest for the buck--Just because I like to eat. What do you do when the bucket is full? What do you do with an artichoke? Am I regular? I've been here for 21 days and the bucket isn't full yet. I'm running out of lime. If you can't flush it, you gotta dowse it with lime. In other words, keep your shit covered.

* * *

The Sunday morning sun brought us closer together. We made love on a sailing ship of desire out past the 200 mile limit. It came to me that I was involved in some wonderful dream so far out in space that only a starship could interrupt.

"Ooooh oooh oooh oooh whooosh shooo," came the echo down the hallway and in through the door.

"Horatio, it's too early for close encounters."

"You promised me breakfast at MacDonald's for my birthday."

"They have a MacDonald's in Eugene?"

"Yes. And I promised for his birthday they would do it all for him. Would you rather eat in or eat out?"

"Tell me. Do I get off to get on or on to get off?"

I got off and got off. I was strafed by a starship as I made my way for a morning shower. Refreshed and refined, I returned to the large combination living room-dining room for breakfast in. Melody prepared lox and cream cheese on toasted bagels with an entire pot of coffee for me. We sat on large fluffy pillows on the floor. Her coffee table was a very sturdy, large old tree stump which grew from the floor.

"MacDonald's. What about MacDonald's?" Horatio pestered.

"Don't you want to decorate for your party first? Maybe Sullivan would help?"

"Does he have to come to my party?"

"He's havin' a party? Should I oughta leave?"

"Only if you'd rather."

"I'm having a wonderful time."

Melody left me munching on a bagel. She soon returned with rolls of red and green streamers. She looked like a Christmas tree, complete with angel hair, walking the length of the room from the kitchen to where I sat. Horatio circled her carrying a flying train. "Whoo, whoo," he said.

> Rupert says,
> Please believe in Christmas, Santa Claus and toys.
> Moms make lots of cookies; jingle bells make noise.
> Carry Christmas spirit, each and every day.
> What is Christmas spirit,
> If it ain't having something nice to say.
> Please believe in Christmas--Give your hand and heart
> If you don't believe in Christmas
> Now's a good time to start.
> Christmas is for giving, lots of love and joy.
> It's for all big people, and every little girl
> And little boy.
> Remember all the little things
> That sometimes we forget.
> Just say please and thank you, and never ever get upset.
> Christmas makes me happy
> It's an upper for the whole down year.
> So please believe in Christmas
> And Christmas will always be Cheer.

Rupert likes to chime. Hey, there's money in Christmas. Falalala falala.

* * *

I just had the most wonderful dinner. Rice, green beans, canned tomatoes, mushrooms, peanuts, hot pickled cauliflower seasoned with one jalapeno and soy sauce, all mixed together. I washed it down with coffee and Kamchatka vodka.

Rupert says, "You are what you eat." Am I ever in trouble!

I massage boats for a living. Steinbeck picked grapes. I wax and massage fiberglass boats. "The Wrath of Fiberglass." Grapes are more organic than fiberglass. At least they used to be. Progress is our most important product.

If I didn't have Rupert's rhymes, I don't know what I'd do.

Et cum spirit tu tuo. Tied up in a paper chain, I am. No longer do I remember why I am here. So it continues. I guess anyway.

I'm going out to wallow in the pond. I haven't forgotten my quest, I just must remember how I got here and why I must stay and continue. Parnassus is rising and I'm still connected to the realm of rock and roll. I've been delivered thus far to where I am and can't understand why. Rupert says, "Does it really matter where you are as long as you are there?"

The only thing I'm certain of is that I must buy Tripod a flea collar. In my search for identity, sometimes I forget what it is. Rupert says, "My search for identity is my identity."

Don't you understand, I am God, you know. Don't you see what you're doing?

Slow down, Dude.

What?

Easy Now.

Oh. Yeah.

Rupert says, "God is as much of a creation of man as man is a creation of God."

DAY 22

Ah, sweet melodies of life, this is my 22nd day. Though my volume of words has decreased heavily, I feel as though I'm accomplishing something as a full-time boat waxer. After all, massaging fiberglass boats is for the betterment of all mankind.

Fill the bottom of an oily wok with water and bring it to a boil. Add one handful of wide egg noodles, generic brand. Cook until done. Drain noodles and place wok back on the stove to dry. Add olive oil and mushrooms. Toss in noodles and a couple of whole tomatoes from a can. Break up one jalapeno and open a can of sardines in mustard sauce. Throw in both. A handful of peanuts and a half can of green beans plus a few dashes of soy sauce makes it complete. Eat from the wok; be sure to use a wooden spoon and whole wheat pita bread to scoop it up. It's all very spiritual.

My two empty 1.5 liter wine jugs sure have made fetching water from the spring a lot easier. Now I make one trip every other day if I work all day. Waxing fiberglass boats is such a high. Yeah. Wealth has its advantages. I won't receive my first paycheck for a couple of days; I know it's coming so I can let loose. Tripod had a can of chicken soup with her dog chow.

The worst thing about shitting in a bucket is you never get to flush. I was just out taking a wonderful shit. My hemorrhoids are almost gone. I peered through the opening of the outhouse where there used to be a door. Amongst last year's fallen leaves I saw my own image on the ground. Only my face, but it's still a strange feeling to be sitting in an outhouse, shitting in a bucket, seeing your miniature mirror image in the material of a fallen leaf, staring back and smiling. I smiled back. It's all very spiritual.

* * *

Horatio descended like reality occasionally does. He jammed me in my left ear with his flying train, reminding me of my welcomed obligation to hang streamers in exchange for my bagel.

"Happy birthday. How old are you?"

"I believe in ghosts. Are you serious about my mother, or are you fucking her for amusement?"

Melody was preparing a fresh pot of coffee.

"Do you have a cigarette I could use?" I asked.

"I rub snuff. Cigarettes kill you."

"Oh?"

Horatio's hair wasn't as white as his mother's. His halo was tarnished with streaks of brown. He suddenly appeared to me as a midget working for the CIA.

"Are you going to help me with the streamers, or what?"

"Do I have a choice?"

"There should always a choice."

"How old are you today?"

"I'm eight. How old are you?"

"Much older than I thought. I must have missed something. Where are we?"

"We are in my mother's house. Will you hang the streamers or not?"

We crisscrossed the streamers in alternating colors over top the dining-room table in the dining section of the combination living room-dining room. I had dined on the polyurethane-covered tree stump in the living room section of the combination living room-dining room. Rupert says, "Dining is a very important part of living."

Horatio drank his coffee black when we took a break from hanging streamers. I used milk and honey. Melody abstained. We gained momentum after our coffee with Horatio directing every step of the way. He dispensed the scotch tape and pointed out the exact spots where he wanted the streamers attached. Not in the vicinity, but the exact spots. He even supervised the proper twisting of the crepe. It was his birthday. Melody left us alone.

"I don't believe you have enough stamina for my mother," he said.

"What?" I inquired innocently.

"I watched you last night. You gave out before your pecker did."

"What brand of snuff do you rub?"

"Copenhagen. The kind Bert Jones the football player uses."

Melody was bathing.

"So you live with your father, huh?"

"Yeah, it works out. I don't say anything about his men; he doesn't say anything about my snuff."

"Oh." I was not in someone's home to pass judgment.

"I'll make a deal with you," Horatio said. He smiled like a general in a back room at the White House.

"Yeah, what kinda deal?"

"My mom's taking me and some friends to the Enchanted Forest for my birthday. You don't say anything about our conversation, and I'll get you off the hook and tell her to let you stay here."

"It sounds like fun. Suppose I wanta go?"

"Hey, buddy, I don't want you to go."

"That's all you had to say; it's your birthday. Do you watch a lot of television?"

"Every chance I get," he said with a snicker.

"Educational stuff, huh?"

Melody appeared in a short robe with water still running lightly down her thighs.

"Is everything hung?" she asked.

"I still have a few years to go," Horatio commented.

"Huh?"

"What about MacDonald's?"

"It'll take me a minute."

Once more Melody disappeared into her room to change.

Rupert says, "Life is like a banquet. You take it in, digest it, use some of it and shit out the rest. But what do you do when the bucket is full?"

> Rupert says,
> I think life is such a groove
> Everyday is like a movie
> You play a role and act out every scene
> You enter spaces where you've never been
> BEFORE. . .ONCE MORE. . .AND AGAIN.
> You touch someone and maybe they touch you
> You try to feel what they are going through.
> You share some scenes you think are overdue.
> Sometimes you find they like your movie too.
> The spotlight seems so bright and it's okay

But when you turn your head they run away.
You cry but find you've got nothing to say.
So you wait to see what's in another day.
DEELIGHT. . .with a cast of thousands tonight.

Rupert likes to rhyme.

* * *

I had to shit once more to see if my image was still there on the ground. It's still there—mingled with the earth.

* * *

"That's the basis for many of the world's problems," Horatio informed me. The kid was quick on his feet.

"What?" I had to ask.

"There isn't enough sex."

"What?" I had to ask again. He certainly was a little hell.

"Mom seemed happy for a change last night. I can tell. Her work gives her a lot of stress. I like to see her happy."

"It's just another diversion, Horatio." Our communication was expanding. "Sex causes a lot of problems, too, Horatio."

"Not while you're doing it, I bet."

"It all depends upon whom you're doing it with."

"Dad does it with men. He seems a lot happier than when he does it with mom."

"Oh?"

"Yeah, every once in a while they have to make sure they don't belong together. They give it another shot and hate each other for it."

"See what I mean."

Rupert says, "I cannot be whomever I don't want to be. Some people are meant to be cab drivers."

Melody entered the room. I welcomed her presence. Horatio returned to being an eight-year-old birthday boy.

"Mom, what about MacDonald's?"

"Why, Horatio, everything looks ready for your party."

"He helped," Horatio said pointing to me. "MacDonald's, Mom."

"Can we take Sullivan with us?"

"I guess."

We were off in search of fast food. I attempted to figure out the difference between being led and being manipulated. The sun was quickly burning off the morning cloud cover. The simplicity of life once more smacked me in the face when Melody stopped at a Burger King instead of MacDonald's for Horatio's treat.

"I thought we were going to MacDonald's?"

"It's all the same. The Burger King is next to the Baskin and Robins. I'll pick up the ice cream cake while he eats."

There was also a sundries store next to the Baskin and Robins and Burger King. It was all very convenient. Horatio had his treat— Melody picked up the cake—and I purchased a pair of brown flip-flops for a dollar eighty-nine. My eighty-nine cent flip-flops were becoming tired.

We dropped the cake in the icebox back home; then I was given a ten-cent tour of Eugene: Parcels of meticulously decorated land, jogging and biking paths, and dancers rehearsing in the square downtown. It was Sunday. Most were still at the Country Fair. Easy Now leisure along clean streets with positive movement; there were no helium-filled balloons. They must have been at the Fair. The dancers were elastic, repeating and perfecting with personal style which came from the eye. Each dancer performed his necessary task as part of the whole. It was fully orchestrated with the director looking on and commenting on what he saw. Purple leotards, mingled with pink and white and black, taking on different shapes depending on the occupant, were connected by rhythm emanating from a cassette. The ears heard the same tune and the eyes carried out the individual tasks. My task was to enjoy, along with Horatio and Melody. Though the director sat off to the side, he seemed as much a part of the dance as the music.

Rupert says, "Hard work is good for the soul, once you find your toasted roll."

I felt privileged to be granted the tour. I knew I was only passing through and would never return to Eugene again. My tour guides were gracious hosts—even the worldly eight-year-old Horatio. I certainly had no complaints about the sexual gifts of Melody, but a one night stand is a one night stand—even if it lasts for two nights. We returned to the house where I was given a map of Eugene and the keys to come and go as I pleased. My own paranoia made me wonder why Melody seemed not to have any. I, of course, feared a set up. I fought hard to let that fear go, and simply enjoy what was offered.

Melody and Horatio were soon off to the Enchanted Forest. I ventured out on my own little adventure with map in hand. There didn't seem to be very much to do, and I wanted to be entertained. I had carried one book along with me on my journey. It was *Breakfast of Champions* by Kurt Vonnegut, Jr. I thought perhaps it was about early morning loving, so I carried it along on my walk in case there was no other entertainment to be found. The book had been a gift from Rhoda Apple, the Republican from the Hope Springs Eternal Hotel. She was at the very beginning of the story and won't return, unless she should show up at Santa's cabin to see if I'm still alive. Even if she should show up, I may not be here. I'm not here that much any more. Massaging boats takes me away quite a bit. Have we discussed this before? I don't know if it matters.

* * *

Tripod says, "Each conversation is new—no matter how much it's repeated." Tripod and I have a pretty decent relationship, even though she refuses to become my lover, and I have been leaving her here alone quite a bit lately. Or so it seems. But things aren't always as they seem, are they. Vonnegut quoted Omar Khayam in his book:

> The moving finger writes
> And having writ moves on
> Nor all your piety nor wit

> Shall ever lure it back to cancel half a line
> Nor all your tears wash away a word of it."

Vonnegut said, "Some poem."

I finished reading the book at a girls' softball game I happened upon. I must admit occasionally glancing at the young girls bouncing around the bases. I felt my back heating up in the afternoon sun on my walk back to the house. I carried my shirt in my hand, along with my new flip-flops. They were still a little too stiff to wear and began to cut the inside of my foot. There's always something to carry. I did find enough soft manicured lawns to make the walk enjoyable.

Melody's house had central air; I napped on the living room floor across the large pillows I had sat on for breakfast. It was all very delightful in a casual sort of way. I finally managed to convince myself that if Melody wasn't paranoid, why I should be.

Rupert says, "Vision without strength becomes hallucination in the desert—no one else will ever see it."

I was stirred from my sleep by the car pulling into the driveway. There were other boy voices besides Horatio's. The party was at hand. I rolled from the pillows onto the floor, contemplating suicide and mouthwash in the same thought. I chose Listerine, which seemed the safest and best of both worlds, though I prefer turpentine and a match to the old taste.

Rupert says, "Marketing is a very important part of life."

Dadadalump, dadadalump, dadadalump. In a method offending the sensitive ear, they entered. Moved by celebration and an occasional need to participate in the race and resurrection, I set the table with paper plates. Horatio thanked me for not going to the Enchanted Forest.

"Repay me by seeing to your education."

"Demand your own truth no matter how much it hurts."

Horatio's friends seemed at his mercy, though they were all slightly older. He directed them where to sit, in rank according to the value of the gift. I sat next to Kenny. He had a tablet of blank sheets of paper to offer. Kenny had acne and was lost in his own world. To Horatio's left and Kenny's right sat Algernon. His gift was a large package of Cheetos. Horatio ate them by handfuls, even before the ice cream cake was served. Algernon was plump and ate most of the gift.

To Horatio's immediate right was Ack. He offered an old doorknob. He and Horatio were constantly talking. His bottom front teeth were stained. It was obvious they were snuff-rubbin' buddies.

The mother served. Melody pounded candles into the ice cream cake and poured lemonade for all. She took her place at the side of the oval table between Ack and me, after adding Jose Cuervo Gold to my drink. She was a beautiful woman. I wished to know more of her, but I knew I would be leaving in the morning and I thought perhaps there would only be time for sex. I wanted to confess my murder, at least; the impending reaction always told me a lot about who I was dealing with. It did chase some away. Even I didn't know if I was bragging or complaining or admitting remorse no matter what the circumstance of the event and the situation that had been hoisted upon me.

The festivities were momentarily halted when Horatio blew out the candles. Only a woman from Savannah, Georgia would understand. Melody tried to understand while scraping saliva and snuff from the top of the cake. Horatio was frightened at first, but his mother only wished to see him have anything she wasn't able to give—even rubbin' snuff. I found the reason why Ack was called Ack when he laughed. Ackackackackackackackack, he did. Algernon raced for the bathroom and threw up. Kenny dooddled nonsensical scribblings on lined paper.

After a few tall drinks of lemonade and tequila, I was talked into playing ball with the boys on the front lawn. The grass was a little long. We used a plastic bat and a plastic ball, and Horatio always won. The game was uncertain, but Horatio always won. The single parents of the other three boys began arriving one at a time. Then, surprisingly, Milborne appeared. He had been the bus driver when I first arrived in Eugene. I was more surprised in seeing him than he was in seeing me.

"I thought it might be you," he said.

"Wow," I said.

Milborne still carried his Easy Now smile though he looked much different standing up.

"I knew one of us would get you before you left Eugene," he said.

"What?"

"Have you been enjoying yourself?"

"Yeah."

"You know there's always a price."

"Yeah?"

"Easy Now is contagious."

"Yeah."

Milborne took his son, Horatio, and they disappeared. I was left alone with Melody in her house.

> Rupert says,
> For me there is no other--Time or other place
> Today is just a moment--Tomorrow another space
> The silly game we play here--Will end in just a while
> So while we have to stay here
> We should do it with a smile. I go from day to day--
> My time is standing still.
> And there is another way--& extra time for me to kill.
> Now is but a moment--Before it ever was
> And when now is over--It isn't just because. . .

Rupert likes to rhyme.

DAY 23

FIDDLE!

DAY 24

FADDLE!

DAY 25

FUMP! AAAHHH!

DAY 26

This is my 26th day in Santa's cabin. The past three days I have wallowed. It's a big pond. They let me away from my boat-massaging duties early Friday. I called Damien Rumsford in Baltimore at his sister's house. A new shipment of Easy Now had just arrived. It was my intention never to sell drugs again—even Easy Now. I seriously thought I could achieve the enlightenment it provides in other ways. I still feel it's possible through hard work and silence.

On my drive to the city I picked up two sailors in uniform, hitchhiking on top of a mountain. They were headed to Washington, D.C. to participate in some sort of demonstration for peace. They were both "bomb-makers" on board the aircraft carrier Kennedy. It seemed rather odd that they would be coming from Norfolk on their way to D.C. by way of the mountains of western Maryland; I have learned to accept such occurrences as a part of it all. Who am I, a common man, to question any movements of our military.

Algernon sat munching on a bag of Cheetos in the back seat with Tripod. Ack sat up front with me.

Algernon had joined the Navy to escape a prison sentence; Ack joined to run away from a woman. One of the reasons for my timely visit to the city was: I was down to my last two joints. I shared them with the sailors.

Both Algernon and Ack claimed to be conscientious objectors in their own right. They make conventional bombs. They both claimed to have refused to have anything to do with anything nuclear. We became pleasantly stoned on our ride over hill, over dale as we left the country trail and the nation goes drolling along. Give me liberty or give me two dollars. I have not yet begun to figure it all out. I have but one life to give for a while. Ask not what your country can do for you, ask what you can do for the corporation. Praise the Ford. Buy Blondes.

Ack had eyes that were very far apart. He and Algernon were buddies of the road. They hitchhike everywhere together. Most of their shipmates are afraid to hitchhike anymore, they told me. "There are too many crazies out there."

Yeah.

* * *

At first it was strange being alone with Melody. Horatio's absence was as imposing as his presence. Melody fixed things quickly by removing her top. Her breasts were large and firm even out of bed. They needed no support and one was quite independent of the other. Each of her breasts seemed to have a personality of its own. We sat sipping Tequila on the large pillows at the polyurethane coated tree stump.

"Sullivan," she said seductively, "the desires that each person feels fall into several categories."

I touched her right breast lightly and it wiggled.

"Some people feel making love is the ultimate act of communication."

I touched her left breast and it stood at attention. Her hair shimmered from the light of one lamp lit in the dining room. All the curtains were drawn.

"Others say it taps them into a positive experience shared with the rest of the world."

I touched her right breast again and it wiggled.

"Still others say it's giving in to the devil."

I kissed her right breast and it wiggled.

"Personally, I enjoy fucking."

"Why does your right breast wiggle?"

"It's done that ever since I nursed Horatio."

The distance of the stars seemed closer by the light around Melody's head. Her platinum halo enticed me to the point of continuation. The music was "By the Light of the Silvery Moon," with the Mitch Miller Singers. I became emotionally involved with her right breast.

"Have you ever consulted a chiropractor?"

"He became emotionally involved with my right breast."

The wiggle was an enticing wiggle. It wasn't a nervous wiggle. It wasn't as if it was trying to shake something off. It was like jello. It said, "I am here for your pleasure." It said, "There are many things in the world that are frightened." It said, "I am not afraid." It gave itself to me and Melody carried the tune.

We found ourselves "enveloped in the splendor of the moment." We found ourselves on the top of the polyurethane-coated tree stump. Many limbs and an unending search for completion carried me to blossoms in the spring, not caring about the winter.

"Sullivan."

"Yes, Melody."

"I have to tell you something."

"Yes, Melody."

"This afternoon while you were playing with the boys."

Her right breast vibrated violently.

"I had a phone call."

I pursued my ultimate devastation building to a crescendo crashing with cymbals and the scream of a maniac. "AAAAGGGGHHHH."

"It was from a friend of mine—Carolyn—and she's entertaining a lawyer from Portland for the weekend. I invited them over for a drink."

"Sure babe. You want I should leave?" We fell to the pillows on the floor wrestling with thoughts of who should be the aggressor. Melody assumed control.

"I wish only for you to be comfortable."

"Do I have time to shower?"

Writhing and contorted in perpetual motion, we made our way to the bathroom, not bothering to separate. We showered. I expected kinkiness on the horizon. Melody's thirst for sex seemed unquenchable. I, being a mere mortal at the time, was open for anything. Melody popped some popcorn.

Her friends arrived shortly. We sat around the polyurethane-coated tree stump, sipping tequila and eating popcorn. Carolyn was another single mother. I was curious as to how the film would develop. Melody was very affectionate to everyone, even the lawyer. I sat quietly observing, and speaking only when necessary, hesitant to confess to so large a gathering. The lawyer produced a vial of fine cocaine. Line after line was laid on the polyurethane-coated tree stump while the women read dirty jokes from Hustler magazine. We took turns snorting the coke while the two women took turns reading between the lines.

Melody was wearing a tight-fitting tee shirt with the words "I AM" scripted across the front. But I wondered if she believed it. She suggested a game once the mood was lightened by the coke. I was ready. "Aha," I thought, "here it comes."

A deck of cards was produced and we played pinochle until after 11:00. Carolyn and the lawyer left. I was once more led to Melody's brass bed in a land where my every suspicion seemed to dissolve with other moments taking over. I didn't have time to confess my murder, and the need disappeared like a helium-filled balloon when you let it go.

Seven o'clock Monday morning there was no need for an alarm. My eyes popped open, looking directly into Melody's opened eyes. We made love. She fixed me a light breakfast while I showered and dressed for the road. She gave me a light blanket and three joints for the trip.

We left her house and found 11th which led into 126. Lalalala lalala. Melody took me back to where the Country Fair had been near Elmira and we drove past the east entrance to the fair. I found myself standing next to a blackberry bush. I was headed for Winchester Bay to go fishing. How simple everything is.

DAY 27

Oobladee, oobladah. I've been here for 27 days. I'm wallowing and frolicking and working and waxing. I rubbed boats until 7:00 tonight, making fiberglass into a mirror so fish can see themselves is what I'm doing. Smile.

For dinner I had rice, peanuts, fancy mixed Chinese vegetables, one jalapeno, chunk pineapple, pink salmon and soy sauce mixed in the wok and sopped up with a bagel. I replenished my wine and vodka and walked to the spring for fresh water. I fed Tripod. I'm even too tired to masturbate.

When I was a good Catholic going to confession, it always upset me to tell the priest how many impure acts I had committed with myself. My stuttering was very recognizable. I imagined the priests sitting around drinking wine and swapping stories. "The dududdduda kid jerks off 14 times a week."

* * *

The afternoon in Winchester Bay passed quickly and pleasantly in the company of Brad and Theodore. For some strange reason I knew I would be on a boat soon enough, though there were no immediate prospects. Brad constantly acted as my agent—whether he was trying to help me or get rid of me made no difference. By doing one, he would accomplish the other. The name Emmett began popping up.

DAY 28

Rice, peanuts, minced clams, fancy mixed Chinese vegetables, chunk pineapple, one jalapeno and soy sauce, sopped up with a bagel and washed down with white wine. If I wrote as much as I eat and ramble, I'd have *War and Peace* completed twice over. This is the story of my journey and it's my 28th day—not into the journey, but in this fucking shack. Not only has my t never quit sticking, but the p and the k are doing the same.

"Sounds like a personal problem."

* * *

It was after 7:00 when we were leaving the Pub. I rode back to the peninsula with Brad and Theodore to investigate the distinct possibility that Emmett might need a puller. I didn't know who Emmett was. At the time he was merely a thought linked to a slim chance of becoming reality on a journey where anything seemed possible. I was into the third day of my journey, caught up in a web of connection, sailing along on a thin thread of positive energy where Murphy's Law usually applies—if anything can go wrong, it will.

Rupert says, "Anything that goes wrong is for the best in the long run, although it may not seem so at the time."

Ahead of us, next to an old Chevy pickup truck with a homemade camper, stood a man straight from the movie screen. He looked like Doc from Snow White and the Seven Dwarves. But then again, he didn't look like Doc. He was short. I'm straining my brain over here for that first impression, give me a minute. Dadadalump, dadadalump.

Red and white, that's it. He was red and white and he looked like Doc. His hairline started in an arch, somewhere near the top of his head. His hair was curly and white and looked like a snug fitting hat. His high forehead and face were red. He wore blue jeans and a blue flannel shirt.

Moments of positive electrical energy danced around the car as I became aware of my need to carry a positive impression strong enough to pierce the initial armor of a complete stranger without defeating my own purpose by being obnoxious and overbearing. I had been with Brad and Theodore for several hours, and a limited relationship already existed between me and the small fishing port of Winchester Bay. I desired the partial fulfillment of a former night wandering dream—no more, no less.

"Emmett," Brad called out as we came to a stop, "you headin' out tonight?"

"I'm tryin'," Emmett answered with a puzzled look on his face. He had been pacing without obvious purpose to the rear of the black Chevy pickup.

"You have a puller?"

"No, I'm goin' 'er alone."

I felt high and desired to be complete in my present ambiguous state of being. I remained silent and smiling, waiting for my moment.

"This is Sullivan Duda from Baltimore. He's a writer and he's as strong as an ox. He helped me hook up my tanks this afternoon. He's looking to sign on a boat for the experience."

"I can't afford no puller. That's why I'm goin' 'er alone."

There he was, the beleaguered Doc, offering me a ticket to an adventure about which I had only dreamed. Even his pacing made me think he had been waiting for me. He smiled exposing a gap in his front teeth. There he was—next to a beer truck in the middle of the desert, waiting for me to come and drink. I remained silent.

"He's not looking to get paid. Feed him, and if you make out on your trip, slip him a few bucks," Brad said.

Emmett leaned over and peered through Brad's window to get a better look at me. As if on cue, I climbed from the VW and walked around to where this curious little man came up to my shoulder. I extended a smile and my hand, and Emmett drew like a desperado with an imaginary gun, reaching for my hand and grabbing it firmly. He was small, but his strength was real and not pushy.

"I wish I could help ya out. I just can't afford to take on a hand right now," he said. I took it to mean he wanted the offer from my lips.

"Emmett, an apple this big."

"I'm not sure my insurance would cover you."

"I'll sign a release."

"Where you say you were from?"

"I am from the realm of never-ending passion, desiring to taste more than fast food."

"Yeah, I don't blame ya. I think they use horse meat at most of them places."

"I'll work hard and if I don't work out, tell me and I'll go."

"Can you swim?"

"I can tread water for days."

"As long as you can tread water, you can learn how to ride the tide. I gotta ride into town for a minute. Let me think about it."

"That's all I can ask. I'll wait here for your answer."

"Ya might get run over here. Those steps over there lead to where I'm docked."

Boing! It was happening. Emmett hopped in his truck and clanked down the peninsula towards town. I thanked Brad and he smiled. "Son of a gun," he said, "I think you've got a boat. Good luck, Sullivan."

"Good fishing, Brad."

Emmett was docked on the opposite side of the peninsula from Brad, where the older wooden boats on the east swayed to a slightly different tune than the newer fiberglass boats on the west side. I pulled my gear from Brad's VW and waved as he and Theodore disappeared. I sat on my duffel bag next to the steps leading to the dock. I worked at not trying to figure anything out. In a short time I saw and heard the old black pickup heading up the peninsula and coming to a stop among the trailers and campers and pickups and many cars, which were scattered over the huge manmade structure. Two brick buildings, housing showers and toilets and telephones, were all that was immobile on the surface.

Emmett crossed over to me carrying a cardboard box. He looked like a piston with his shoulders pumping with each leg movement. I stood to greet him.

"Mine is the Mary Patt," he said. "Stow your gear and we'll go pick up some grub."

I followed his perpetual motion down the steps to the dock. We turned at the end and walked along another dock parallel to the peninsula, passing Elizabeth and Burgers with their bows resting on old tires. We came to Mary Patt, all green and white and chipped, with two unpainted trees for outriggers. They stood at attention on either side of the cabin amidships on the 52-foot schooner.

She rested against two old tires, and her beak, rusted and chipped and open, extended over the dock, pretending—in my eyes—to be a hand-carved wooden figurine of a naked lady. We walked down the finger extending from the dock alongside the Mary Patt on her port side. We boarded her by climbing up wooden steps that matched her paint job—chipped. We entered the cabin through a sliding door; I stashed my gear on the top bunk.

"Can ya cook?" he asked.

"I love to cook."

"We'll get along fine," he said, then let out with a chuckle that sounded like chopped pecans—earthy but minced.

* * *

This is disgusting. Sigh. I'm dressing for bed. It's freezing tonight, outside and in. I can't find my gray sweat pants. I wore them last night. I took them off this morning. Sigh. They were in my red suitcase, where else.

I was just out taking a pee, standing on the front step of my cabin. Shadows in the night are intriguing with the help of a high-intensity lamp. They're so much larger than life.

I've just dusted my hair with baby powder to clean it. I must smell bad, but I have a cold; I haven't bathed in four days. My reflection looks strange; I'm getting baby powder all over my typewriter. Occasionally there's opera in the background. I'm getting fragmented again. I've eaten a Quaalude. I'm creating a swamp from pissing so much. I think I have too many I's.

* * *

I showed Emmett my driver's license with a picture, to reassure him that I was who I said I was. We left the boat and walked back to the peninsula where we hopped in the truck and clanked off to town for supplies. I began filling Emmett in on my story as we drove. We stopped at a place that was a combination grocery and fishing tackle store. Emmett said the prices were a bit higher than elsewhere, but they advanced him credit when he needed it and always cashed his checks. He began shopping while I used the pay phone outside the store to contact Ermonie back at the camp.

"Hello," the deep sexy voice answered on the other end.

"We have a collect call for Ermonie Hunter from Sullivan. Will you accept charges?"

"Yes."

The sound of that voice brought rolling hills and life without guilt to my brain. And a touch for the heart from so far away gave me reason to continue wanting intimate moments we had shared.

"Sullivan!" she shouted. "Where are you?" Her voice changed to the sound of youthful innocence and expectation as it always did once the guard was let down.

"I'm in Winchester Bay and I'm about to get on a boat and go fishing for salmon. How are you?"

"What!" she screamed and laughed a self-assured laugh like it was exactly what she expected to hear.

"It's been an incredible weekend. How are you? How's everyone?" I said.

"I'm fine. Everyone's fine. It's been a relaxing weekend here. A new group of campers arrived today. We have 25 children who are nonverbal. It should be a challenging week. How's your head? Do you feel right?"

She always asked me that. She had this thing about rightness. She said my life made sense to her, murder and everything.

"I feel I'm in a movie."

"You are, Sullivan. Enjoy yourself."

Now there is no Ermonie.

After the call I entered the store to find Emmett pushing a tiny cart around the one circle that made up the grocery section. In his cart already were a chunk of cheddar cheese and six large red delicious apples. He selected a case of beer. It was brewed and can only be found in Oregon. We picked up a loaf of whole wheat bread and a dozen eggs. I selected wide noodles and rice and packaged luncheon meat. A pound of Folgers coffee and a half-gallon of milk, along with a six-pack of Coke found their way into our cart. Emmett found the butter and a jar of strawberry jam. Around the circle we walked until the bill came to $53.42. Emmett paid in cash from a large roll of bills he had stashed in his side pocket. We carried three half-filled bags, a small box and the case of beer out to the truck and returned to the peninsula to the Mary Patt.

Rupert says, "Sometimes each day seems like a lifetime. Each day is a life line."

It was nearly 10:00 that Monday evening. We were seven miles out into the Pacific. The sun was melting into the ocean. The Oregon coast became a whisper in the twilight. Emmett set the wind sail for the evening's drift. We had no anchor. With her engines cut, the Mary Patt rolled like the malfunctioning horizontal hold on a TV screen.

I was excited, yet exhausted in a world of fog. I knew only that I would sleep in the top bunk with the blanket from Melody to keep me warm. Emmett and I were still strangers and he had the companionship of the Mary Patt. There was time for me to get to know them both—gradually.

"Emmett," I asked, "what do you do besides fish?"

"I been workin' with asbestos for 23 years. I like to live

dangerous," he said, and then chuckled his chopped pecan chuckle.

I climbed onto the top bunk where a dishrag covered the porthole and both my head and feet rubbed walls.

DAY 29

On my 29th day my desire to continue with this project is faltering quickly. Waxing boats is hard work. Dinner tonight was lousy. Rice, peanuts, fancy mixed Chinese vegetables, zucchini, pinto beans, chili sauce, pink salmon and soy sauce, mixed together and sopped up with a raisin and cinnamon bagel. That's what happens when you try to go international. Maybe I'm becoming ill from all the boats I've been massaging.

Rupert says, "When a man speaks of his realm of continuation, usually he does not desire pity, but continuity in the sharing of his experience. It's the listening that takes work."

* * *

Emmett continued doing odd jobs as I lay there in the top bunk and the world outside became totally black. I heard him in the cabin.

"How did you come up with the name Mary Patt?" I asked.

Again he chuckled. "That's what she was called when I bought 'er. It woulda been too much trouble ta change the name."

I felt a certain sense of security from his chuckle and his honesty. I was quickly rocked into a deep unconditional sleep.

DAY 30

Rice, hot pickled cauliflower, tuna, cream of mushroom soup, mushrooms, one hot pepper, crushed pineapple and soy sauce, sopped up with a bagel and washed down with Schmidt's beer. The amounts of each are however you feel. I've always wanted to write a cookbook, but I've always been confused by the exact proportions they instruct you to use. A quarter teaspoon of thyme has never aroused my curiosity. Now, a pinch is another story.

I was very tired last night. My bones ached. Today is another day, and my 30th day of exile. It's all only a pinch of thyme.

* * *

It was still dark when the sensation of being in an unlit popcorn machine struck me. My eyes popped open like kernels of Orville Redenbacher popcorn! The violent roll of the Mary Patt and Emmett's dry hacking and wheezing intensified the feeling. It had been a comfortable sleep, though short. The bunks were wooden and the mattress was as thin as rice paper. It was still a bed with a roof.

Before I realized where I was, I rolled from my top bunk on the backside of a wave—lost in space momentarily—I found myself—stunned by the material of the small dining booth across the aisle from my bunk. The abrupt movement from port to starboard awakened me-- Left to right for landlubbers.

"You up already?" came the short happy unperturbed sound from the front of the cabin.

"Yeah, yeah. It's time to get up, ain't it?"

"I can never sleep the night before a trip."

"You all right? That cough don't sound none too good. Are you a heavy smoker?"

"Naw, Ah quit 10 years ago. Ah got a slight case of asbestosis."

"Sounds fatal," I said jokingly.

"Heh-heh-heh," he chuckled. "Can be."

"Shit."

"Visited a friend of mine last week. He's probably dead by now. Asbestosis can lead to mesothelioma. That's a cancer."

"Shit."

"Symptoms begin to show up after 13 or so years a workin' with the stuff."

"Shit."

"It's a good job though. Ah work when Ah wanta. Good money."

"Shit."

"Yeah, maybe Ah should mention. If ya gotta piss, do it over the side, but be careful or you're gone. If ya gotta shit, there's a bucket. Don't use the head. It ain't hooked up."

With the engines still silent and only the sound of jars rattling in the night, suddenly there was a drum roll.

"But, Emmett, what do you do when the bucket is full?"

"Ah never wait that long. Dump it over the side after ya use it, and don't ferget ta rinse it out. Paper's in back a the old john. It ain't good ta leave old shit layin' around too long. Causes a personality deficiency."

DADA.

Rupert says, "Get it out—get it out of the way—and continue."

It was definitely a morning of exploration. Emmett showed me where the tank of propane gas was located, right outside the back door of the cabin. "Always turn it off after ya use it. Leaks if ya don't.

If ya don't hear a pffft when ya turn it on, we're either out a gas, or ya left it on and we'll be out soon enough. I don't mind uncooked food, but uncooked coffee gets in yer teeth."

He showed me where the old head was located behind a curtain. That's were the bucket was, between the bunks and the rear wall of the cabin. The toilet seat was still there. He mentioned his plan to make it usable with the bucket. "Hard to keep balanced over an open bucket when yer a rollin'."

There was a $500 fine if your head was connected, I was told. "She's an old boat and ah caint ford no holdin' tanks."

Across from the head in the rear of the cabin was a sink with running water and a Formica counter along the wall between the sink and the gas stove. Dawn began to break. Emmett climbed downward through a hatch in the cabin into the hold and pounded his Chrysler with a hammer. "Sometimes ya gotta do that," he said. The Mary Patt started right up. I brushed my teeth and walked out back in the morning air and listened for the pffft of the propane tank. "Pffft."

"I forgot to ask," he chuckled, "Do ya get seasick? Ah guess Ah shoulda asked ya before. I musta forgot."

"I don't get seasick."

"Ya ever been on the ocean before?"

"My father was a sailor in World War II and he crossed the Oceans Blue and the equator where they smacked him on the ass as a right of passage. Yeah, I've been on the ocean before."

"Okay," he chuckled.

We had been drifting south all night and as dawn became certain we headed north. I got my first clear view of the Oregon coast. The white sand met the tree line and melted into the ocean with two large breasts called the Twin Knolls. I attempted a pot of fresh coffee held in place on the stove by crisscrossed springs, the kind found on old-time screen doors to pull them shut.

Out at sea, the outriggers of the Mary Patt became wings held by rope, extending from the deck by their weight, remaining rigid in the wind. They were wings nonetheless.

I lit the stove with a wooden match and destroyed perfectly good water by an overabundance of Folgers and too much time on my hands. Emmett busied himself with the automatic pilot, instructing it to hold a northerly course by attaching a chain between a gizmo with gears hooked to a compass and gears on the wheel at the front of the cabin.

* * *

Excuse me. My bucket is just about full. When I sit on the hole over it, my ass is tickled by the paper and nearly sneezes from the lime. How I wish I could dump it over the side. It seems far too much to carry.

The arched tree on the edge of my knoll has larger leaves than any other trees. Maybe they merely seem that way because they're at eye level. My colorless rainbow blossoms.

Escapes are such a necessity at times. I've ingested a Quaalude and an unhealthy ration of alcohol to open up the hemisphere of my brain which taps me into that other place and allows me to forget I'm massaging fiberglass boats for a living. I only wish Ermonie were here or I was there in her beautiful Valley, sharing the lights in the sky and the mellow ambience of her presence.

Damien Rumsford, who is now involved in selling women's shoes, says, "Love is like a butterfly. It's beautiful to see and experience. Whenever it comes around and lands on your shoulder, it's a wonder to behold. It flutters away and disappears, making room for the next."

Rupert says, "Sometimes, letting go isn't meant to be easy.

* * *

The coffee, even after an overabundance of milk, tasted like a sandpapered tin can. Emmett was very worried that I might fall overboard and warned me continuously that if I did I would probably never be seen again. After I threw up over the side without falling over, his confidence in my sea legs and balance soared. I began noticing, however, a look of harnessed skepticism as opposed to concern, though he watched me less frequently. He allowed me to handle no lines. It must have been the coffee, though he merely smiled when he drank it. I attempted to redeem my culinary skills by preparing neatly folded cheese omelets for breakfast. They tasted delicious, though afterwards I became unable to retain them. Halfway into the second pot of coffee I commented, "Emmett, I believe I need a little practice on the coffee."

He chuckled warmly, exposing the gap in his front teeth and said, "I wasn't gonna mention it, but ya do need a little practice with the stove." He enjoyed the cheese omelet, however.

Emmett confided that he had never been fishing for silver salmon before, though he had fished for tuna. "Maybe we'll both learn something," he said. I was impressed by the enthusiasm and total involvement he had for his boat and his own created world, while the shoreline and other boats and the sky and the ocean became merely photographs to be enjoyed at another time.

He remained in the dugout across the stern of the Mary Patt, selecting lures and flashers, connecting nylon leaders to wire lines wrapped around cylinders and held out from the boat by wings and 30-pound lead balls. The balls were the last things to be connected and dropped and the first things to be pulled in and reseated on their little bowls on either side of the deck. They were positioned slightly forward of the dugout.

Rupert says, "Balls are a very important part of life."

I stood on the deck to the rear of the cabin, aft, watching for traffic and observing his technique as much as possible, hoping to learn something. After two hours of watching him tangle lines and curse at his pulleys, I learned that I would learn much.

Finally, after much persistence, Emmett managed to have four of the six wired lines in the water at once, fully loaded with lures and leaders spaced by little beads. There was a set of two beads, 18 inches apart, every fathom. He ran a leader every three sets of beads. We were running consistently at a depth of 50 fathoms.

That is the only fucking fishing lesson I intend to give.

With the pulleys and the levers and the outriggers and the gears, it was all too mechanical for me. Above my head, where I stood, was a tiny speaker, spitting out tinny sounding voices, talking shop and cracking dry jokes with an occasional heh heh. I really didn't push myself to the limit in trying to understand any of it. I did enjoy the movie. I felt quite privileged. Emmett was a pleasure to watch with his natural, easy uneasiness, plunging totally with his desires and relying on instinct, but not mechanical at all, cursing constantly at his lack of knowledge, but gaining it continuously by trying. His determination amazed me. Meanwhile the voices over the speaker babbled on in different tones and pitches, but all very nonchalant, like Steinbeck describing death.

Emmett and I each drank a beer once the four lines were submerged. The lures took part in a totally related but completely separate drama beneath the surface, their sexual, needle-sharp, ledged hooks hidden, giving them an appearance of vulnerability, hoping to prey on the unsuspecting aggressor. Such is the way of the everyday housewife.

On the first round of pulling in the lines, surprisingly, there were two salmon hooked. I was allowed the honor of manning the large net. Much to my surprise I was successful in bringing the two pierced victims aboard. We celebrated our accomplishment with a beer. Emmett was very involved in the realm of now, either celebrating or cursing, but always enjoying each individual moment. I could tell by the look in his eyes. It was quite different from the look in the eyes of the fish, although they were also involved in the moment.

The fish had the same look my victim had had—after he became attracted to my lure of vulnerability and he tried to filet and eat me—and the aggressor became the victim. We were eye to eye. He blinked.

DAY 31

A sincere hope is that when the assassin performs his duty, he looks the victim in the eye as he sends a spirit on its way. Last weekend when I picked up the two bomb-making sailors on their way to the peace demonstration, they spoke of surface-to-air missiles with video cameras and telescopic lenses. They said that the purpose of the telescopic lens is to photograph the expression on the face of pilots about to meet their doom--Prime-time fare, no less.

Murder is a concept that should be experienced totally. I spoke with my victim—about life—before his death. The choices were clear. Nuclear weapons take so much of the personal touch away from murder. Perhaps it is in line with the trend of the world: Substitute quantity for quality.

That is why I wish I had my gun—for the personal touch. I would love to see the expression on my face as I pull the trigger. A button seems--so indifferent. **Absurdity** is a trend. **Irony** is a way of life. **Death** is a very important part of it.

DAY 32

This is the 32nd day of my actual existence. I can not deny my intense love for Ermonie and a need to be with her, anywhere— even for brief moments on paper.

I've eaten half a Quaalude and drunk a half-pint of Windsor Canadian whisky and a pot of coffee is on the stove. I have eight large Hefty trash bags of garbage waiting to be delivered to the dump, and, possibly, one bucket of shit. I may save the bucket of shit for posterity. Some things are hard to let go of.

I learned little about fishing from Emmett; there were many distractions. For dinner I cooked fillets of brown rockfish he had caught. Emmett taught me the proper way to fillet a fish by hanging on to the tail. Pffft. I fried the fillets in butter in a big black skillet with just enough lemon.

Emmett was from Oregon originally. He was the first person over twenty-five I met in Oregon who was actually from Oregon. I napped briefly in the afternoon while Emmett continued fishing. I became slightly ill once more. I don't know whether it was from the sea or from fear of shitting in a bucket on the deck of a rolling boat in the open sea.

Rupert says, "Shit is a very important part of life. Without it, cultivation and growth would take longer than the cycle allows. Give a good shit for life. Stay regular."

After my nap and my illness I once more stood on deck beneath the rear speaker. I was ready for everything. The boat steered itself and Emmett played in the dugout. Some boats came and went, and other boats followed or led. And the coastline began to take on different dimensions from different, slowly obtainable angles. But I was ready for anything.

Occasionally, I was even called on to dip the net and grab the pierced victims from the ocean with my extension, dumping them on the deck. When I dipped, Emmett stood aside.

Emmett had been a merchant seaman before he became involved with asbestos; he fell in love and needed a job that would keep him near. He had been through two marriages since. His first love was the sea, and now the Mary Patt. The Mary Patt, though chipped, had a character all her own. She was like a happy old dog, struggling by on three legs, enjoying being a boat with a skipper.

The crackle and the tones over the speaker became music as the day progressed, though the only words I heard were the ones in my head and an occasional instruction from Emmett. He never stopped moving. He worked with the lines and the boat; he adjusted course and changed lures constantly. I observed in a dreamlike state, feeling like a smile.

"Calling the Mary Patt," echoed in my brain. "Another thought," I thought.

"Calling the Mary Patt. Emmett, you turned on?"

"Aha," I thought, awakened from my trance.

"Emmett, Emmett, are ya there?"

I informed Emmett that he was being paged by the gods; he climbed from the dugout and listened for the voice. It didn't return.

"Musta been Otley," he said. He walked through the cabin to the front and called out over his radio, "Burgers, is that you, Burgers?" There was no answer; Emmett returned to the dugout. A short time later, once again came the voice. "Emmett, it's Otley. When ya get a minute, call me back." The voice sounded much different from any of the other tones I had heard all day. It sounded like unstable barometric pressure. It needed studying to really know where it was coming from.

Once again I informed Emmett of the voice; leaving no particular task unattended, he climbed from the dugout. "Callin' Burgers. Otley, it's Emmett."

"Emmett, Emmett, is that you? This is Burgers here."

"This is the Mary Patt."

"How ya doin'?" I couldn't figure out whether it was a deluge or a drought coming on, but the voice ruled the airwaves. It seemed like suddenly everyone else abandoned ship.

"We got a few; those rock fish won't leave us alone."

"I know what cha mean. Ya stayin' out tonight?"

I wanted to stay.

"What's the weather?"

Everything was beautiful.

"Might get rough."

"Might go in."

"See ya later."

End of conversation. Emmett returned to the dugout and no particular task. He didn't ask my advice. Pffft. I made a pot of coffee. After the coffee was finished cooking, Emmett took a break from the dugout; we both sat on the hatch of the after hold and sipped coffee which was improving. It had graduated to the flavor of slightly soiled flannel.

"You enjoyin' yerself?" he asked. He seemed sincere. I got the immediate impression that I was along for the ride—as a witness. I didn't know if I was supposed to learn something through observation, and suddenly begin doing things on my own or if I was there simply to enjoy myself without expectation.

"I'm having a good time. I want to do more, but you're the skipper. If there is anything that you may want me to do, tell me. Otherwise, I'll try to stay out of your way."

"Okay. Everything seems to be under control," he said. I knew to continue doing only what I had been doing. It was his boat. "Coffee's gettin' better, still needs a little work." His eyes shone like happy little droplets of blue splashed on a canvas by an artist for a reason. And he knew he was dying.

"That was Otley Mowbray called before," he said with an affectionate tone. "Lives down here all year 'round in a trailer. He's from New York original." Emmett wheezed and coughed whenever he tried to bring out what was in. "Used ta own a hunert hotdog carts. Helped him retire here and he's only forty-two. He breaks out in hives though—whenever he eats anything with mustard on or in it. Fishes alone and takes his time. Don't catch much. He don't need to. Claims there's money in hotdogs."

Emmett continued and told me a story of how Otley had been fishing for tuna, alone, 200 miles off the coast. Burgers had been set on automatic pilot while he was below untangling lines. There was a sudden jolt that knocked him off his feet. He scurried to the deck to find he had nearly collided with a Russian freighter, coming close enough to have one of his outriggers sheared off. He feared he had started a war, but the crew of the freighter, seeing no severe damage was done and no one was hurt, leaned over, waving and laughing, making sure everything was okay. Otley laughed back. It's a good thing there were no generals around.

We finished our coffee break and Emmett returned to the dugout where he pulled in a few more salmon between untangling the lines. I returned to my post. The voices continued commenting on how easy everything was—though fishless.

* * *

I'm not sure whether I'm looking forward to massaging fiberglass boats tomorrow. I'm glad it's only a temporary job.

* * *

We turned and headed south as clouds began to appear from the west. Emmett decided it best not to stay out another night. The lines, being controlled by pulleys which failed to respond on several occasions, began to be a burden because of the lack of salmon and an overabundance of minor ailments, like kinks and twists and tangles, which would mean nothing if there were more fish.

* * *

My fear of being alone is intensified by the mind-altering substances which I have inflicted upon myself for escape. The rock group the Eagles say, "Every point of refuge has its price." What would I do if I had to pay rent? The epitome of masochism is putting oneself in a position with high expectations where there is no logical satisfactory conclusion.

You hung up?

No, I'm working.

Ramona Pearl sang, "Sometimes the lights all shinin' on me. Other times I can barely see. Lately it occurs to me, what a long strange trip it's been."

Rupert says, "Fragmentation is a very important part of life; everything is nothing more than pieces brought together."

I'll buy that. I've been listening to the public radio station out of Pittsburgh. They're having a contribution drive. It's all very religious. Rupert says, "Religion can be healthy for many; there is no one way. Besides, if you ain't got no money, you gotta keep the faith."

Go drive your cab, why don't you, Rupe?

* * *

The sun began to sink rapidly. Emmett pulled in the lines and neatly stowed the tackle for another day. There was a proper place for everything. He taught me the proper way of cleaning salmon for sale, also. I felt privileged; I had something to do. I stood in the dugout, astern, where a special wooden tray was mounted. I scraped and gutted our catch of 26 Salmon, pushing the innards down a chute which emptied into the ocean.

We headed quickly for home and soon the lighthouse came into view. The beam became brighter as darkness approached. The silhouette of a large crane looked like a giraffe in the amber twilight. It stood motionless at the very end of a large stone jetty, still being constructed at the entrance of the bay. It nearly connected to an older jetty.

They formed an arrow, pointing westward. The north side of the entrance was a peninsula of sand and vegetation which sank into the ocean, forming a hidden bar which had to be crossed to gain admittance to the bay.

The gutted fish were placed aside to be hosed and stored once we were docked. We ran parallel to the coastline until we reached the channel markers. Emmett turned hard to port and headed for the jetty.

"Now we gotta cross the bar," Emmett said with tension in his voice.

The huge boulders forming the jetty and the silhouette of the giraffe seemed to take on life. We were moving, but they approached. It was a life and death struggle with the crash of the surf and overindulgence in foam.

The Mary Patt became a reluctant surfboard as we made our way through the narrow channel. Emmett kept her balanced. He rode the crest of waves while the surf crashed into the jetty on one side and broke over the bar on the other.

Then there was calm.

The lights of the basin became a glow on the other side of a rise as the engines were slowed to a putt-putt, once inside the bay. Emmett instructed me how to change the outriggers from wings back into limbless trees. "We gotta hurry," he spit out, "got no rear runnin' lights. Coast Guard'll give me a ticket." We each drew a line constructing a tree, fastening it in three separate places on the boat.

There was the sound of a bell and a horn, and then a whistle above the smooth silent hum of the Mary Patt. Emmett stood smiling and silent at the helm, directing her ever so gently alongside the rise toward the sound of the whistle. "Whoooo. . .whoooo. . .whoooo. . ." I stood halfway in and halfway out of the cabin, to Emmett's left. We turned the jetty and passed through an inlet, while sounds went and sounds came and a sign whispered, "You are responsible for your wake." Amber lights appeared like a festival in the forest.

We passed where I had been with Brad the day before for bait, where the sweet-tasting bait dipper was docked. And we turned to the row of old wooden boats, where some ticked and others tocked to the gentle rhapsody of the basin. Emmett squared the Mary Patt easily into her berth against the old tire defending the dock. A truce was made in reverse.

Burgers was already docked next door to port; Otley Mowbray took the bow line. I recognized the voice. Emmett showed me the stern, and we hemmed her in neatly for the night. I didn't know what I was supposed to do. Suddenly, I felt perhaps my adventure on the Mary Patt was coming to its conclusion. There had been no mention of the length of my stay. I didn't really do anything except brew some bad coffee. So, I dipped and cleaned a few fish. I was wrapped in a blight not wishing to assume anything. I didn't know what Emmett's intentions were. I was confused. Then it came to me—maybe I should ask.

"Emmett, do you suppose I could use your bunk for the night?"

The perky little dwarf, who didn't want to be grumpy at all, flashed at me crossly as if I had said something wrong. We had spent the day on a boat together and communicated. Still we were each wrapped up in our own little worlds.

"Not with me in it," he snapped.

The sexual innuendo flashed in my brain. "Assume nothing," I thought. "Why would he think that," I thought—the earrings—the typewriter—perhaps, because I was from Baltimore.

I coughed and laughed and covered up. "An apple this big," I said. "Hold on, Emmett. I don't want to sleep with you. I only want to use one of your bunks."

"Oh, ho," he coughed and laughed and covered up. Then he wheezed and spit. "Sure, that's fine. I mean just don't mess up ma roll. I go into Reedsport to ma trailer." He walked into the cabin and felt his sleeping bag on the bottom bunk. "This should be comfortable fer ya."

"I'll use the same one I've been sleeping in."

"I thought. . .well you said you're a writer and some a dose guys are weird" he stuttered.

"That's okay."

"There's a space heater if it gets cold. Ma trailer—I stay in ma trailer."

Thoughts of Ethel's instructions had never crossed my mind. But suddenly I realized I was not the only paranoid person on the face of the earth.

"You're more than welcome to stay here. I forgot to bring ma TV with me though. Hooks up here across from the bunk." He even appeared to be embarrassed.

"Everything's fine, Emmett. Thank you."

We squirted down the gutted fish and stored them in the forward hold, over and under ice. "If it turns out to be a nice day tamar, we'll go out again. Shower's in the north buildin' on the peninsula. Flush toilets, too."

Emmett quickly gathered a few things and was soon off, down the dock with Otley. I heard Otley laugh, sounding like a chicken with a broken wing as they disappeared up the steps from the docks. I was alone with the Mary Patt. I rummaged through my duffel bag, which was stored under the table in the booth, for a clean towel and clothes. I changed from my Nikes to flip-flops and strolled up the dock to the peninsula and over to the brick building, hearing whistles and bells and horns.

After my shower, I returned to the Mary Patt where I became restless and walked into town for french fries and gravy and coleslaw with a small Coke at an all-night café. Silently in the night, not seeing a soul, I returned to the Mary Patt for the sounds of the whistles and bells and horns and the amber lights of the festival in the forest, and sleep.

DAY 33

I've come to the conclusion that suicide is a matter of mood and a customer of convenience on this, the morning of the 33rd day of my deliverance. It's Monday. I type while the coffee boils and I prepare to go massage boats. GRUNT! It's a gray day.

* * *

Rice, zucchini, tomato sauce, hot pickled cauliflower, one hot pepper, hot pickled onions, Jack Mackerel and cranberry sauce, sopped up with a cinnamon and raisin bagel, washed down with pineapple juice and Windsor Canadian. I can't forget to mention the Hershey Almond bar for dessert. There's a tornado watch out for the area tonight. If I see it, I'm going to look for OZ.

* * *

Wednesday morning, the fifth day of my journey, one week and one day before I became God, I was awake before Emmett arrived. Pffft. I prepared some coffee. I couldn't understand what I was doing wrong. I make good coffee now. Unless it's just that I've gotten used to bad coffee and I can't tell the difference anymore—programming. It coulda been the water.

The skies were clear; there was a very brisk wind blowing in from the ocean. Emmett decided it best not to fish that day.

"You're welcome to stick around and see how she breaks."

"Why not?"

I didn't like to smoke around Ermonie's children, and I hadn't been smoking for some time, but I needed something to do with my hands. I asked Emmett if he wouldn't mind picking up some Prince Albert in a can and some rolling papers on one of his trips into town. I promised not to smoke around him if it was a nuisance. He coughed and wheezed and said, "I like the smell of pipe tobacco. Make yourself at home."

I guess he popped over first thing to see if I was still there, because he was soon on his way back up the dock and into town. I tried to relax and figure out what I was and wasn't supposed to do while I drank the lousy coffee. I skipped breakfast though; I felt a need to earn. Emmett soon returned with the tobacco and I reimbursed him the money spent. I began rolling. My hands were happy.

He started up the Mary Patt after banging his Chrysler engine three times with a hammer. He cussed at it, and then thanked it when it started. I still didn't smoke in the cabin when he was around.

"I gotta pump out the bilge; watch out fer helicopters," Emmett said with a mischievous gleam in his eye. I didn't ask. I didn't mind either. He rummaged below in his engine compartment and I watched the sky. And then I began watching seagulls. They were playing tag on top of the pilings, or maybe it was "Chicken." One would land and one would take off and hop to the next, where one would be sitting until the other one came, and it would take off, and the other would land. Occasionally a piling would be passed where one was sitting. It would remain. Whether it was comfortable or didn't want to play or ignored seemed to make no difference. It was all part of the game, and I got to watch. I saw no helicopters.

The slow rumble of the Mary Patt didn't seem to disrupt anything. It blended into the scene. Its music caused Emmett to dance, or so it seemed. Like an Indian, without paint, from one side to the other, he hopped, leaning over the side and back to the other, leaning over the side.

"Look out for the Coast Guard, too," he said. "They have a station right across the way." He danced into the cabin and back out, carrying a plastic bottle with a squirt top and a trigger. There was a sky blue liquid in the bottle. He danced to one side and shot at the water. "A fisherman's ritual," I thought. He danced to the other side and shot at the water. There were no helicopters, coming or going. I watched him cautiously from atop the cover of the dugout. He walked back to me, taking a break from his dance.

"This stuff really works," he said, chuckling as if he had discovered a wonder of technology. "A lotta boats use it; it's an industrial degreaser. I gotta oil leak. If ah don't pump out the bilge, we'll sink. I hate dumpin' oil in the basin; besides, it's a $500 fine if they spot a slick comin' from a boat. Watch out for helicopters."

He continued his dance. A rainbow, nearly surrounding the Mary Patt, appeared in the water. Emmett danced around, looking up every so often, then down, shooting the blue liquid into the rainbow. The rainbow was eaten, with another soon taking its place, and again, Emmett would dance until it disappeared. This went on for some time—Emmett's rainbow dance. Finally the bilge pumped clear.

"I've been meaning ta fix that leak, but the engine still works. There are a lot of things around here that don't. If it works, don't fix it." It was decided, since the pulleys and spools of wire line didn't work well the day before, to repair them. Some had nicks and were sure to break; others were too loosely wrapped. We spent the rest of the morning unwrapping, re-wrapping and splicing where needed.

For lunch we drove in the black Chevy pickup through town and a little north on Highway 101. We stopped in a restaurant-bar and had burgers and a beer. I confessed my murder while waiting for my burger with raw onion and pickles. It seemed like the thing to do at the time. It just sort of came out while we were discussing apples. The subject continued.

After lunch we drove back through town and out to the Mary Patt where we finished working on the lines. With the task completed, we gathered up the previous day's catch and drove down to the weigh station. The legal minimum for silver salmon is 18 inches; for Chinooks, it's 24. We each carried two burlap sacks with the 26 fish. We proudly dumped our catch on the trays at the station; the young boy promptly re-sacked eight. "These are illegal Chinooks," the boy said.

Emmett was more nervous than upset, though the price from the eighteen legal fish would hardly cover fuel. "I'm going to have to learn how to tell them apart," he said. "Keep 'em outa sight. They give you a heavy fine if they catch ya with any illegal fish."

"What do you want me to do with them?"

"Eat 'em. Makes no sense lettin' good food go to waste," he chuckled. Pffft. The day was coming to an end. I returned to the Mary Patt. Emmett returned to his trailer near Reedsport. I had four 1-1/2 inch thick salmon steaks for dinner.

DAY 34

This is my 34th day of confrontation. I worked today; I will work no more. I've been fired from my job of massaging fiberglass boats. Goodbyes are such a trauma. I did enjoy the physical activity, though it kept me from my obsession.

I worked hard, and all who worked there were pleasant. I cannot be a company man for only $3.35 an hour. I wasn't as emotionally involved with the company as they would have liked me to be. I didn't feel overtime was necessary, especially since it kept me from my words. Now I am with my words and they are with their fiberglass.

Rice cooked in pineapple juice, peanuts, one jalapeno and refried beans, sopped up with saltines, washed down with coffee and spring water, with cling peaches for dessert. "What we have hya, is a failya ta communicate." I am not a quitter, and my priorities were becoming confused. So, here I am, once again, without gainful employment. I still have my wok.

This may sound strange: I find myself laughing out loud hysterically over being fired. For some odd reason, I think my boss knew he was doing me a favor. (He wore a billed cap.) At this point, it really doesn't matter. After all, I did come here to die. Now, perhaps, I can again enjoy my reflection in the fogged mirrors. How I've missed my hollow point. It's never moved; now I can see it again.

Rupert says, "Confrontation is a very important part of being alive.

* * *

I woke up Thursday morning on board the Mary Patt. It was the sixth day of my journey, one week before I became God. Pffft. I cooked two salmon steaks for breakfast, with coffee. My coffee was improving.

Emmett arrived at 9:30. "It's still too rough to head out. I think it's time to hook up ma anchor," he announced.

A gathering commenced. Otley Mowbray arrived, carrying a very large drill, which could handle a one-inch diameter bit. In the daylight, he looked as I had envisioned him by his voice over the speaker and his name. He wore a billed cap and a red face. Otley had labial Herpes. He covered the spot on his lip with cream and complaints of exposure.

The day was windy, yet sunny and dry. Otley was wearing calf-high wet boots. His pants and shirt were uniform gray; his thick spectacles made his eyes seem like solar-powered pinwheels, always turning by the rays of the sun.

A large hole had to be drilled in the Mary Patt's bow mount, so a new roller could be attached. The bow mount consisted of two half-inch thick plates of steel, painted green and chipped. It still looked like the hand-carved figurehead of a naked lady in my eyes, but then I am very nearsighted. It extended over the dock as proudly as any hand-carved figure of a naked lady I had ever seen. An anchor was necessary, I was told.

"So this is your crew?" Otley squeaked observantly.

Rupert says, "There is beauty in imperfection."

Three more resident fishermen of Winchester Bay arrived on the scene, while Emmett, Otley and I were contemplating the task at hand. One of the three could have passed for the twin of the man I murdered. He was broad-shouldered, barrel-chested and big-bellied. He wore a white tee shirt and his black hair was cut short, exposing oversized ears. But this man was quiet and spoke only with his eyes that searched my being for a motive. Everyone liked Emmett; all were curious about the stranger—me.

Another of the three was very thin, with a large Adam's apple and the eyes of a hammerhead shark. He was the mouth and the brains of the larger man. His thin lips were those of a skeptic and a troublemaker, as was his tongue. The third was a mere shadow who left no impression.

I was the outsider and I was a shadow myself. I tried to sit back and be an observer, though I knew, next to the task at hand, I was the focus of attention. Eyes are never quiet; vibes are part of the ever present beat, and the beat goes on, with heavy bottom.

Rupert says, "Bass is a very important part of striving."

I was asked various questions, which I had answered over and over again since my arrival in Winchester Bay. I answered again.

"I'm from Baltimore."

"I'm a writer."

"I'm hitchhiking down the coast."

"An apple this big."

There was a conference on the angle of attack. It was decided that a crate, farther down the dock, should be used to stand on to reach the hole in the bow mount with the drill. No one moved; I went for the crate.

There were actually two crates, one on top of the other. The one on top was battered and seemed unfit to stand on. The bottom crate was filled with assorted things. It looked to be in much better condition than the one on top. I proceeded to remove the things from the bottom crate and place them in the crate that had been on top. It was all very time-consuming. There seemed to be nothing else for anyone to do while I was dealing with the crates. They watched me. I wasn't particularly interested in their conversation. I was involved in moving things, listening to the bass; I heard a pedal steel guitar.

"He's nothin' but a big fuckin' faggot." Then, laughter.

I dragged the crate back to a position below the bow and stood back, smiling and oblivious, though I knew my test was at hand. I had propositioned no one and had no intention of doing so. I could think of no reason for the comment, other than exploratory surgery—or the game that seagulls play. I was very comfortable on my piling.

Rupert says, "Don't take my kindness for weakness."

There was a job to be done above all else—games could wait. Emmett stepped up on the crate, while Otley boarded the Mary Patt and leaned over the bow. The large drill was started by Emmett; he aimed it at the hole on the port side plate. Otley held onto the drill also, from above. Perspiration filled Otley's spectacles, making his eyes look like starfish in a bowl. Both men applied pressure, attempting to force the dull one-inch bit into the half-inch hole. There was a lot of noise, but not much action and very little headway. The pedal steel guitar with the Adam's apple took over after a few minutes. His slight frame could barely keep the drill afloat, even with Otley helping from above and Emmett pushing from behind.

My reincarnated victim and I looked on, though we were obviously the bulkiest of the lot. The shadow remained a shadow. Emmett, Otley and the Adam's apple shortly ran out of juice; my ex-victim took a turn on the crate. He was very big and very strong; he made an indentation, but he had no staying power. He blinked.

Rupert says, "It is said for my existence that I'll always need persistence, or so it seems, my role in life is like a serf."

I took my turn on the crate and felt the need to complete the hole, no matter how long it took. I did. I felt comfortable on my piling and played the game as I saw fit. The game ended. The mood became easy and fun. Otley retrieved a smaller but sharper bit from his boat next door; we took turns on the other plate and it was pierced in half the time.

Rupert says,
I heard a different drummer
A long long time ago
I was told a different story
But you see, it ain't necessarily so.
Perhaps we can't see I to I
Sometimes it's doggone rough
But yet there's no real problem, friend
Cause I'm only semi-tough.

Rupert likes to rhyme, but don't let him kid you, he goes for the jugular.

* * *

Once the task was completed, my ex-victim and the Adam's apple finally introduced themselves and shook my hand. The shadow had disappeared. Otley had some work to do onboard Burgers and went about it. The easy little fishing village of Winchester Bay remained that way. I understood the reason for the test once Emmett and I were on our way to Reedsport to pick up 300 feet of steel cable to use as an anchor chain.

"Somebody's givin' me this here cable," he said. He seemed a lot more comfortable and began to speak more freely. "We all try to help each other out when we can. With the way things are out thar, that's the only way a little guy can make it anymore. We got a community."

Fat Grew says, "There's no business like your own, so mind it."

"Who's that?"

Don't worry about it; that's what he says.

After picking up the cable, we stopped by Emmett's trailer; we shared the bottom of a bottle of brandy; he showed me souvenirs he had picked up around the world when he was a merchant seaman. His first wife had run off with a truck driver and his second left him for another woman. Emmett was happy in his trailer and on board the Mary Patt. There seemed to be no conflict of interest.

"Ya know," he said, "if in the course of a man's life he finds one true friend, then that man has led a good life.

We returned to the Mary Patt, where Emmett dropped me and met up with Otley; they went on their way. Pffft. I had salmon steaks for dinner. My reflection in the mirror is yawning. I think it's time to dream of Ermonie and how it could have been.

DAY 35

Such a joy it is to sit and have breakfast this morning, now that I am once again among the ranks of the unemployed: Fresh hot coffee and cream of wheat with cocoa and peanut butter and honey and cling peaches. It's all so wonderfully insane, this world we live in. Where else but in America could a man lose his job and lay in a week's ration of booze and hide out in a cabin in the woods deciding whether to take his own life, or perhaps join the marines. I took my trash to the landfill which is plastered with POISON signs; my knoll is beautiful on such a bright sunny spring day.

* * *

On the seventh day of my journey, Friday, pffft, I had salmon steaks with coffee for breakfast. It was windy and I was sure it would be another day of no fishing. I had spent $20 since I had left the camp; there was still $31 left in my fund, with still a long way to trip to LA. I felt my time on the Mary Patt growing short. Emmett arrived later than usual on Friday, allowing me time for a morning shower.

On my return to the boat, about 10:00, he was there. I didn't discuss the prospect of my leaving first thing; I was enjoying myself too much, and thought I'd see how things went.

"What's on the agenda for today, Skipper?"

"I'd like to try gettin' the anchor hooked up. First ah better pump out the bilge."

With the new roller mount in place and the cable on deck, it seemed like the thing to do; what better way to start the day than with a dance. Emmett climbed into the hold in the cabin and started his ritual by pounding some sense into Chrysler. The Mary Patt coughed a few times and then hummed; so did Emmett. He became "Emmett of the Mary Patt and his Rainbow Factory" featuring ZAP-dried rainbows. After watching him again, I soon realized what happened to the rainbows he sprayed—he carried them in his pocket. I enjoyed him.

On the forward deck there were two hatches, both leading to the forward hold which was the cold-storage compartment for ice and fish and beer and other assorted perishables. One hatch was more forward than the other. Directly between the two hatches, which were painted some sort of coarse-textured gray along with the forward deck, was an oversized chipped green winch. Actually, it was a large cotton spool made of iron. First, we took the 300 feet of cable down on the dock. I walked with the end, while Emmett checked it out for quality.

"Have you ever stacked cable?" he asked.

"I think so."

"Just remember, every other turn is opposite," and he demonstrated. Once the cable was re-stacked, I lugged it back on deck to the very front of the boat, where one end was attached and we witnessed the power of the winch. A slow-moving salt water taffy machine is the impression I got; it took an entire minute for one loop to be pulled from the stack. I volunteered to direct the cable in neat rows on the spool, since it had no automatic leader. I wore gloves for the task and sat on the forward hatch of the forward hold, watching the wheel and pulling taffy. Emmett busied himself in the cabin, running wires for the rear running lights.

Listening to the Mary Patt sing and watching the winch slowly turning, I deeply desired to have one more day out on the ocean. Occasionally I would remove a glove to roll some Prince Albert.

Rupert says, "Some things which are perfectly natural and normal in one realm may seem odd when viewing from afar. There is no one way."

I felt very relaxed and at ease, holding the cable taut and allowing it to creep through my hand. At the time I was quite unaware of the drama taking place behind me. Though the winch was rolling ever so slowly, progress was being made. Every so often, I would be nudged between the shoulders by the cable. I turned and shook it straight and easiness prevailed. After a while, the nudge became more frequent and the cable harder to straighten. No longer did it need a shake, but a shove, to correct the turbulence. I first thought it rather amusing, the once neatly-stacked steel cable performing a snake dance to the hum of the Mary Patt. It soon began to attack me. I called out to Emmett. I merely provided unheard words to the melody of the motors already being performed.

The steel cable began to caress me and wrapped itself in my hands. I was slowly being dragged by the heels of my hands toward the massive, creeping, powerful roller. I pictured myself a giant polish sausage, stretched to infinity, to be used as an anchor chain for organic fishing. I had always fantasized my life being ended by being gunned down by machine guns in Times Square. The concept of meeting death has always bothered me more than death itself. If I were to die on a boat, let it be at sea, scooped up by a giant squid or swallowed by a whale. I was to become taffy, wrapped up in a giant cotton spool, drowned out by a Chrysler engine with no chance for a rebate. I kicked off my flip-flop and lunged for the lever to turn off the winch with my foot. It worked. I untied my hands and gazed at the mass of linguini, wishing I could cover it with a white clam sauce and eat it instead of messing with it anymore.

Rupert says, "Look in, but watch out."

I attempted at first to untangle things by moving a loop here and a knot there. I soon came to realize that my lack of knowledge on the subject of tangled steel cable would only make matters worse if I persisted in my cover-up. I felt I was floating on a raft of shit. Then I remembered, "Dump it over the side." But it wasn't my raft. I prepared myself for the consequences by rolling some Prince Albert. I walked through the cabin to where Emmett was concerned with wires.

"Emmett," I said, waiting for the proper moment to avoid anyone's electrocution.

"Is it done already?"

"Boy, is it done."

"Oh-oh."

"Remember the way you taught me how to stack steel cable? It wouldn't by any chance have to be un-stacked the same way, would it?"

We left the wires hanging, returning calmly to where the smattering of influence was photogenically poised about the deck. It all looked very artistic. Emmett didn't think so.

"Aw, shit," he said. My very thought as I waited and watched helplessly.

He turned the machine on, to unwind. Ever so slowly, a few turns unturned, giving him room to work. He pushed at the knots and twisted at the loops, causing other knots and other loops to twist and turn and dance.

"What did ya do?"

"Emmett, I fucked up."

"Every other one, I told ya every other one." He began to lose his cool.

"I'm sorry, I thought it was only to stack it. It seemed to be coming along fine."

Rupert says, "Sometimes, there is only one way. There are exceptions to every rule."

More and more came unwound. Emmett stretched and cursed and coughed. I was waiting for an explosion. He turned purple, but still the cable prevailed.

Then, all at once, it came to him, his own words. With a feat of superhuman strength, the tiny man outstretched his arms and swooped down like an eagle, grabbing the unruly serpent in his mighty talons. He raised it in the air and stormed to the bow and dumped it over the side onto the unsuspecting dock. "Kashcoshabbabbabalcabonkthud" was the reply of the shit.

"Do you always turn purple when you're upset? I made a mistake. I'm sorry."

"It's not yer fault."

"I know, but you coulda killed somebody."

"Ah guess ah do get carried away a little. It works. I feel much better now. Ah used ta hold everything in. Didn't work."

* * *

Rhoda Apple from the Hope Springs Eternal Hotel was just here. We had coffee. She stopped in to see how I was doing. I told her I was fine. She told me Ermonie married the Marine. It happened last week. Oh, well.

Refried beans and cranberry sauce, washed down with grapefruit juice.

* * *

Once more we stretched the cable on the dock, removing all tangles and knots. Instead of stacking it, we rewound it on the roller, straight from the dock.

Afterwards, Emmett was a little reluctant to oblige me with any new tasks. I finally approached him. "You know, Emmett, once I was working with a carpenter friend of mine. I discovered my mechanical aptitude is zilch. It might sound like I'm boasting, but it's only grasping at straws. I'm going to tell you the same thing I told him. I can't do much, but I've fucked over a hundred and fifty different women. I don't see any women. Give me something to do, please."

"That's something." He chuckled and coughed and smiled and after searching, handed me a can of green paint and a brush.

I very carefully painted over the chips. I flattened some wrinkles with a scraper in places. And I stroked the Mary Patt gently with my extension and the fresh paint in an attempt to give her the illusion of youth for her master. She needed it, and so did he. He only comes and goes.

Rupert says, "Watch out for helicopters."

Yeah, that's right. We finished the tasks for the day and Emmett took me on a tour of the area where I hadn't been. We left the peninsula and instead of driving through town, we turned up a narrow road and headed south. Emmett pointed out Otley's trailer and we continued uphill, past the lighthouse where we came to a spot called "Chicken Point." I was told it received its name because many fishermen drove up there the night before a trip to get a look at the bar at the entrance to Winchester Bay. Once they see the surf breaking over the bar, many decide to wait another day. The twin jetties were pointing out to sea, towards the purple sky and the setting sun. It looked as if a front was moving in; I felt my time was growing short. I mentioned if we didn't fish the next day, I'd be on my way.

He dropped me back at the Mary Patt, where I sat and thought and listened. I had a Dungeness crab for dinner. Pft. It was given to me by the young man on the boat next door. His boat was called The Hunter. And I used my typewriter for the first time on my journey also. I used it to compose a letter to Ermonie. Now I know I'll never see her again. Maybe I wasn't romantic enough? Perhaps that's it. I've been practicing on Tripod. She doesn't think I'm romantic enough either. It doesn't matter. She won't screw me, but she still sticks by me.

The absolute freedom I feel. I won't have to punch a clock tomorrow and grunt for $3.35 an hour. I have all the time in the world to think about what to do with my bucket of shit.

I just came from a walk to the top of my hill. The colors have changed dramatically since my last walk. I even stopped and talked with my neighbor Clyde. His lawn is so perfect. He removes all the rocks and even chips off the tops of the ones he can't move.

"Clyde," I said, "rocks are good."

"Can't mow a rock," he answered.

* * *

The night I became God on Monastery Beach, I read a Rupert rhyme.

> Rupert says,
> I woke up this morning
> And didn't know what to do
> So I drank a cup of coffee
> And I smoked a joint or two
> I ate a jelly doughnut
> I thought about a job
> I jumped right back into my bed
> Cause I'm fearful of a mob
> I've got the cop-out blues
> I take life simply as it comes
> Philosophizin' with the other bums
> I'm going nuts.

Rupert likes to rhyme. It's longer than that, but it's boring.

Gosh. It's all very strange. I think I'm even losing Tripod. She has another friend. I wouldn't have believed it, but there's another three-legged dog in the neighborhood. She's missing her left hind leg. Clyde said her name is Corners. She shits on rocks. Maybe that's why Clyde removed all the rocks from his lawn. Why didn't he say that? Maybe that's not why. I'm glad Tripod found a dog friend.

But then, on my journey, I was in tune. Everything was so simple. But now, a tribute to Duke Ellington is coming over the radio by way of public broadcasting from the Kennedy Center in Washington. I intend to enjoy it.

DAY 36

Cream of wheat, cocoa, honey, peanut butter, peaches and evaporated milk with hot coffee and grapefruit juice on the side, just like uptown. Welcome to the 36th day of my everlasting meal. I'm running out of drugs; I can no longer take an overdose. There are so many birds singing outside this morning, it must be spring or some other communicable disease.

* * *

Pffft, Saturday morning, the eighth day of my journey, I had coffee and was all packed and ready to hit the road. Emmett arrived at eight, pumping like his piston self.

"You ready to give 'er another go?" he called to me from the dock without boarding.

"Yeah."

"I'll be right back," he said, ready to rush off.

I called for him and he took my letter for Ermonie. Off he shot like a mechanical toy, wound to the max. I was overcome with joy. I filled the water tanks with a hose running from the dock and changed from my flip-flops to my Nikes. Emmett returned in a few minutes with more beer and bread. I stashed the beer and he beat the Chrysler. We cast off the lines and the Mary Patt was under way, all watered, wired, anchors aweigh and smelling of fresh paint. I waved to the coast guard and the sweet-tasting bait dipper, whistled at the whistle and tooted at the horn. We left the basin and drifted in the bay.

"Lower the outriggers!" Emmett commanded.

I let loose the lines with a jerk and the trees became wings once more.

We ran alongside the rise and turned at the jetty, heading out to sea. The Mary Patt crossed the bar like a hooker taking a drink; we ran at the channel and headed north at 30 fathoms. Emmett set the automatic pilot, we uncovered the dugout and he began preparing the lines. I once again assumed my role of standing on the deck under the speaker, watching for traffic and helicopters. Emmett pumped the bilge.

I soon removed my shirt to fully enjoy the ultraviolet rays of the sun and keep in line with my death wish as the morning wore on and the sun grew hotter and stronger. There was no threat of *mal de mer,* since I felt totally at home on board the Mary Patt, who was now my friend. Preparation and comfort were our forte. Of course,

Emmett did the preparing while I was comfortable, enjoying his boat and his presence and our surroundings. I wasn't allowed to handle any lines.

> Rupert says,
> Parsnips are hanging--On a line
> Perhaps the thought was
> There was no other place for them to go
> But then again they didn't want
> The roots to show--It doesn't matter
> I'll eat them anyway.

Rupert likes to rhyme? Don't always analyze, realize, fool. Oh, okay.

Everything took on new meaning. The adventure was still there, but the fact that I could associate different voices over the speaker with different faces or spot a boat like Burgers or The Hunter or Do It Again and know who they were, made things seem more real. Emmett pointed out the boat of my reincarnated victim and that of the Adam's apple. He even smiled at my coffee and said, "This is good."

The sight of my first whale in the wild made me jump for joy and point out my discovery. Emmett chuckled from the dugout, more at me than the whale. He had seen many whales. Its gray smooth wetness slid into our circle and then out, saying "Easy Now." Our circle was so much larger that day; my responsibility of easiness didn't change, but became more just the same.

We celebrated with a beer when Emmett managed to get all six lines in the water. He cursed when a large brown seal began to follow us. I thought it was one of the most beautiful sights I had ever seen, swimming casually on the fringe of our wake. Then I remembered signs in several of the local stores which pictured the seal taking chunks out of hooked salmon. The signs read, "Fisherman's Enemy." The seal said, "We eat here too, thank you very much."

* * *

Rice, cream of mushroom soup, peanuts, corn, tuna, celery, bean sprouts, water chestnuts, bamboo shoots, one jalapeno, soy sauce, cranberry sauce and peanut butter mixed in the wok, scooped up with saltines and washed down with Schmidt's beer.

* * *

Fog banks began cropping up everywhere. The world once again became focused.

"Look ahead and listen," was the order. Didn't matter, couldn't see a thing. The fog became weighty and thick like refried beans. The trolling hum of the Mary Patt was all that could be heard. The air became chilled; I re-shirted and sweatered. Emmett continued fishing. Every so often the seal would swim very close to the boat to let us know he was still there.

We continued sailing north; the fog became heavier, even the seal disappeared. Emmett decided it best to turn and head south. The fish were few. Pffft, we had salmon steaks for dinner. Sixteen salmon were landed before the lines were pulled in. Once again, Emmett was surely losing money. We were having a good time.

I gutted the fish on the tray from the dugout and hosed them down with the onboard hose. Occasionally there was a break in the fog; long enough to spot the coast. Then there were no more breaks. The sea became as heavy as the fog. Blue skies and the serenity of Winchester Bay became a memory. The fish were stored in the forward hold. The dugout was covered and all the hatches were battened down. The Mary Patt seemed like she was strung out on speed at a rock concert. Her wings even began flapping.

Emmett urged me to stay inside. I didn't even argue. At the front of the cabin near the helm, he unhooked a rack and lowered a chart table. A digital screen was switched on. Numbers appeared on the screen. Emmett retrieved a pair of spectacles from a shoebox.

"Picked these up for $2.89 in a dime store," he chuckled. He looked at the screen and then examined the chart. He looked at the screen again. Then he turned on the light and examined the chart again. The screen changed numbers and the Mary Patt danced. "I can't figure this thing out," Emmett finally admitted. "Ah never used it before. It's nearly new, cost $3500."

"Did it come with instructions?" I inquired.

"I think they're in ma trailer."

"Oh."

We were lost in the fog.

"Ain't no sense headin' in if I don't know where we are," he said. "Hate ta run aground." Emmett cruised her out to a depth of 50 fathoms and cut the engines. "Now maybe ah can hear if a boat's a comin'."

"Oh."

I figured we were going to die; it had been a long, exhausting day. It was growing dark. I went back and stretched out on my bunk. The rest of the world had disappeared. The neutron bomb had done its bidding, I thought. Emmett still examined charts. The radio had even been silent.

Suddenly with all the subtlety of a hot fudge sundae with Tabasco sauce, the blistered-lipped, red-faced, wet-booted, gray-suited, bill-capped, pinwheel-eyed voice of Otley Mowbray broke the silence. "Callin' the Mary Pat, callin' the Mary Pat. Emmett, can ya hear me?"

Emmett sprang to his phone, to his team gave a whistle.

"Ah hear ya, Burgers."

"Watcha doin'?"

"I'm a driftin'."

"Lost are ya?"

"It's this goddamn fog; ma machine's all screwed up."

"I thought ya might be lost."

"Where are ya?"

"I'm docked. Looked like it was gettin' foggy. Headed in. Fog's a liftin' here. Ya might try headin' east. If you're close, you'll see the light. Better hurry. It's getting dark. Storm's a comin'."

Emmett sprang into action. He tried starting the Mary Patt. It sounded like phlegm being dislodged. He tried again, same thing. He raced to the rear of the cabin and climbed below. Clank, clank,

clank, he smacked the engine with his hammer. Once more he turned the key. The Chrysler obliged. Now that he became stationary at the front, I climbed from my bunk to see what was the matter. The fog lifted just enough so we could see a storm fast approaching and the setting sun being devoured like a hard-boiled egg with salt.

Full tilt, due east, we headed, riding the crest of many waves. I stood by, watching for the light in the distance through a haze of cataracts and too many beers. It seemed a whisper, but loud enough to be heard. I pointed to the light, well off the port bow; Emmett adjusted course and we began to listen for the jetty. The fog bank, taking on the appearance of curdled milk, hovered above the wings of the Mary Patt. The whites of the waves became more and more frequent; the Mary Patt rolled into the meringue but still beat its way forward. I had the strangest feeling we were about to become egg custard against the rocks of the jetty. Emmett switched his depth finder from fathoms to feet and finally remembered to turn on the running lights.

The lights in the rear worked, none of the others did. I looked for the flashlight to check the fuses. It was nowhere to be found. It seemed to be lost in the cosmos. So was I. Emmett screamed orders that didn't mean anything. I looked for hatches to batten down.

The silhouette of the giraffe came into view. It was surrounded by the Vienna Symphony Orchestra, playing Wagner's *Die Walküre*. A fat lady in a blonde wig was singing and Rupert conducted. We followed the music.

We cleared the jetty and came about in the channel. Emmett balanced the Mary Patt precariously above the surf, avoiding the rock and the bar like a spinster crocheting an afghan due for a luncheon the next day. The curdled milk above fell like a curtain and the rain came. We were over the bar and in the bay and listening to the rock from a distance. "Watch out for the Coast Guard. Don't wanta get a ticket for not havin' no runnin' lights."

The curdled milk evaporated and darkness prevailed. The rain whispered against the gentle swells of the bay. We ran alongside the rise; the amber glow of the basin could be felt along with the bell and the whistle and the horn.

The wings were pulled in and fastened; we turned at the jetty on the end of the rise and through the narrow inlet—"you are responsible for your wake"—past where the sweet-tasting bait dipper had been docked, and around to the festival in the forest. It was night when we drifted into the berth; Otley was there to catch the bow line. The only sound became the rain on the water and the thunder. A light show performed in the sky while the Mary Patt rested against her tire; the lines were fastened, fore and aft.

"I guess I'll be leaving in the morning, Emmett."

"Ah'll be by."

Emmett and Otley disappeared up the dock into the rain. I stretched out in my top bunk and thought about the day, knowing the next day would take care of itself. It was time to go.

* * *

It's time for a recap. In the beginning there was a thought. It grew and compounded and evolved into many thoughts, with each taking on its own life and shooting off in different directions, growing and evolving and multiplying. Some became mighty in their own right, forgetting where they had come from and their relationship with the other thoughts. They died, losing their might and retaining only the significance that they once were. Others never got that far. Still others continue. Parnassus is rising.

I haven't seen my penis-shaped light bulb in days. I just found it under a pile of papers I haven't moved in days. I must be horny again. What a simpleton. He'll never get it.

A fire burns against my rock on the knoll. The Philadelphia Orchestra performs for me by way of public radio. The moon is three-quarters full and is slightly distorted by a haze and a good portion of a bottle of brandy. Tripod is already asleep; I'm ready to do the same. My reflections say, "Easy Now," and I wish I had some. Why did she have to go and marry the son of a bitch?

DAY 37

Cream of Wheat, cocoa, honey, peanut butter, evaporated milk, cling peaches, coffee and grapefruit juice. If it works, Do It Again.

This is the 37th day of my non-hunger strike. I'm feasting because I still have food to eat--Better eating through chemistry.

* * *

Sunday morning, the ninth day of my journey, I had no time to rest. I showered and prepared for the road. Pffft, I had salmon steaks and coffee for breakfast. My fishy clothes were stashed in a plastic trash bag; my blanket was re-crumpled and packed. I wanted to see Emmett before I left; I stood waiting on the after deck staring at the water. The week raced through my mind. Emmett of the Mary Patt and his Rainbow Factory: ZAP-dried rainbows. Just add water with a little salt. "If it works don't fix it." Goodbyes are such a trauma.

He arrived with a chuckle and I was leaving with a smile. I felt like a man who had earned a million. Emmett agreed to give me a lift out to the highway. He carried my axe and I lugged my bag over my shoulder and winked at Otley Mowbray as he passed. We walked up the dock and onto the peninsula and over to Emmett's black Chevy pickup. Everything fit up front. He drove through town and out to 101 and headed south up a hill. We came to a scenic overlook, where Emmett pulled to the side and I got out.

"This is a little newer and higher up than Chicken Point; you gotta better view of the bar if ya want it. It's been a pleasure," he said. "I mean it." He flashed his grin with a gap and didn't chuckle.

We looked at each other in the eye, shaking hands.

"You better see a doctor about that cough."

"I don't trust 'em. They fine ya if yer sick."

I could only smile with distorted eyes while he was there. He reached in his wallet and pulled out a twenty.

"This is for Prince Albert. Burn the boy," he said.

"Socks and all--Thank you."

He disappeared. I cried like a baby. I walked to the edge of the scenic overlook and took my last twisted glimpse of the bar and Winchester Bay. I momentarily felt like a pretzel dropped in a pitcher of beer. But I was back up to $51 in my fund, and it was a new day. I stood by the side of the road and waited with my protruding thumb and very pleasant memories.

* * *

Rice, peanuts, corn, cream of mushroom soup, one jalapeno, soy sauce and cranberry sauce, sopped up with whole wheat bread and washed down with coffee and brandy.

Suicide is a challenge. I've just now come back from running off the road twice. Once I went into a ditch and the other time I ran into a tree. It didn't work—I'm still here. I guess I didn't run into it hard enough. Perhaps jogging to death isn't the right way. From all the smoking I've been doing, I was only able to run halfway up the dirt road and back. It isn't very far. I think I'm freaking out.

* * *

Eternity, one would think, lasts forever. But a ride always comes along. I waited for eternity at the scenic overlook. Many cars stopped—only to look. Thoughts of returning to the Mary Patt barraged my sharecropper's mind. I've always been a little bit scattered and slightly disorganized, but I do believe there's a proper place for everything. My proper place at the time was standing at the scenic overlook with my thumb sticking out—waiting. In conditioning my brain for the unknown road ahead, I constantly told myself, "Wow, look how it's been? The best is yet to come." I attempted to manipulate my own mind into being ready and open for anything. I was quite aware that there is usually some sort of a let down whenever things are moving along smoothly. In fact, I'd always thought when things were going right, "This is too good to be true. Something's got to go wrong." Strangest thing, I didn't feel that way at any time on my journey. The mind I was in told me, "If anything goes wrong, it's for the best."

What does any of this mean? What? What are you talking about? What?

What does any of this mean?

Who are you?

"I am but a psychotic reaction, digging through the lime, enveloped in the pleasure of the torment, pushing the hate and drawing flies."

Son of a gun.

Right.

A skinny gray-haired man looking to be in his nineties came along. He was driving a pickup and was only going a short distance. He took me eight miles, which was far enough away from Winchester Bay to keep me from turning back. Sometimes it seems the safest and easiest thing to do is turn back. Thank God for short rides.

You're welcome.

I was left off by the side of the road where I immediately stuck my thumb in the air, and a Datsun pickup stopped. It was dark green and there was a young man and woman in the cab. I was somewhat unsure of where I was to ride. Without saying a word the man driving thumbed me to the rear. I tossed on my gear and followed. I felt like a king, driving along, watching where I had been. We crossed some bridges and were soon in Coos Bay in front of a Mustang being driven by a beautiful young girl. I waved and she waved back. I fantasized that she would be overcome by my animal magnetism and charm and realize I had been on a boat for the past week and take me to where the flowers grow. She turned off.

We passed through Coos Bay. I wondered what would have happened if I had followed the advice of Dave, the PR man from Georgia Pacific. But I didn't wonder very long. I had time to notice Coos Bay was much larger than Winchester Bay. The young couple dropped me at the southern edge of town, where I thanked them and they replied, "Jesus Saves."

I was still on Route 101; there was a bend in the road, a bad place to hitch. I walked around the bend and came to the parking lot of a school. Two boys were riding bicycles. One car was parked in the lot. I became very caught up in "Easy Now;" it didn't detract from my desire for sex. Next to the car stood an older man and a very beautiful young woman, who seemed to be the daughter. One just knows such things. He was waiting for a ride; she was waiting. Once again I began to fantasize that when he got his ride, I would get mine--Can't stop a thought. I spoke to them briefly.

"Hi."

"Hello."

"Nice day."

"Yes, it is."

He got his ride. She drove off. The fantasy had kept me amused and easy while I stood on the side of the road, some 3,000 miles from home with $51 in my pocket and my thumb in the air. I waited in a maze of mystery, wondering, what's next?

A young girl came around the bend. Her flannel shirt was rolled to the elbow. Her stride was that of an urban cowboy who didn't like to ride horses. We exchanged smiles and greetings.

"Are you going far?" she asked, still striding, noticing by my gear that I wasn't a local.

"LA," I answered, pleased by her friendliness.

"Good luck. Coos Bay is a good Christian town. Good Christians don't pick up hitchhikers on Sunday," she said.

"I don't know about that. My ride into town here told me Jesus saves."

"Looking for converts--See if any help you escape."

It seemed an ominous warning. Once again, with no fantasies to amuse me, I was wrapped up in eternity. It came to me, standing on the fringe, that heading out is certainly an eternity. It's not here nd you never know if you'll ever get there. And then, just as quickly, "Easy Now," wherever you are--Son of a gun.

Right.

Shit.

Dump it over the side.

I was picked up by a shirtless heathen driving an old battered Chevy.

"Ain't goin' far," he said, as I crammed my bag into the cluttered back seat.

"Far enough," I answered, noticing we were pointing in the right direction.

He looked to be about nineteen, with a beer between his legs.

"I'd offer you one, but I got no more."

"Ride's fine."

"Hitchhike much?"

"Only when I have to."

"I was hitchhiking in southern California once. Got picked up by a beautiful girl; she took me home. We got naked. She said if her boyfriend walks in don't get excited, he'll join us. I put my clothes on and left. I don't go for any freak action. Where you headed?"

"Southern California. Do you remember her address?"

"Aw, you're kidding."

"I just like to watch--Like in the movies."

"You ever get picked up by any women like that?"

"I haven't been to southern California yet."

"Whoa, I mean to tell you, they're crazy down there. Which part you going to?"

"LA."

"That's where they're the craziest."

"Good."

"You a little weird?"

"I'm not sure. Sometimes it feels natural."

"You a faggot?"

"No, I don't think so. I enjoy fucking women."

"Okay, then you're all right with me."

We came to a cloverleaf where my friend turned towards Coquille and left me with a pleasant goodbye. If I amused him as much as he amused me, the world became a better place because of a short ride on a late Sunday morning. I walked up the ramp towards the 101 continuation and stopped for fresh ripe blackberries by the side of the road. In my quest through the thorns, I came upon a round white reflector—the kind found on unlit roads at night. It was just lying there on the side of the road. I stashed it in my bag for possible use.

I munched on blackberries and waited for my next ride. I removed my shirt to enjoy the early afternoon sun. Munching on blackberries by the side of the road helps give eternity movement. The length of time is the same, it just tastes better.

Rupert says, "Tasting is a very important part of life."

Equal time, equal time.

No way.

There weren't as many blackberries there as there had been where Melody Lingers had dropped me near Elmira. These were also harder to get to. It was a matter of stepping over a rail and making and effort, whereas, in Elmira I turned where she dropped me and there they were for the plucking, with only thorns to deal with. I did manage to leave some for the next passer-by at both locations. The blackberries near Elmira seemed much sweeter. The ones where 42 and 101 were sweet also, but not as sweet as the ones I had had the previous Monday and maybe my tastebuds were confused. After partaking of my share of blackberries, I lingered with a smile, thinking I had better call Damien Rumsford and Carla Smersh in LA and mention I was still on my way. There was no phone in sight.

Another shirtless heathen stopped for me. He appeared to be in his late twenties and very caught up in Easy Now. I climbed into the gray Chevy Impala which looked and felt like it was from the late sixties. The heathen offered me a sixteen ounce can of Budweiser beer the moment my door was shut. The cold wet taste seemed to mix well with the aftertaste of the blackberries on an afternoon that was heating up quickly.

The driver was a surveyor. He was in the process of building his own house on five acres he had recently purchased back in the hills; he hoped to become as self-sufficient as possible. He was on his way to play volleyball with some friends and drink some beer.

"If you have the opportunity and the time, you should pass through Bandon, slowly," he suggested. "Two of the people I'm playing volleyball with today were hitchhiking through about a year ago. They had the opportunity and time to spend the day; they haven't left yet. It's a nice mellow town."

There was a sign, BANDON 4 where he dropped me. The surveyor turned east and headed for the hills. On the other road, which went westward, the sign read DUMP. There were also fresh, ripe blackberries along the side of the road. They were easy to get to than the ones at the 42-101 connection, but still took more of an effort than Elmira. I had to walk a few feet for these. It was on ground level. I merely munched a few for effect. No longer was there any eternity. It was only a pinch of thyme.

Standing there by the crossroads, I still didn't have a shirt on. I thought perhaps I would increase my chance of the right ride coming along if I put my shirt back on. After all, many still judge a book by its cover. The traffic was very light. I also prepared my first sign on a sheet of typing paper. I had no heavy marker. The word BANDON was blocked in purple ink. It wasn't a very pretty sign. I'm not very artistic. It did say what I wanted it to say, and it certainly could be seen. Whether or not got the proper message across depended on the skill of the reader who was simply passing by. It was only a six letter word. I even tried to make it easier to read by hyphenating the syllables. It read "BAN-DON." It didn't say "HELP." I knew I would get to where I was going. I was quite aware of my own need to continue. I must admit, the paper did have a tendency to flap around a bit.

I waited for a good while before finally deciding a slight change in position might be in order. I flip-flopped and flapped across and small intersection where I once more took my pose of flapping and thumbing. I didn't particularly care for the sign. I felt perfectly content with my thumb in the air; I did have an urge to stop in Bandon, and the sign could prevent any horizontal U's from being flashed in my direction. It had taken me a long while to figure out what that sign had meant.

I held the sign in my thumbed hand and raised it in the air each time a car would approach. I thought perhaps it was a little too much of an overly enthusiastic attitude; I was trying different techniques for curiosity and amusement's sake.

A very large, very blue, very old Oldsmobile with fins whizzed by without really slowing or reading. For some reason it caused me to follow it with my eyes, not allowing it to escape so easily. I watched it swerve slightly, kicking up gravel on the shoulder and then crossing the yellow line and back to the shoulder with the brake lights coming on. With a mild effort, it turned around and returned to the crossroads where I was standing; once again it made a loop and stopped beside me, still in the lane of traffic. But there was no traffic.

A balding, palomino-haired man stretched across the seat, unlocked the door and pushed it open. The familiar smell of whiskey assaulted my senses like eating barbecued potato chips after popcorn without anything refreshing in between. He seemed a nervous, sad-eyed man. "I don't usually pick up no hitchhikers, but something told me I should give you a ride," he said with a slow drawl, almost as if he were apologizing for stopping.

"Are you going as far as Bandon, sir?" I asked, a little apprehensive about accepting the ride.

"Yeah, yeah," he said, "It's not too far, it's not too far."

The seat was pulled forward, allowing me to stash my bag in the rear; I held my axe up front with me. No sooner had we pulled off when I noticed that the swerve of the Olds was its natural state of being, not just excitement over picking up a hitchhiker. I felt no immediate need for alarm. The night before I had been lost in the fog on the ocean with a man who knew he was dying from the effects of asbestos. We found our way home. This man simply had a little too much to drink; though he swerved, we were headed in the right direction and Bandon was only four miles.

"I'm, I'm Oliver," he said in a seemingly very confused state of being.

His entire face was wrinkled, like he had been crumpled and packed away once too often.

"I'm Sullivan. Pleased to meet you. Is everything okay?" There seemed to be bewilderment in the air.

"Yeah, yeah," he hesitated. "I just, just, don't usually pick up hitchhikers."

"If you feel uncomfortable, you can drop me anywhere."

"I, I. . .didn't say that. I. . .I just meant, there was something about you that made me stop."

I wasn't sure whether to feel honored or damned. His tough-skinned hands took turns holding the wheel, adjusting each time he switched. I thought about asking for a sip of whiskey to help blend into the scene. I decided it wasn't my place.

"I'm headed. . .for Port Orford. . .if. . .if. . .I live on government land, back in the mountains. Building roads. I. . .I. . .like to get away. . .away on weekends."

I didn't know how far, but I knew Port Orford was much farther along in the right direction. I became aware that Oliver was just a lonely old man who wanted someone to speak to and maybe I should ride with him.

"My last ride mentioned I should stop in Bandon and see what it's like."

He began to grow more secure and spoke more easily. "Yeah. . .Bandon's a nice town. They must have meant the rocks. You should see the rocks at Bandon."

"They have rocks in Bandon?"

"Yeah. . .yeah. . .it's quite a sight. I have some time. I'll take you to see the rocks."

"That's not really necessary."

"No, no, you don't understand. I must show you the rocks." He pulled out his driver's license and showed it to me. "I'm okay, really. I just feel I have to do something for you."

"Why not."

We drove into Bandon and through the old town section, out past the docks and down a narrow winding road, until we came to the ocean. There was an old lighthouse; the wind was whipping in like an unsettled spirit crying for mercy. We parked near a small building above the beach. It housed restrooms. I had a tremendous urge to pee, more so than to stand in the wind watching rocks. After relieving myself, I stood outside for a few minutes—in the wind—

watching rocks.

I was very impressed with the formations and the lighthouse which seemed to have withstood the powers of nature for many, many years, and Oliver, who was granting me the privilege. I still had no intention of driving all the way to Port Orford with him. I wanted to, I even felt it was my duty. But I didn't feel comfortable enough. We got back in the car; he tried to make me feel comfortable.

On the way out from the rocks, we stopped by a trailer. Oliver got out and knocked on the door while I waited. He had mentioned that a friend lived there whom he hadn't seen in a long time. A large man wearing a cowboy hat answered the door. I was invited from the car and introduced, and made to feel like an old acquaintance. Oliver and the man spoke while I played catch with a very large, long-haired Belgian shepherd called Duke. I liked Oliver. I liked his friend. I liked the dog. I couldn't continue on with him. I don't know why. I felt like I wanted to continue on with him. I even felt I'd be disturbing the forces of nature if I didn't continue on with him. I couldn't continue on with him.

After the brief visit we drove back along the narrow winding road past the docks and into the old town section. I insisted on getting out to have lunch.

"Look," he said, "I don't usually pick up hitchhikers. I saw you and I stopped for you."

"Thank you. I really appreciate it," I said. "I have to stop here. I have to eat."

"Okay. . .okay. . .don't get me wrong."

"Oliver, thank you."

He disappeared. I still don't understand any of it. I didn't feel comfortable enough with him, yet I felt like I committed some sort of sin by not riding with him. I overcame my guilt by stopping in a small restaurant and eating the biggest hamburger I have ever experienced in my entire life. Along with french fries and a large Coke, it cost $2.25. It was a little after 2:00 in the afternoon of the ninth day of my journey.

Rupert says,
Come talk to me--Just say hi--If I like your smile
I'll teach you to fly--If you don't wish to fly
We'll go for a walk--If you don't wish to walk
We'll sit down and talk.

I hope you like my smile--I want to walk with you
Please like my smile--I have to talk with you.
Don't turn around--Don't walk away
I like your smile--I need you today.
You don't like my smile--Goodbye.

Come talk to me
Just say hi. . .

Rupert likes to rhyme.

DAY 38

This is my 38th day of exclusion. Space colonies are being inhabited
by chosen people in preparation to blow up the earth to ease the
problems of starvation and unemployment.

Noodles, bamboo shoots, bean sprouts, water chestnuts,
celery, one jalapeno, sardines, mustard sauce, soy sauce, and
cranberry sauce—and I've located one clove of garlic—sopped up
with whole wheat bread and washed down with white wine and
instant coffee.

* * *

My hamburger finished, I left the old town section of Bandon
and pointed myself back in the direction of 101. I climbed a small hill
and walked a few blocks to where the road became a double lane
going in each direction. I realized standing by the side of the road I
would have been approaching Port Orford if I had stayed with
Oliver. I attempted to make myself feel better by countering,
possibly not. It didn't matter anymore: what was done was done. I
stuck up my thumb with no flapping sign, and waited, and waited,
and waited. There was an ice cream store not far from where I
stood. Family upon family stopped in for Sunday afternoon treats. I

thought how much I wanted a family—with Ermonie.

I had to settle for a ride in an old battered station wagon. The driver's hair looked to be an enormous battery-powered wig. He'd turn his head and the hair would pause and then follow and then focus with him. His hair stood on end and touched the ceiling of the car with its curls. The only clean spot in the entire car was the little patch of cloth directly above his head.

"I'm not going very far," he said.

"I know," I answered, holding up the sign of the horizontal U. He laughed and his hair swooped.

"People have a tendency to flash that sign to ease their guilt for passing," he said.

"At least they acknowledge your presence."

"Is that what it is?" he questioned with a smile.

"Maybe."

"Maybe not."

His program seemed different than the others. My guilt for ditching Oliver was momentarily erased. I felt very comfortable, perhaps because my benefactor reminded me of a flower. I spoke of my path, fore and aft.

"The coast is beautiful. Take your time," he reminded me. He said he was living on a farm with a woman who was writing a book on meditation. I mentioned I also was writing a book.

Learning that I had never made the trip down the coast before, he said, "I can only think of two places off the top as goals to shoot for, and possibly spend a little extra time. The cliffs at Mendocino shouldn't be missed, a place to crash if you should find yourself without shelter for the evening. The women in Mendocino still walk the streets barefoot." I made a note as a reminder. "Another place," he said, "is Arcata." I had heard of Mendocino. "Arcata?" I asked.

"Arcata's a college town. They have their own symphony and chorus; strange, pleasant things happen in Arcata. It's happened to me twice, once headed south and once headed north, and also to friends of mine." He spoke very softly in a strong sort of way. "While hitchhiking late at night on the Arcata on-ramp to the freeway, someone has come up from town, different people on each occasion. Speaking for myself, I've been taken to their homes and fed and given a place to crash, and depending on the person, given a buzz and in the morning left back on the highway with a smile. Nice people live in Arcata."

I wrote the word Arcata next to Mendocino; my ride dropped me at an exotic animal farm and continued on his way. Once more I regained the feeling of being on a cloud, following a natural course with direction and goal. I waited on the edge of the parking lot of the exotic animal farm and watched the families come and go. I used the public facilities available to rid myself of the excess of my meal after it went through its process.

There is still no doubt in my mind that my next ride was Wallace Beery "The Champ", driving a late model pickup truck. He was on his way to Port Orford where Oliver had said he was headed a few hours earlier. He smiled at me skeptically when he noticed the two earrings in my left ear, the way Wallace Beery would smile, being tolerant. He realized I meant no harm. He was wearing a flannel shirt with suspenders and a red bandanna around his neck. On his head was a too-small slouch hat, tilted slightly to the side.

I felt a strong need to converse with Wallace Beery. I got caught up in myself and it became a monologue as I related the story of my journey. He relaxed with a raised eyebrow or a quiver of the lip, or a tilting of his head with a slight shrug. He listened with abstract ingenuity, and allowed me to continue believing he would be at all interested. So caught up I was in my own self-importance, I didn't hear his voice. But I know he was a retired logger, still only in his fifties. He probably walked with a slight limp and drank lemonade. He left me off at the southern edge of Port Orford, across from a bar next to a parking lot, overlooking the ocean with a view of large rounded rocks coming from the ocean. The rocks looked like the snouts of gigantic whales, springing from the depths, looking to see what progress would be inflicted.

I left my bag and my typewriter near the edge of the lot where there were no cars; I used the facilities provided. After washing my hands, I returned to my things, to find a silver Lincoln Continental backing over my bag.

Another car had arrived in the lot and a photographer walked by with his model and smiled while I flapped my arms and yelled for the driver of the Lincoln to stop. The old man driving looked startled and his wife turned her head and looked at the floor. I finally got my point across and he stopped on top of my bag. He looked at me. His wife still looked at the floor.

"Sir," I said, "your car is on top of my bag."

He was silver and trimmed and he laughed an embarrassed laugh. "Oh, I'm sorry, I didn't see it. I hope nothing's broken."

"It's only the edge. I believe it's a blanket."

He shifted into forward and drifted to the asphalt. "I was just turning around," he said.

I saw an opportunity. "Which way are you headed?" I asked.

"South," he answered.

"I'll accept a lift."

"We wouldn't be of any help," he said. "We're only going to Gold Beach. It's a short ride."

Aha, I thought, the sign of the horizontal U, verbalized. I smiled at my own arrogance. "Okay, enjoy."

The woman never raised her head; they drove off. I was a sight and didn't expect a ride, but the harmless game amused me. I walked back to the top of the parking lot, onto the edge of the road and once more stuck out my thumb. There were distractions to make the time pass.

The photographer and his model were playing on a rock so I could watch. Of course, I felt they were doing it for my benefit. The model posed like a fresh blackberry, waiting to be plucked; she seemed like a yodel, echoing from the buttock-shaped rock she perched on, while the man stooped and walked and snapped. They walked along a path to another rock, large enough to accommodate a path and people, and up it, giving me a better view, posing and snapping. The silhouette of her body through the thin material caused me to believe they were going to approach me to make movies wearing a mask. They disappeared on the other side of the rock. I kept the thought and was merely waiting for their return.

Three young maidens passed, wearing very shiny short shorts, pushing ten-speeds uphill. I followed their progress until they disappeared. I was ready to screw a chicken.

Rhoda Apple says, "Buy guns."

Ethel Much says, "There are three ways to make money in this country: oil, steal and truckin'."

Damien Rumsford says, "I don't fuck wit no slouches."

Ermonie says, "The stars ease my night, when the night makes me nervous."

Mick Jagger says, "You can't always get what you want, you get what you believe."

Equal time, equal time.

Shit.

Dump it over the side.

A silver Toyota with a bike strapped to its back stopped in front of me. There seemed to be a large pair of eyes sitting in the driver's seat. The eyes covered the earth. They were wearing a tiny hat. Seeing it was a girl, I hesitated momentarily. The idea of being picked up by a woman in my present state of mind was like an invitation to dine. Remember, I felt as if I were following a wonderful star where everything was being done for my benefit. Was I being handed a woman in a silver Toyota, I wondered? Her big brown beautiful eyes seemed like a pair of overdone, sunny-side-up eggs, sizzling on a grill. I wanted to eat her eyes.

The pause seemed extended. I was waiting for her to pull off. She didn't. She unlocked the door. I hustled my gear and got in. Her hair was pulled back and touched the floor behind her seat. We exchanged names as we pulled off, headed uphill. Hers was Rosa.

"My radio doesn't work," she said.

I pointed out the phallic whale snouts, attempting to unleash a connection before its time. Once again I was caught up in my own self-importance, rambling on about my journey. But I caught myself, remembering another person was present.

"Where are you headed?" I inquired.

"Fort Dick," she said. "I've passed many hitchhikers and decided to give one a lift."

That did it. I told her I was hoping to reach Arcata because one of my rides had suggested it. But visions of a motel room with soft lights and a California wine, easing into a gentle dance with long hair and universal eyes, caused me to inquire further. She was coming from the eyes. I didn't want just another surface-to-air relationship.

"Well, Rosa, where you from?"

"Boston," she said. "My radio doesn't work."

"Well, I'd sing, but—well, maybe later. What brings you out here on the coast?"

She looked at me rather strangely, but I didn't mind. Oh, those eyes.

"I'm an environmentalist and I've been working to clean up the Charles River and I needed some time off. It isn't working out."

"An environmentalist?" It struck a nerve. I remembered Dave, the PR man from Georgia Pacific, and herbicides and clear cutting and emotions. "Are you emotional?"

She looked at me. Oh, those eyes.

"My radio doesn't work," she said.

"Maybe I should explain. I had a ride with a fellow from a lumber company, and he claimed that environmentalists only dealt with emotions and not in scientific fact. Are you emotional?"

She seemed puzzled and very emotional. "I'm on vacation, and my radio doesn't work."

"Oh," I answered. I figured maybe she was just embarrassed because she was into rivers and didn't know nothing from trees. After all, this is the age of specialization.

We passed a field where sheep were grazing. Some clouds were partially shading the sun. The lighting was unique, like a refrigerator with a pink light bulb. Rosa pulled to the side of the road and got out with her camera. Watching the sheep, I remembered instructions from a farmer on how to screw one. Either put its legs in high boots, or place it on the edge of a large sloping rock; they keep backing up.

* * *

I have a craving for apricots.

* * *

Once more we returned to the car, and I changed the subject, not wishing to embarrass her anymore for fear of blowing my shot in the dark room. I did, however, continue to ramble on about anything that came to mind.

"I'm sure you're a very nice guy," she said, "but my radio doesn't work. I know hitchhikers like to talk. I usually turn my radio up. But my radio doesn't work. I want to enjoy the ride."

"Oh."

We continued driving along. I became humble and insecure. It was absolutely disgusting. I also over-apologized. In fact, my apology became a soliloquy. Then there was finally silence. Occasionally I would point out a beautiful view and then catch myself. The silence became dismembering. I still thought I was going to get a ride to Fort Dick. I was no longer cocksure of afterglow, but a ride is a ride—and oh, those eyes.

Rupert says, "We must keep our rivers clean."

You blew it, buster.

Shut up.

You shoulda pulled the trigger.

Shit.

Dump it over the side.

Fog began to appear in patches, making silence even more distracting. We crossed the Rogue River Bridge, heading into Gold Beach; Rosa seemed to hear my words, though there were none.

"I think I'd like to stop and take pictures," she said. "Back there, at the state park. I think I'll be awhile."

"Sure." What could I say.

By now the fog was so heavy, if one was outside, one could not see the proverbial tip of one's nose. Rosa was kind enough to drop me at the southern edge of Gold Beach, where she went through the action of making a loop and heading back in the direction of the bridge. I once more apologized for running my mouth. I found myself across the street from what seemed to be a very nice restaurant called the Captain's Table. The air was chilly and damp, and the fog was like an overbearing Duda, crowding out the rest of the world. There was very little traffic. Ten minutes passed. A silver Toyota whizzed by. There was a bike on its back. The car was being driven by a very large pair of eyes. Oh, those eyes. I laughed for laughter's sake, shaking the earth around me, and inhaling the fog.

Rupert says,

> We all talk in riddles--Or so it seems
> Never saying much— What we intend to say.
> Causing things to come--Then go another way
> To pick and choose some fond regrets
> That are hustled with a smile
> Embellished with some mindless threats
> Which are gone-- In just awhile.
>
> Speak for yourself.
> Who is that guy?

Rupert likes to rhyme.

DAY 39

This is the 39th day of my involution. I am, however, relieved to say I am immensely enjoying laughing out loud at myself and the world right now as I look at my distorted reflections in the oval mirror to my right and the fogged mirror before me. Birds are singing in harmony outside my door.

Instant coffee is absurd. Thank God I have to at least boil water. You're welcome.

* * *

The air became rather chilled in the moving wetness of the fog. It wasn't nearly as heavy in town as out. I had the patronage of the restaurant to keep me entertained as I was perhaps entertaining them. I partially changed clothes while standing on the side of the road. I removed my four-pocket safari shirt in exchange for one that was easier to tuck in. I attempted to tuck in the safari shirt, but two half-pockets protruding from the top of my jeans seemed unbalanced. I changed shirts and added a sweater, along with my tweed slouch hat and a bandanna for the upper parts.

Enveloped in the splendor of a moment and a sweater, how strange it all seemed. The day had been warm and sunny. The haze was intriguing as opposed to frightening. I did entertain some thoughts about walking back into town. My glimpse had been brief in the company of Rosa, but I had noticed a few bars that had possibilities. After all, I felt a rich man with the extra money from Emmett. I felt no anger towards Rosa. There was no reason to. The timing was off; such things happen. It hit me that it was merely the reverse of what happened between Oliver and me. Such is the balance, I thought.

Rupert says, "Timing is a very important part of life."

I bet he doesn't even know how to tell time.

There was also a large hotel within my sight and reach. I think it was a Ramada Inn. The lack of traffic gave me ample time to use both hands in rolling Prince Albert. Thus I could chain smoke. When distractions ran low, I fought off the temptation of wandering back into town by being entertained and amused by my own peculiar self, dressed like a vagabond, smoking hand-rolled cigarettes in the fog, with the sound of the surf in the background. Occasionally people crossed from the hotel to the restaurant or vice versa. I was ignored by most; it didn't matter, but I still noticed it.

Two chubby fortyish women didn't ignore me. In fact, they approached me, smiling. I was already smiling. I simply focused in their direction.

"We've been watching you," one said in passing, "from the restaurant."

"Oohh?" I chuckled, quite pleased.

"You've been putting on quite a show," she said.

"I'm just waiting for a ride," I said, smiling. I felt like a flower.

"We're staying at the hotel here. We walked down the beach earlier and found an old shelter. If you shouldn't have luck, you may wish to keep that in mind."

"Why, thank you, I just may do that." I was pleased by their concern. They made me feel better than I already felt. Eons passed. I couldn't decide whether to choose the bars or the shelter. The fog made the hour seem quite late, though I had no idea of the time. Thoughts of Arcata simply disappeared. My confidence began to wane, though I still entertained the idea of something very pleasant happening. I wasn't sure whether I was to seek it out or allow it to find me.

Once more, the short ride made the decision for me. The omen delivered, seemed rather reluctant. He was certainly sent from somewhere or by someone in the form of an uncovered jeep with a roll bar, sleek and new and painted with a surf board sticking out the rear, and a bleached blonde, speechless teenage boy, sticking up behind the wheel.

He didn't look or speak when he stopped. It was as if he appeared directly in front of me, pointed in the right direction. I smiled once more at the Captain's Table; off we drove. We cleared the outskirts of the town; once more the fog became as heavy as oatmeal. That's when the boy said, "I'm only going to Kissing Rock."

"Where's that?"

"A few miles," he said.

I felt absolutely blessed. Thoughts that I was in a movie had constantly been cropping up in my mind. Everything had seemed so planned, so directed by someone other than myself. Now I was absolutely convinced I shouldn't toy with the natural flow, for surely the boy had been sent by the Captain or someone to take me down the road, out of sight and out of mind, at least far enough out of town so I couldn't turn back.

We stopped in a lunar parking area very near the edge of the earth, next to enormous rounded rocks, caressed by the fog as if it were a leech, sucking out disturbed blood. A strange feeling of weightlessness came over me; the sound of the surf became cymbals. A few other cars were already there. The young boy jumped from the jeep and disappeared into the fog before I had a chance to thank him. The weightlessness in no way affected my bag and typewriter. In the long run, it was for the best; it kept me waiting as opposed to wandering.

I stood at the edge of the parking area by the road. I realized no one would see me to stop. The grayness was confining. I dug in my bag and located the little white reflector I had found earlier in the day. It served as a crutch rather than a signal, for surely no light from the oncoming traffic, which was almost nonexistent, could even come close enough to reflect. Once more my enlightenment that everything was meant to be began to wrinkle slightly. I heard the sound of laughter on the tip of an occasional breeze of sound, mingled with the surf. Again I thought of the bars and the shelter. Hitchhiking on Sunday night where stretches of wilderness roads ran on and on looked to have no future in it. I left my gear briefly and wandered down to the beach in search of the young surfer.

I found him and some friends playing in the sand among the huge dancing rocks. They paused and mumbled as I approached, trudging through the heavy sand and fog like some hairy creature from the sea. I spoke directly to the boy who had brought me. I asked him not to leave without me if I was still there when it was time to go.

"I may spend the night in Gold Beach," I said.

He answered with a mumble; I left them all playing in the sand and returned to my vigil in the fog by the side of the road. Once more, my moment of doubt was answered by a short ride.

A young bearded farmer, driving an old green pick-up, rescued me from the clutches of the clouded air and mind.

"I ain't goin' far," he said.

"It doesn't matter."

It was a very short ride, uphill. We passed from the shroud. Suddenly it wasn't as late as I thought it had been. The sun was still shining. He dropped me where there was nothing around but trees and the sun. The air was warm; I immediately removed my sweater. I was overjoyed. I bent down to repack my sweater and hat; while I was so doing, a Lincoln Continental left over from the 60s stopped directly in front of me. My thumb wasn't even sticking up.

* * *

Brown rice, water chestnuts, refried beans, mushrooms, one jalapeno, soy sauce, cranberry sauce and olive oil, sopped up with whole wheat bread and washed down with Genessee Cream Ale.

It occurs to me I've been here nearly 40 days—without sex. I've been considering unnatural acts with the dog, and performing them with the typewriter and its fucking t. Sometimes it's all so silly.

* * *

But then, the electric window lowered. I looked up from my chore of packing; a person who looked exactly like Dick Clark from American Bandstand was driving.

"A strange place to be hitchhiking," he said, noticing it wasn't the middle of anywhere, or even the edge, for that matter. It was the top of a mountain in the early evening sun. I busied myself, hurriedly attempting to finish packing.

"Take your time, take your time." He was almost cheerful, wearing his white shirt and tie with a checkered sports jacket. Finished packing, I stowed my gear in the rear and we were on our way. The window raised, the air was on low. He immediately turned the radio up, and then down.

"Where are you headed?"

"LA," I answered. "I do have a stop in Mill Valley."

"I found a wonderful station; it's a look at the year 1954 through music." The Big Bopper sang, and Peggy Lee. "I can talk you as far as Arcata."

"Where?"

"Arcata. I have a class to teach there in the morning."

The word struck a nerve. I looked at the slip of paper in my pocket. "Arcata," it read. I immediately associated it with a place to stay for the night. "Someone told me to stop there," I said.

"Good, it's a nice college town."

We introduced ourselves as the sun went down. Dick sang along to the music, bopping down the road. We spoke during commercials about love and life and computer technology. He was involved with computer software research. "My purpose is right in line with nature," he said. "Computers might not seem natural to you."

He gave me no chance to answer. "But you must take a long, hard look at the evolutionary process in history. My purpose in computer software research is to make myself obsolete, where the computer needs no one to program it."

Another man with a death wish, I thought.

"In time, there will be no need for the existence of man in order for there to be an existence."

"There's no need for man now—except for man's need."

"Man is here to progress into the realm of spirit, or else get back to the earth if there's an earth left. The computer age offers the option of doing it or dying to live. And besides, there's money in computers."

"What course are you teaching?"

"Gourmet cooking," he said. "Computers also offer the opportunity to do what one enjoys."

We sang and talked and drove through Fort Dick and a patch of redwoods. My first sight of the giant redwood was in the dark. We continued, arriving in Arcata at 11:00 in the evening. Dick dropped me near downtown.

"Thank you," I said.

"An Apple this Big," he said.

I stopped in a phone booth to call Ermonie. The night was warm in Arcata; there was no need for extra clothing. I reached the camp and spoke with Ermonie briefly. I mentioned I was in Arcata because someone had told me to stop there, and I was somewhat expecting to find a place to stay for the evening; I wasn't sure how. Things had been going well at camp and all were in good health and spirit, including Ethel.

After the short but sweet conversation, I took up my burden and began to search. I wasn't quite sure what I was searching for; I felt I was there for something. I circled a few blocks and saw no hotels though there were a few bars in the square, directly downtown. There were no real high-rises—it was a comfortable, unimposing sort of town. I didn't find what I was looking for, because I didn't know what it was. I settled for a few beers in a few bars. Sunday night, things were slow. I'm not quite sure what I expected, sitting in a bar with my bag and axe next to me. I thought perhaps someone, seeing I was a traveler, would approach me and offer me a bed. I even inquired about a room, with the hopes of being granted a privilege or at least finding a cheap room. I was growing very tired. The mind plays funny games in exhaustion.

One a.m. approached. I realized I was only fooling myself. I couldn't hope to spend any great period of time anywhere; I was on the road with a destination and limited funds. I had enjoyed myself in a quiet sort of way in the downtown bars of Arcata; it was time to go. I received directions from a young lady behind a bar on how to arrive at the freeway; I once more gathered my things and walked along deserted streets.

I was very tired. The beers hadn't helped my energy level. I stopped on a very dark street and eased the beer from my system into some bushes, and then I continued. A car turned slowly up the street I was on. I saw it was a police car. I walked from the sidewalk out into the street and waited for it to stop. I asked the officer if there were any cheap rooms in the area. He said he wasn't sure, but $10 or $12 stuck in his head; it was also unlikely I'd find anyplace open anyway. I inquired about the hitchhiking laws and the very nice man said, "Stay on the ramp."

Rupert says, "Continuing is a very important part of life."

Yeah, asshole.

Shut up.

I continued onto the freeway and up the on-ramp, where I cheated as much as I could so traffic from the freeway would perhaps see me or my reflector, which I put into use once more, again for effect only. I was certain my own image would overshadow any tiny reflector--So there.

I'll get you.

I stood waiting, waiting, convinced of my own rightness, but somehow confused as to why I felt that way. I decided it didn't matter. I was there on the on-ramp in Arcata, very late at night or very early in the morning, coming and going at the same time, but still there beneath the stars, holding up my thumb and a little round white reflector each time a car approached. It seemed so simple.

I was really becoming tired. The idea of sleep seemed pleasant. I began to survey the area along a slope on the side of the on-ramp. The grass was soft and not too high. The air was comfortable so I felt my blanket would be adequate, and I did have extra layers of clothing. I chose a bush to hide me from view and perhaps avoid any misled pleasure-seekers or unsympathetic cops. It seemed the thing to do. There was very little traffic. "I'll give it a little while longer," I thought. I then sat down on top of my bag on the peninsula between the freeway and the on-ramp.

A car came up along the ramp from town. It was the first car to do so during my hour-long wait. I held up my thumb from my sitting position. The yellow Dodge Dart stopped. It was an older car. The driver looked to be from Greek mythology. He had strong dark happy eyes. His face seemed carved from his black hair by the sharp trim in his beard and mustache. He offered me a ride.

"Little late to be hitchhiking--It's not the sixties anymore," he said in a casual way. Though there seemed to be no obvious need to hurry, I gathered my things and rushed to the car. We casually pulled off and I thanked him, explaining that I'd just about given up for the day and was ready to crash under a bush.

"That'd be a little dangerous nowadays," he said. "There are a lot of crazy people running loose." I realized that the craziest ones are the ones who usually say that. But this man seemed very comfortable and secure.

"I've been too lucky," I said.

"Where are you headed?"

"LA—lalalala lalala—with a stop in Mill Valley along the way."

"I can take you about 20 miles to a truck stop in Eureka."

"It's movement."

We spoke, taking turns, sharing the circle. He had been playing cards and lost and was on his way to visit a girlfriend. I mentioned I had been sailing on magic ships and visiting strange festivals in the forest. His name was Fred and he built castles for a living, one at a time. The ride was short, but I was again left with a very nice feeling. He dropped me at the truck stop, where I decided to eat.

The restaurant was bright and crowded with a clientele of people who had been playing and wished to continue doing so. I found a stool at the counter, with enough room for my things beneath my feet, and soon placed an order for biscuits and gravy with French Fries and coffee. While I was waiting, I was overcome by a strong urge to use the bathroom. I left my things and wove my way through the maze of happy drunks and sweet painted ladies. I eased and cleaned for my meal and returned to the brightness of the dining area.

Fred was there, standing near the entrance. I saw him and waved and smiled. "Are you getting something to eat?" he asked.

"Yeah, I already placed my order. Are you?"

"I went to my girl's house and the lights were on and there was a car in the driveway. We have an understanding and she already has company; I thought I'd stop by and see if you'd like a place to crash for a few hours. My mother and two sons are staying with me, but it's a big castle and there's plenty of room for one more."

"Why not?" I felt perfectly at ease--We sat in a booth and Fred ordered coffee. The biscuits and French Fries came. We shared the French Fries; I ate the biscuits and gravy.

There didn't seem to be any walls; we spoke freely about ourselves and left the restaurant after we each picked up our own check. We drove back through Eureka down a maze of streets and boulevards to an area that didn't seem urban in the black of night. The castle was enormous and wooden and new and quiet. We entered and the lights were turned on and doors gently shut.

"Wow," was my reaction to the castle built of matchsticks and redwood, with a spiral staircase and doors leading everywhere.

"Ssshhh, my mom's in there," he said, quietly, and then walked over to the door and pulled it easily shut. "It's okay to talk now. It's pretty solid. I built this castle," he said proudly. "I'm living here until I can sell it."

"Wow," I said, "you do good work."

"It's a little gaudy for my taste. I built it for someone else. Then they couldn't come up with the money."

"I know the feeling."

"Do you build castles?"

"No, I just mumble once in a while. Where am I?"

"High on a hill in northern California--There's a beautiful view from the deck, but the fog seems to be rolling in."

I stepped out on the deck to look at the night; the deck was large and beautiful, the night was black. I had mentioned in our speaking that I was in the process of becoming a builder of novels. I left Fred with a short story about a room while I was allowed to shower and make use of fresh, clean towels. On my return to the spacious drawing room, we sat and talked and sipped brandy from snifters and smoked some fine Humboldt County Bud and relaxed.

Fred had been married twice; his second wife had died; his sons were five and nineteen. The eldest was there recuperating from a broken leg he got surfing in southern California. Fred read some poems he had written for his father, and I read a Rupert rhyme.

Rupert says,
I don't want too much from life--I just want to live

About twelve million dollars
And heart enough to give
I ain't asking very much--Just to take my time
I only want fresh lobster--And another bag of lime
Sometimes it seems so silly--The silly games
We play--We want the things we'll never get
Cause they'd just get in the way.

Rupert likes to rhyme.

He has all the fun; if you want to call it that.

It's longer than that, but it's boring.

I'm sure it is.

We sat for a while and laughed and joked and spoke of philosophies and life. I was shown to my own room and given clean linens for the mattress on the floor; sleep visited me quickly.

* * *

There's no doubt and no question anymore. I'm a prisoner here. They told me today. I was looking in my mirrors and they told me. I didn't ask. I was simply brushing my hair, looking in the mirrors. "You're a prisoner here," they said. I don't know who they were. Neither was familiar. I've never seen them before. They had sharp piercing eyes, enlarged by the reflection, I think. Their eyes looked like pimiento-stuffed olives, floating in a martini. One sat and stared while the other did the talking. The one who stared meant the same thing. I could see it in his eyes. Perhaps one was a woman. They wouldn't answer any questions.

I wonder if Tripod is also a prisoner. "So goeth, so goeth thy dog." I don't think she'll mind, as long as she has a stick to fetch and an occasional can of chicken soup. If she would only screw me, I wouldn't mind either. I'm not really sure I do mind. It's peaceful here usually, at least outwardly. Such beauty surrounds my knoll. There's a patch of beautiful white trilliums just over the edge, of few of which now decorate my littered table.

Corners visits occasionally for a cookie. Perhaps it's not so bad being a prisoner here. I still have my journey. Ermonie has become an unrealized dream.

* * *

Daylight arrived; I came back. I had slept soundly and comfortably, though the mattress had rocked all night long. I had been gone from her for many hours and many miles and many new faces, but the MARY PATT was still with me. All night long, the mattress had rocked; Emmett's cough was my call in the morning. I stayed stretched out for a few extra moments, once my eyes were open. So good, I felt, and ready to continue.

I cracked open my door and waited for the sound of someone awake. I prepared for the road and joined Fred downstairs in the kitchen for quick coffee and a cold meatloaf sandwich. His mother had made the meatloaf. There was still too much fog for the view; it was time to go.

We left the house and drove back down the hill and through the maze of streets and boulevards.

"Fred," I looked at my benefactor and stared when the thought hit me.

"What?" he said, somewhat confused by my obvious look of "WOW."

"Yesterday, outside of Bandon, a million miles away, someone told me this would happen."

"What," he said laughingly.

"The on-ramp in Arcata--Someone told me this would happen."

"Remember," he said, "when you become who you wish to become, and I can read your novels, I want to hear your voice."

"Listen for it." He dropped me back on 101, a little farther along than where we had coffee the night before, at another truck stop.

"A star is shining on you," he said. "Enjoy your trip."

The magic in a firm handshake, when it comes from the eye, is enough to cure the measles. He disappeared. It was Monday morning—the tenth day of my journey.

DIRTY WORDS

DAY 40

They have the audacity to call this a prison. I have no more drugs and there aren't even any young boys to fuck. This is my fortieth day in the desert of sporadic desperation.

Brown rice, one jalapeno, mushrooms, refried beans, olive oil, soy sauce and herring are mixed together and at my disposal, along with lots and lots of coffee. I need my caffeine.

* * *

But then, I stood on top of the world, watching the traffic whiz by. So caught up in Easy Now, I was waiting and waiting and waiting—enjoying every precious moment of it, enveloped in the splendor of life, no doubt, no question. I was. I am.

So am I.

Me too.

Son of a gun.

Right.

Shit.

Dump it over the side.

Perhaps.

I was traveling a road so many others had traveled; I was there now, and it belonged to me while I performed my simple task of being. There are always others.

You said it.

The morning rush hour was at its peak, while cars and buses and trucks carrying enormous trees paid me no particular mind. It simply didn't matter. A young man with hair draped over his shoulders, wearing an Easy Now smile, came strolling down the highway while I stood there with my thumb sticking out. We exchanged smiles and greetings.

"Where you headed?" he asked.

"Mendocino. How 'bout you?"

"Florence, just up the road."

"Here, take my spot. I'm in no hurry, and I could use a cup of coffee."

"Sure," he smiled.

I gathered my things and walked to the restaurant of the truck stop and purchased coffee in a Styrofoam cup. I left it on the counter while I used the bathroom. I came out of the bathroom and picked up my coffee and the young man I had given my spot was gone. Once more I walked to the road and took my position in the world. I looked down the road ahead and saw someone hitchhiking in the distance. I thought it was my long-haired friend deciding to give me the right of way. I waved and turned back and stuck up my thumb.

I was standing on the shoulder of the road. Suddenly I was face to face with a battered gray Volkswagen, slowly walking towards me. One step at a time it came, smiling and trudging and continuing, like any old trooper following his orders--Doing his duty. Another young man with hair draped down to his shoulders—this one had a beard—was smiling behind the wheel. I thought perhaps the car didn't have enough energy left to keep up with the normal flow of traffic. I stepped back up onto a small curb surrounding a tiny grass plot, to allow it to trudge on by. They stopped for me. The door cracked open; the driver asked where I was headed.

"Mendocino," I said.

"I'm only going to Florence," he said calmly, "just up the road." His phrasing struck a nerve and I remembered the hippie up the road.

"This might sound strange," I said, "I don't mean to impose. But that next hitchhiker is going to Florence." I sounded baffled and confused to myself, but I still got the message across.

The pleasant driver looked around at his already cluttered VW and then back at me.

"I'll squeeze in the back," I said.

He sort of chuckled and pulled the seat forward. I shoved my large green duffel bag and my axe and myself into the rear in the company of many books and blankets. We pulled off and I quickly explained my reasons while we coasted along the shoulder up to the next hitchhiker, who turned out to be a young Asian man who looked like an orange carrying a number ten brown paper sack containing things.

"That's a different guy," I laughed.

We stopped; the Orange Man climbed in the front seat. The driver shrugged and smiled; the VW BUG kicked up its heels and jumped into the line of traffic. The Orange Man reached into his bag and pulled out a hand-rolled cigarette.

"Reefer," he said. The joint was lit and it became a nice quiet short ride. Not another word was spoken.

We soon approached signs for FLORENCE. "Gotta let y'all out here." Orange Man smiled and didn't say a word. The driver obliged both of his passengers, by first dropping the Orange Man, and then me, a quarter mile down the road.

Rupert says, "Sometimes it's best to go it alone."

Who's he trying to kid?

Stoned and amused by the side of the highway, I stood counting pebbles and tugging on the good-luck star which dangled from the back of my earlobe. The star disconnected and fell to the gravel mixed with the earth. The star was only as big as a match-head, but its gold gleamed in the sun and I found it without looking. Soon a car stopped for the Asian and continued along the shoulder for me. He was already sitting up front in the Honda station wagon. The back seat was folded down; I was allowed to squeeze into the rear deck with my things. The driver was quiet and wore a cowboy hat and a bandanna along with his goatee and mustache. We were pointed in the right direction. We pulled back into traffic; before the speed limit was reached, we came to another hitchhiker.

The driver looked back at me. "Got room?" he asked.

"Sure."

"May as well filler up in one swoop," he said, stopping for a young cowboy in boots and a hat and vest, holding a sign "PHOENIX."

The blonde teenager shoved his saddlebags into the rear and followed behind. I pulled my things towards me and scrunched up like an accordion across the back. We were under way.

"I'm going to Garberville," said the driver.

The Orange Man reached in his bag and held up a hand-rolled cigarette. "Reefer," he said.

The driver held one up also. "Try one of these. I grew it myself."

We smoked the joint and then another. I became lost in the splendor of a compact car. I promptly fell asleep. I woke up at the off-ramp in Garberville. No one had to wake me, I just woke up, knowing we were there. At the top of the off-ramp was the beginning of the on-ramp.

"This is it," said the driver. We stopped and the Orange Man immediately jumped out and ran down a hill for the shade of the overpass above the highway. There was already a young couple standing at the top of the on-ramp under a tree. The cowboy climbed out and walked halfway down the on-ramp, where he took his position, holding his PHOENIX sign.

I unfolded and rolled to the door, shoving my bag before me. I felt rested and pleasant and willing to wait in the sun. I carried my burden on down the on-ramp, past the couple under the tree, past the cowboy. I glanced at the Orange Man sitting in the shade of the bridge and continued from the on-ramp, up a slight incline on the highway. I walked to a spot before which there seemed to be a parking lot. It was actually a flat, dirt and gravel-covered plain, extending from the highway like a sort of growth. There was a black man wearing a denim vest and one motorcycle and two women parked in the lot. They weren't hitchhiking. I don't know why they were there; I didn't ask. I felt it was okay to stop in front of them. They looked at me curiously. I waved and smiled and stuck up my thumb.

The sun was very hot; I was achieving a refried brain. It didn't matter. I was very pleased with everything. I became very caught up in looking without taking pictures, allowing my brain to scan without focus, without purpose, enjoying.

I suddenly felt it was time to move. I did. I walked past the three with one motorcycle and through the pretend parking lot. "A view," I said, pointing ahead, stopping at the top of the lot where there was a view. A beautiful river valley was below me, green and alive, with a singing bridge. Each time a vehicle passed over the distant bridge, I could hear it sing. "OMMMMMMM," it sang, like a poet forgetting his words, but delivering a message all the same. "How perfect everything is," I thought.

The cowboy on his way to Phoenix rode by in a van. He waved and I answered. I removed my shirt to take on the sun. My dry mouth wasn't a hindrance. Back on the distant on-ramp I noticed a person walking down. He continued. The Orange Man was still in the shade of the bridge. The person left the on-ramp and walked up the incline of the highway towards me. The vision was more than a sight to me, it became a presence and then a momentary threat.

I was perfectly happy alone. Yet, he continued, up to the parking lot, stopping momentarily to speak with the three on a bike.

"He's wearing a hat," I thought, "in this fucking hot sun, he's wearing a fucking hat. Not only do I have to deal with somebody, but he's a nut."

The person left the three on a bike and continued on towards me. The hat he wore was one like my own. It was a tweed slouch cap. I could tell by the cock. Mine was packed away.

The cap was removed and the head was shaken, exposing shoulder-length dark wet hair with a glow of red. I am being delivered a woman, I thought.

The vision was indeed a presence and no longer a threat but a delight, looking like a boy on purpose, traveling alone on the road. I beamed like a lighthouse, not thinking of sex, merely looking for companionship with the possible challenge of a sexual adventure.

"Hi, mate," she said. "It's a bit hot, but a lovely day for a walk."

"It's beautiful," I said, momentarily stunned. "Are you from England?"

"Naw, Australia, mate."

"Hi, there. I'm Sullivan Duda from Baltimore." I was extremely happy.

"Seems to be a bit crowded around the on-ramp. I was hiking up the road a bit. Mind if I break?"

"My pleasure. Hold on," I said, and immediately dug through my bag and showed her my Big Apple and put my shirt back on. "Who are you?"

"They call me Ramona Pearl," she said, amused by my hat. In all her splendor and glory, she appeared before me. I felt perhaps she was some sort of legend. She pulled a canteen from her backpack and offered me a drink. Her ukulele was immediately slung back over her left shoulder. We began taking turns rambling about our journeys, where we were coming from, how we got to where we were, and where we were going. She showed me a sign. BERLIN it read on one side, FRISCO on the other.

"They hate it down there when you call it Frisco," she assured me. I was absolutely enthralled with her voice and her Easy Now manner. Traffic passed. We just talked. We spoke of our first buzz of the day and wished for a joint.

We noticed a large four-wheel-drive vehicle accelerating up the hill in the passing lane and swerving in front of a car with ample room, into the right lane. There were two young boys in the front seat. The passenger yelled something and threw something as they passed us very close. It was the joint we had wished for. We looked at one another and laughed, and promptly picked it up off the ground and smoked it. We were having a party.

I told her I was a writer and showed her my typewriter. She said she was a plumber and showed me a small wrench she always carried. The rest of her things were being bussed down from Seattle. She prided herself in her little blonde mustache and sideburns.

"Lots of crazies out there, mate. Sometimes it's good to pass for a boy on the road."

She explained how she was married to a gay man in Seattle. The marriage allowed her to stay in the country for five years and travel, plumbing when necessary. Something very pleasant was happening. I rustled through my pack and pulled a paper from my briefcase. This amused her. I sang her one of Rupert's rhymes while standing there, enveloped in the meandering of focus. And she listened and laughed.

Rupert says,
I might not have no position
I might not have no fame
But I've got my ambition
It's that things don't stay the same
But I think I'll keep my names
I don't like no roadmaps
I don't want no clock to punch
I'd rather just go hungry
Than to be told when to eat my lunch
I don't mind a workin'
I know you gots to pay your way
There's certain things I won't do
I don't care what you say.

I can't stick to schedules
I won't live by your rules
And I might end up diggin' ditches
Like a lot of other fools.
I hope you hear my story
I hope you understand
To me you are important
But on the other hand
I admire you for who you are
What, I just don't care
And it's really been a pleasure
We've had this time to share
Yes, it's always been a pleasure
Just to have some time to share.
Rupert likes to rhyme.
Parnassus is rising.

There, now, are you happy?

It'll do in a pinch.

* * *

I explained to Ramona that one of Rupert's schemes was to locate a tribe of aborigines and have them carve little sayings in rocks and have them shipped to gift shops all over the world. They would be called "Rock and Rupertism." She laughed.

Pretty soon, Ramona began holding up her sign to passing traffic. "No sense lettin' all the traffic pass without a flash," she said. Suddenly, we were hitchhiking together, taking turns holding the sign and laughing and talking and she sang to me. She strummed on her ukulele and sang, slightly off key, while I listened and her freckles danced.

> Truckin' with the Duda man
> Who once told me you got to play your hand
> Sometimes your cards ain't worth a dime
> If you don't lay 'em down.
> Sometimes the light's all shinin' on me
> Other times I can barely see
> Lately it occurs to me
> What a long strange trip it's been.

* * *

Such a glorious day it was. We were both headed for the same area, I to Mill Valley, just north of Frisco. But we were more than a day's journey away. I didn't wish to appear forward and say, "Let's do it." I still had intentions of stopping in Mendocino to sleep on the cliffs. After all, I still had two slips of paper in my pocket. One said Arcata and one said Mendocino, and the same trustworthy flower had given me both names, so long ago. Ramona was on her way to Ukiah and then Hot Springs at Orr to visit a friend. I had forgotten that such minor complications have a way of taking care of themselves and getting straight while on the road, especially on my journey—a journey that was surely scripted by the gods.

And we played, speaking of hopes and dreams and visions while we waited for the ride to take us apart. The couple who had been sitting under the tree up on the on-ramp finally passed in a van. Ramona waved to them. She said she had a chance to speak with them along the way. The Orange Man was still under the bridge, sitting in the shade.

Hoping to put off our inevitable separation, we decided to walk back into Garberville to have a beer. The three on a bike were still there—waiting. I didn't know what they were waiting for. I put on my shirt, gathered my bag, and Ramona, her pack; we each took our axe and walked towards town. Ramona continued holding up her BERLIN sign. If a ride came all the way to Frisco, we'd stay together for a while. I had been wearing my eighty-nine cent flip-flops. Ramona called them thongs. A strap broke on one while we were walking. We stopped for my other pair, the brown pair I had bought in Eugene. She laughed and said, "I don't believe it. I met a man who carries a spare pair of thongs." I didn't think it was funny.

A pick-up truck stopped. It was being driven by a young blonde boy on his way to Ukiah. We took the ride. Ramona and I carried on, not thinking of the road, but playing and singing while the young boy drove. We all three shared the cab with Ramona's uke; my bag and axe were in the back, along with Ramona's pack.

But then, uncertainty, uncertainty, searching for the answer--I was headed for Mendocino on the coast. Ramona was off to Ukiah inland and the Hot Springs at Orr. The coastal highway cutoff was still a long way away, so we sucked every ounce of joy in every moment. "We ain't got a barrel of money," we sang as the boy drove, stone faced. Ramona plucked her uke. "Maybe we're ragged and funny. But we travel the road sharing the load, side by side."

We stopped in a store and picked up some beer and the couple who had been under the tree at the on-ramp in Garberville. They were headed to Mendocino; the same place I was going. They climbed into the bed of the truck.

"Plumbing?" I asked between songs.

"Your shit is my bread and butter! One thing leads to another, Mate, if it's all connected properly." Ramona sang, "The hip joint's connected to the thigh joint. And then there's always the air holes."

Ramona stopped singing abruptly and asked the boy, "Doesn't the road from Ukiah to the Hot Springs continue on to Mendocino?"

He looked rather puzzled. "Yeah. It's a long way."

"How long?" I asked.

"It's only about twenty miles past the springs, isn't it?" she said.

"I guess," he agreed.

"That's not far, it's all connected," I enthusiastically complied.

So it was decided. I would continue on to Ukiah and accompany Ramona to the springs and then continue to Mendocino. The couple in the rear enjoyed themselves as we drove through the giant redwood forest.

"Holy shit!" I said on my first daylight viewing of the giant trees.

"They're just really big trees, mate."

Ramona had wonderful sparkling eyes that always laughed and sang like a soprano in a happy moment.

We dropped the couple where Route 1 meets 101 and continued. Like children, learning a new song, we played, not really sure where it would lead, nor caring. We were dropped in Ukiah by the young boy. We thanked him; Ramona carried my typewriter and her pack and uke, while I constantly switched shoulders with my now overbearing burden that seemed to become heavier and heavier with time. The walking and carrying were beginning to catch up to me, as was the pot smoking and beer drinking. We walked to the Orr Springs road.

"It's a dirt road," I said, feeling duped.

"Only in part," she said with a snicker.

"How far is Mendocino?" I asked my sly companion.

"Oh, thirty or forty miles."

"Oh," I said, and then hiccupped.

Then, a dream occurred.

We walked a city block on the dirt road to the Springs before a beat-up pickup picked up Ramona, me, and my hiccup. There were two smiling Easy Now ranchers in the cab on their way home from wherever. Not a word was spoken since everything was surely planned. Ramona and I hopped into the rear with our gear. We drove uphill for a short time; the dust engulfed our seeing; bumps nearly forced our peeing. We came to a stop at an aluminum gate that Ramona hopped out and opened.

We waved goodbye and our spirits let fly as another car shortly approached. We squeezed in the bug, to our arms gave a tug, while we wound up the marvelous mountain. Just another short ride and our thirst didn't hide; then we searched for a spring-like fountain. We still walked for the sky, when along came a guy, in another pickup truck. He carried us still to the top of the hill, and we thirsted from dust and the muck.

We began walking down to the valley and spoke of our plans for the day. Then we turned round a bend for a message, godsend, LEMONADE, the sign did say. It seemed all unreal, though our pulses did feel, and we pinched one another with passion. We entered with ease. They said, "Drink, if you please." We were served and felt quite the fashion. We sipped on our drinks at that marvelous place, the only one on the road. We waved, as we left, to that wonderful space, while in two faggots strode, from nowhere. We continued on our journey. Thirsts quenched, with it all downhill. Then along came a ride on a flatbed truck, which took us farther still. The road turned to black and asphalt; we drove through an open gate. Ramona turned and looked at me and said, "An apple this big. Go for it, mate."

Thanks Rupe.

Rupert says, "Is it narcissism or is it schizophrenia? Doodle-deedoodleeedoduda."

We entered Paradise. The driver of the truck asked me to lock the gate behind; they were closing for the evening. I had told Ramona if she found her friend I would disappear. There was no need; he didn't live there anymore. I followed the truck, on foot, across a wooden bridge, down a narrow dirt road, to a large cabin that housed the "office," which didn't seem like an office at all. Ramona remained on the truck until it stopped.

She inquired about camping and baths for the night. Eight dollars a person, we were told. We each had a twenty. The sixteen dollars was taken from mine. Ramona agreed to repay me in the morning. I had been spending money like an oil sheik since the Mary Patt; even eight dollars for a night's lodging and a bath seemed a bit extravagant at the time. But there was a softness in the air. "A cushion," I was told, "from the rest of the world."

I didn't know what the Hot Springs were. I was along for the ride in the company of a very pretty lady who possessed the beauty of a child climbing a familiar tree. We were told to wait and we'd be given a tour and shown to the campgrounds. I helped the driver of the truck unload some lumber while we waited for the drug to take effect. A drug it was, in the air. "A palace of relaxation," echoed from every crack and crevice and person and flower and even the lumber we were carrying and stacking on the soft earth. Then I began to notice things.

The driver was thin and blonde and gave the appearance of someone working in the mines. And then he spoke. He had soft blue eyes that whispered contentment and lived in a dream, once the lumber was stacked and the truck was pulled to the side among the other cars; it seemed less a parking lot than the growth on the side of the road near Garberville. The ships were docked in a basin, in no special order, but a basin still the same, like the festival in the forest, without lights.

"May I show you around," he said.

All around was a celebration of peace. Gardens flowered on the side of a hill, while silence bathed in warm waters from the earth, and nakedness was natural and not naked at all. Like a glow on the horizon of a fresh new dawn, causing birds to sing, came the quiet laughter of children bathing in pools and tubs and pleasantness, with other young and old and many desirous bodies together, giving cause for celebration of peace enveloped in the splendor of the moment as unexplainable as enlightenment.

All around me was a temple of mellow adjustment. All who were there wanted to be there, lost and found or wandering. Silence became a memory while the music of life played on, singing in complete harmony, with a truck-driver from the mines as the tour-guide. "easy now."

Rupert says, "As we each continue—I will grow, so will you. I wish to grow with you, not away from you, but in harmony."

Through gardens we were led, some with the feelings of wildness and others of controlled cultivation in quadrants of privacy much like the Biblical Paradise without the animals that never shit. We walked through gateways, to a pool, etched into the earth and fed by rocks. A big, fat, old, beautiful naked lady was standing there, not naked at all. She was wearing a bathing cap. She spied my axe and looked like a perpetual giggle, all wrinkled and rolled.

"Is that a typewriter?" she asked, in a voice of momentary interruption.

"Yes, ma'am," I answered insecurely.

"I hope you don't intend to use it here," she said.

"I'm here to bathe; it would get wet."

Our guide led on; Ramona and I giggled with our bodies, like children being scolded, knowing they had done nothing wrong. Past the pool, up a path, into the forest where an orange tent with a pair of feet sticking out was growing, we walked. Ramona chose a spot beneath a large tree above the path, overlooking the stream. Our guide left us with a smile and a welcome. He disappeared. I never saw him again. Ramona quickly shed her clothes. I was there; I didn't know what to do. I watched and puffed on Prince Albert.

"Watch the butt," she said.

"I am."

"Naw," she smiled, catching the pun, "the cigarette."

"No filters. It disappears." I stripped it to demonstrate.

"Aren't you going to bathe?"

"Oh."

Her naked body was soon off down the path. I quickly followed, carrying a towel, and exposing my dignity. The woman by the pool had disappeared. Through a gate and gardens, and another gate, we walked, witnessing each other's body without shame. It was the natural thing to do. We crossed along the edge of the basin and over a bridge to the baths.

There were two empty rooms available. We showered and cleaned and each took a room. The strangeness soon became familiar, as distant thoughts of being told what to do, perhaps by the tour-guide, crept into my brain. I had no fear of this control over my actions. I was in "Paradise." I relaxed, alone, in water which was warm and opened my pores and felt like a blanket, though it overflowed from the tub and splashed against the cement floor, applauding. Anxious to explore, I soon drained the tub and scrubbed it and plugged it up for the next visitor. The tubs were always filling with a steady flow of natural hot spring water and applauding from overabundance.

I looked in on Ramona, who was at home on her sailing ship, perhaps a thousand miles away. I followed my instructions and washed once more in a room with stained glass and concrete, and ventured to a tub of redwood, big enough for people stew. The moist heat made me float like a feather in the wind; I was joined by a goddess and her child. We shared a bath. Others came and went, then Ramona, filling the tub with silent life, because I knew her.

Ramona and I returned to the pool where no one else was around. We played and we swam and hugged in the water, with our naked bodies feeling and tasting.

"I wish to make love with you," I said.

"But we hardly know each other—what about sex?" was her playful reply.

Echoes of laughter filled the earth, removing all time from its face. We splashed and we laughed and played tag in the rain, then bathed again in the dark.

It was time to rest; we returned to our tree. The air became chilled at night. We shared her sleeping bag and my blanket, enveloped in the splendor of movement—and we danced.

Rupert says, "Life is planting seeds, for pleasure, for thought, and for the harvest."

Rupert is a letch.

Enough of that.

Parnassus is rising.

That's better.

* * *

The sleeping bag was comfortable to lie on, with the blanket covering us, at first. The blanket became adequate, though uncomfortable to lie on with the sleeping bag covering us later. Add a pair of jeans and a shirt and a sweater and another body just as chilled as your own, and it becomes a very long night. With the first tinge of grayness, we rushed to the deserted baths and shared a tub of very warm water, waiting for the sun. There was no hurry. It was the beginning of the 11th day of my journey.

The morning passed too quickly; soon we were preparing for the road. Ramona used the communal kitchen to grind black coffee beans with a tiny mill she produced from her pack, along with two mugs. We sipped coffee on the porch of the cabin where we began; then I helped a beautiful woman move dirt from one pile to another. The woman was there learning the art of massage. I didn't remember seeing her naked.

Soon Ramona and I were off, back up the road to Ukiah, walking in the hot sun. I blew off Mendocino without any thought of failed expectations. I changed quickly from jeans to cutoffs allowing my lower legs to breathe again; we shared a joint Ramona had been saving for a special occasion. We had survived Paradise.

Back along the winding asphalt road we walked, uphill, until the fence from the Springs disappeared. Before the asphalt ended and the road once again became packed dirt and dust, we were picked up by a Volkswagen bug and its driver. Ramona sat in the back with our things as we chugged along watching the beautiful landscape. We laughed together when we passed the house where we had lemonade the day before.

The driver of the VW was a photographer on his way to town.

His eyes kept darting off in different directions, taking in the view. "I live down here," he said.

"It's beautiful," I said.

"I've driven this road hundreds of times, and it's always different—it's always different—the lighting or the shades—or the time of day."

The photographer dropped us in Ukiah. Ramona treated me to cinnamon toast and coffee and repaid me the eight dollars that I needed badly. I called the number in Mill Valley that Carla Smersh had given me.

Ben answered. "Call me when you get close," he said. "I'll come for you."

I had never met Ben. I hadn't even spoken to him before. He was a friend of Carla's. Remember, Carla was one of the three big loves of my life. She was now a semi-famous movie star. I was looking forward to seeing her once I got to LA—lalalala lalala.

"Come on down," Ben said.

Ramona and I were soon on the freeway on-ramp, holding up the sign BERLIN. A woman in a compact car stopped for us. She was on the way to Berkeley. Ramona sat in the back; I stretched out in the front and was quickly overcome by a very deep sleep while the women were actively pursuing a conversation, with the likes of which I couldn't keep up. I felt like a conquering hero of old, when such things were in vogue, having passed from Lords to Ladies, over the oceans, across the plains, and under the spreading chestnut tree, surveying the kingdom, with it dying to meet my approval. I was a snob in my good fortune.

By the time I woke up, Ramona and May had become fast friends, talking about the things women talk about, I guess. I didn't eavesdrop, I slept. We were soon approaching the Petaluma exit, where I would have to be dropped. The women intended to turn off and approach San Francisco through Oakland. I was to continue on to Mill Valley to Ben's. Ramona and I planned to get together the very next day, we just weren't sure how.

Suddenly the traffic seemed like an infestation of bloodthirsty mosquitoes compared to the Easy Now rambling further north. May took the Petaluma exit and dropped me on the street, immediately returning to the freeway with a wave. I took my place in the pecking order at the ramp, where no less than a half-dozen other hitchhikers of various shapes, sizes, colors and sexes jockeyed for position in the free-ride market. There was no walking down the road to break away anymore. Though I wasn't into the obvious competition of it all, I soon found a place to squeeze in and stood there in my safari shirt and red bandanna and cutoffs and flip-flops; I stuck out my thumb and smiled my ass off.

Girls obtained rides very easily but the guys had to work a little harder with semi-perfected techniques; a ride always comes along for everyone. Some have to wait a little longer than others, but the right ride always comes along. My benefactor had the rear of his compact car loaded with scuba-diving equipment. He knew exactly where to take me—with a smile. We spoke briefly and joked and he dropped me at a lounge in Mill Valley.

"You think they'll let me in to have a beer while I wait for my friend to pick me up?" I asked. I looked a sight and it looked to be a fine quality joint.

"Just tell them you're a millionaire," he said.

I was anxious to try the technique but the place was closed due to fire. I called Ben from a service station next door to the lounge and he was there in a flash. He looked like a flash. He drove a silver Mercedes and was wearing white pants and a shiny white shirt. His hair was white, as were his shoes and socks. His smile nearly blinded me. "You must be Sullivan Duda," he said in a tone that made me believe it. "I'm Ben. Dear Carla's told me so much about you. Dear Carla, don't you just love her?"

"Yeah."

"How has your trip been on that frightening road?"

"Wild."

"I'm sure it has been," he said in all his whiteness.

Ben had to return to work for the rest of the day; he dropped me at his apartment, or should I say, he left me in his cloud. I was afraid to move at first, stepping in through the door. Everything was mirrors, glass, and white plush. It was absolutely, obscenely beautiful.

"Don't worry about your dust," he said. "The maid comes in tomorrow."

"Yeah."

"Dear Carla said to give you the finest of treatment, and I intend to. I must be off. The guest room is over there," he said, pointing with a dramatic fingernail. "There's white wine in the fridge. There's also a lovely pool out back through the maze. Apartments can be so complex, but convenient just the same. You should find an assortment of lovelies to feast your eyes upon to pass the time."

He left and returned in a few minutes. I hadn't moved.

"I almost forgot. Here's the key. If you should venture out to the pool, please lock up. There's also some wonderful Mendocino County Bud in the fruit dish on the coffee table."

So fitting it was that my road led to heaven, I thought. Saint Peter seemed a bit strange; it really didn't matter. There was no doubt in my mind that nothing should be questioned. What it is. I found the white wine and then the guest room. I was very pleased that it was purple. Ah, sweet variety, I thought. I soon showered and, wearing my cutoffs, carried my axe out the back to the comfortable pool where a number of nubile young maidens were walking out with pubic hairs and firm young buttocks peeking from their wet bikini bottoms. It all seemed rather tempting; I was burnt. I sat there alone and typed a nice pleasant overly-informative unromantic letter to Ermonie. I took an occasional dip in the pool for effect.

I was attacked by the hot sun and white wine and fatigue, and returned to the cloud and pleasantly passed out in the purple room. I was awakened by a gentle tapping on my door. "Yoo-hoo, Sullivan, dinner's ready." It sounded like a melody of cream on top of the grape jello I was sleeping in. I gathered together my momentum and etched myself into the cloud very carefully, being sure not to spill anything, though I was carrying nothing.

"I do hope you like broccoli and fish?" he said. "I have my own special cheese sauce." He had relaxed to jeans and slippers along with his shiny white shirt.

I was still in somewhat of a daze, finding it hard to shift gears because my transmission fluid was very low. "I, uh, hope you don't mind. I gave your number to an Australian girl. She'll call me later. We hope to get together tomorrow. It is the same number I reached you at today, isn't it?"

"Yes, yes, I don't mind at all. The number follows me wherever I may be."

We dined with white wine and white candles.

"Ben," I said, "this is quite fucking wonderful."

"Oh, come, come, dear boy, your brain is still dusty. It's no more fucking wonderful than anything else. Think about it."

I thought about it. He was right. I sat there and enjoyed the dinner and pleasant conversation; I expressed my desire to write novels.

"My dear boy, I once intended to be an artist. I painted and starved and eventually found my way into interior design. I'm living rather comfortably; I still get my creative gratification throwing other people's money around. That artistic shtick is by the wayside; one must survive in today's world. Speak with Carla. She'll get you into television."

"Videotape?"

"It's a living."

Ramona called and we made definite plans for the next day. She would meet me at the ferry.

I enjoyed the company of Ben without any misgivings or paranoia; the fantasy I had discussed with Ethel in the teepee remained a fantasy when I was confronted with it. We did, however, venture to the Bars of Tiburon and elsewhere for the evening. Ben and I even danced together at one little pleasant place of loud disco music and lights. "There are so many different planets to explore," I thought, "One needs only the open mind and the balls—space travel for the common man."

I slept alone in my purple room, enveloped in the splendor of grape jello. The morning came and Ben drove me to the Ferry on the Marin Peninsula. I spent the 12th day of my journey in the company of Ramona Pearl and San Francisco.

Rupert says,
The gay scene has never been
So much in the spotlight
But the bodies move and the people groove
When the music and the spot's right.
If you laugh at them, they just laugh back
And say, I need to be me.
Don't interject, but have respect
The world is full of lifestyles.
If you don't agree, you must feel free
To live your life as you need
So don't demand, just understand
There's more to life than one breed.
Rupert likes to rhyme.
Parnassus is rising.

DAY 41

Rice simmered in seawater in an old aluminum pot over an open fire. The pot was dented and black and looked like it had been worn by a solder who had gotten his head blown off by a bazooka. Crazy Tom had built the fire and was minding the rice. His boniness made his ears appear larger than they actually were, though I'm sure I saw him swatting flies with them.

I sat on a very large rock at the edge of the circle of sand that was bordered by rocks and high salt grass. It was the kitchen of sorts, much like Myron's kitchen in the Haight but without a roof, where Tom was cooking rice in a smaller circle of rocks in the center. Off to the side, one circle led to another circle of sand, the upper ring that was also bordered by rocks and high salt grass.

There was some sense of order in the natural chaos of these rooms without roofs. The sun had gone down, but the sky was still gray; two sleeping bags were already laid out, an extra one was on the side. My axe was next to me on the rock and my bag at my feet.

Red helped Tom with the fire, while Woody rolled cigarettes from a can of TOP tobacco. I offered my Prince Albert. "Leave 'im in his fucking can and let 'im smother," Tom commented and laughed like he wouldn't breathe again.

The cardboard box with pictures of apples and bananas was opened. "I told ya we had plenty a food," said Woody. He smiled with his deep blue eyes and rusted face with wrinkles that seemed like etchings found in some uncovered cave from a past civilization. Woody didn't speak much and kept his distance, rolling cigarettes and drinking wine and passing the bottle. His bright Hawaiian shirt did most of his talking. We had two bottles of Gallo White Port. I had paid for one of the bottles. Before the second bottle was opened, Indian appeared as if he had materialized from sand. He was dark and mysterious and trudged like an omen.

Indian sat next to me and talked from down deep in his throat without breathing through his nose, ever. Crazy Tom added a can of cream of chicken soup to the rice; Red kept watch over the wine so no one took more than his share, while he looked through the box of goodies.

"Hey, man, we got this stuff from dumpsters," he laughed. "Yeah, these people are crazy." He spoke like a situation comedy with his own laugh track, but easier. "They throw away good stuff just because it's got a little piece of mold on it." He listed the booty as if they had pulled off some great heist from the Queen's own kitchen.

"We got cheese and bread and potatoes. We bought the rice and the can of soup. We don't steal," he assured me. "We even got butter and ham hocks and a fuckin' artichoke."

The Indian sat quietly between Woody and me while Red gave his presentation. The artichoke was tossed into the pot with the rice and soup to boil. The potatoes were wrapped in used foil and tossed on the fire to bake. The mold was cut from the cheese and we chewed what was still good, while we sipped on the port wine.

We drained the first bottle of wine and the second was opened. Hard and quick, but short gulps were taken from the last bottle for the wine to do its duty. There was little for many, and an altered state was desired.

"You know," the Indian exhaled, "you might not know where you are."

"They said Monastery Beach."

"This is Steinbeck country, and Miller and Brautigan and writers come and go. This is Steinbeck country. Monterey—Cannery Row. Steinbeck made it famous. Now it's a tourist trap. That's where you are," he said. "We're the bums of Cannery Row. We had to move."

Crazy Tom rinsed the artichoke in seawater and carried it to us. He displayed it on the point of a knife, and placed it on a tine plate in front of us.

"What do you do with an artichoke?" I asked.

"You boil it, strip it down, and get to the heart, but don't disrespect anything," said the Indian with the conviction that he had just solved the puzzles of this world. "Yeah, then dip it in melted butter and eat the good parts with care."

We did.

It puzzled me at first when Slim appeared, pushing a ten-speed bike through the sand. The right leg of his jeans was tied tight with a white sock. He was thin and pale and wore a white tee shirt. He claimed he was a cook at an organic restaurant. The grayness of the sky became a misty otherworldly backdrop, giving the sparks from the fire the color they deserved.

Slim produced a quart of warm beer and passed it around. I soon discovered the reason for his presence--Music. An oblong black box was strapped to his bike. He soon produced a silver tube in three sections and screeches, once it was connected. Like air bubbles coming from the depths of the ocean in a cartoon, he spit and sputtered until they popped.

"We need more wine," said Red with his long hair draped over his shoulder and the only beard besides mine. I chipped in two dollar bills, leaving myself with change, and Slim kicked in a handful of small coins. Woody and Red disappeared into the sand in search of more wine. Crazy Tom kept checking the rice and took his turn on the flute. He could only spit and sputter without pops.

"We enjoy ourselves," said the Indian. "It's a brotherhood. We work when we have to for a bottle of wine. Food!" he said. "This is America. They throw away enough food to feed the world twice over. We don't worry about food. If it gets too crowded here, we move on."

The sparks danced in the black of night to the note popping and spitting and sputtering. Tom turned the potatoes. The Indian told me of the games he played with the deer as a child. How privileged I felt.

Red returned without Woody. He did have a large bottle of Thunderchicken.

"We got stopped by a cop for no lights. Woody was tryin' to save the battery. They took him to the Salinas jail. He was driving on a suspended license. He'll be okay. They'll feed 'im and he can watch color TV."

Tom broke up the burnt potatoes and tossed them in with the rice and added cheese and wine. We passed the jug and dinner was served. We were each handed plastic spoons. I sat next to the Indian, who, with his dark features, seemed like a shadow with a voice. We were joined by Slim and Crazy Tom with the dumpster stew, and Red, with the wine. Everyone circled the pot, breaking every rule of etiquette possible, and dug into the Epicurean delight—by that time we were pretty stoned from the beverage and herbs. Yet, it was tasty and filling. We came up with burnt potatoes and left stringers with the cheese. The pot was scraped of everything scrapable and then cast aside for another day.

Tom and Red danced around the fire to the music of Slim's poetic license. They kicked sparks into the air and Tom's pants caught on fire. Red beat it out with his flannel shirt, and they wrestled like swordless gladiators in the three ring circus.

I sat in the sand with the rock to my back, and gave Indian my copy of *Breakfast of Champions*. The shadows and the sparks and the music presented some kind of distortion that seemed holy and simple, with echoes. Red came over and looked at me closely.

"Are you enjoying yourself?" he asked.

"Yeah."

"You're a good guy, too, I know," he said quietly.

"No, you don't, you don't know me."

"I know of you."

I became God. There was clarity. Whether it was the wine or the feelings or my own self-inflated ego, it didn't matter. I was God. The fire began to die; the Indian disappeared back into sand. Red brought me Woody's sleeping bag. Woody was warm in jail, he didn't need it. Slim had his sleeping bag strapped to his bike, of course. He took it down and picked a patch of sand to lie on. Tom and Red disappeared into the upper ring where their rolls were already prepared. I used my bag as a pillow and quietly accepted the role as the one true God of the moment.

At first I thought being God was a big deal. There I was: GOD. The sound of the ocean was singing to me. The sand was soft and comfortable. I watched the stars above me. A sleeping bag belonging to a prisoner was keeping me warm. I had less than a dollar in my pocket. I was God. It was no longer such a big deal. I did like the idea of being God, the second time around. It was much more pleasant than the first. I felt I would be better at it this time. And I did have a wish to remain God. Again, it was no big deal. I felt the sand and listened to the ocean and looked at the stars and tasted the dampness in the air and sniffed at the dying cinders of the fire. All the hard work was already done. "As God," I said, in a loud thundering whisper, "I allow everything to continue on its natural evolutionary course with all its beauty and pleasure and pain."

"That was easy enough," I thought. "There's got to be a catch."

Sleep was pleasant as God. No more than usual, nor less. I didn't lose any sleep over it.

And then it came to me, on the fiery tail of a comet I saw in another galaxy. "I accept the full responsibility, business as usual." I looked at my qualifications. I have killed someone. That certainly didn't put me out of the running. My entire journey I had continuously allowed things to happen with an occasional forcing of my will and ego, like a blight or a blunder that usually comes about by some divine intervention that is no longer in the hands of God but in the hands of technicians of ego. When the steel cable was screwed up, I told Emmett I fucked up. God's an idea guy with a sense of humor, not a mechanic. God's an Idea. Things happen with wonderment. Man has to build things—he's the technician—so many unfulfilled can-do spirits. I realized God is forever and always has been. 'I am water from the well with lemon and honey added.' THE WELL. The well? WELL, there's money in GOD.

> Rupert says,
> I smoke and drink and curse and swear
> And I don't use no underwear,
> But I'm at one with the universe.
> I rant and rave, don't cut my hair
> Ain't got no bucks, but I don't care.
> Cause I'm at one with the universe.
> The point that I am makin' here
> Is more than often said.
> The images you've taken here
> Are gone when you are dead.
> Rupert likes to rhyme.
> Oh, come now.
> What did you say?
> Parnassus is rising.
> That's better.

* * *

The morning came on the 14th day of my journey, my first morning as God. The air was chilly and damp with a heavy mist. I allowed it to stay that way. I dug in my bag and found my toothbrush and toothpaste. Slim was a clump in the sand, as were Tom and Red. The Indian was the Sand. I got a good look at what was left in the pot we had been eating from the night before. I thanked myself for night. I knew it all hadn't been a dream. The bottles and cans and cigarette butts and clumps of burnt potato strewn about certainly gave evidence to a happening. The fire, which had been so magical the night before, looked cold and obscene. A pair of unused dry ham hocks took on the appearance of over-used gonads from a castrated warrior.

Rupert says, "Make love not war."

Easy Pieces.

I walked barefoot in the sand to the ocean, where I made my first attempt at walking on the water. I needed practice I learned. I rolled up my wet jeans to the knee and allowed the ocean to revive me. I tasted the salt and added Crest and wiped the blight from my mouth. Such POWER I felt. I took a leak where I stood, and laughed, remembering how the seas were created; back to the scene of the grime I strode—feeling like a sheet of celestial parchment etched from the tree of living—scripting myself as God.

I scribbled a thank-you note and left it folded in the sleeping bag and gathered my things. My burden was still heavy; I carried it up to the road, and positioned myself on the south side of a big black Oldsmobile with dew-covered windows. The morning fog was thick and chilly and damp; I wore my hat and bandanna and a smile. Like a curtain, the fog suddenly raised. Across the road, at the top of a hill, a beautiful whitewashed structure appeared like a whisper, giving its name—"the monastery," I heard. The curtain dropped and chimes rang out from everywhere, like an echo that breathes the air.

Then, as if on cue, painstakingly slowly, a rod appeared from an ocean side window of the black car. It was attached to a thread-like wire, and a red feather was at the very point of the rod. The rod grew until the wire was tightened, and then it waved, and then froze like an eternal erection. Except for the feather—it tinkled to the chimes.

"Thank you," I spoke.

"De nada," was the reply from the magic wand.

My laughter became competition for the chimes. I felt there was no need to investigate; the wand remained, at least until I had disappeared down the rode with the first ride of the 14th day of my journey.

* * *

Sometimes it gets downright weird. My hollow point has done a turn. It's been sitting there, laughing and staring at me for centuries, looking self-righteous with all its potential in an abstract state of being, speaking occasionally through its nose, but never breathing. My hollow point has done a turn. My hollow point is sitting on its hollow point. It looks as if there is no point at all. HAH! My feet are cold.

My sincerest wish is that someone would tell me how long I've been dead. Perhaps, then, I could rest for a while. I know death came to me. It wasn't in a dream. The only difference between life and death is realization, when someone finally says, "YOU'RE DEAD." Of course that could just be an opinion to be ignored or debated. Self-defense.

Rupert says, "If you have to feel your pulse to know you're alive, you ain't living at all."

The first day I arrived at this cabin in the woods, I found a little house in a tree, farther back in the woods. I hadn't been able to find it since then. It's used for stalking deer. I just now came from it. I'll never forget where it is again. It's also a neat little tree house. It's allowing itself to go far enough and taking the time to do it. But now there is no Ermonie.

* * *

I didn't mention to Hank, the black man in the Chrysler, that I was God. I didn't think he would understand. He had enough weight on his head already. We sped away from Monastery Beach in a kind of blazing glory. Hank was young, and a jive nigger, the way I remember a jive nigger to be, but a good guy just the same. He was very nervous and spoke constantly about big cars and fucking women.

"Cain't take ya foe. Got some people."

"Hey, man, anywhere."

"Big Sur."

"Fine."

"Jus' had a fight wit ma old lady. She jumped from the car. Ma foot slipped to da gas an Ah knocked down a wole."

I noticed his left front fender was a bit crumpled. "Wow."

"Yeah, she crazy. Ah ain't fuckin' wit dat young shit no moe."

He spoke of his many options with older women and showed me what his Chrysler could do. There was no other traffic on the road; the ride to the River Inn in Big Sur was quick. I thanked him and walked to the bathroom of the River Inn to use the facilities and look in a mirror. I wanted to see if being God made me look any different. I was one anomalous deity. I cleaned up a bit for my proper presentation to the world and returned to the parking lot. Excitement was in the air; several official-looking vehicles were scattered about the lot, along with a few uniformed men.

I was surprised, somewhat, to see Hank sitting in the back seat of one of the official-looking vehicles. I approached an officer with a smile.

"Good morning, sir. The gentleman in your car picked me up at Monastery Beach and brought me here. I was hitchhiking. Is there a problem?"

The officer looked at me and chuckled; others were standing around. "You've lost your ride. It's a stolen car."

"Oh, Hank seemed like a nice fella."

"His name's David."

"Oh." I thought about mentioning the fact that I was God, thinking that that might make them go a little easier on David; I remembered a very important part of being God, the second time around and knowing how it should be done, is not to pull rank. I decided to remain partially incognito. They asked to see my identification.

"Look at the sky and the trees and the birds," I said, and then promptly handed over Sullivan Duda's driver's license. I was allowed to continue hitchhiking; the officer was God also.

I waved at Hank or David or God as they took him away. I purchased a pack of cigarette papers from the store and positioned myself at the southern end of the lot, once more with my thumb sticking up, occasionally holding up the LA sign which Ramona had drawn for me.

I waited and waited and waited. God finally stopped for me. She had beautiful long red hair. She was attempting to pull from the lot and pass me. I looked at her long and hard and smiled.

"I don't usually stop for hitchhikers," she said. "You looked right through me."

I was pleased with my power and knew that I would arrive in LA, lalalala lalala that evening.

My beautiful benefactress told me how wonderful Big Sur was. She was on her way to work and the ride was short; she dropped me on a curve at the entrance to the restaurant where she worked. It's hard to thumb on a winding road; only bends and hills were in sight. However, this particular curve was adequate. I stood on the back side and outer edge of a very large space for stopping. If I had seen a plaque of some sort it would have been a scenic overlook. There was a beautiful view from where I stood—of fog.

Cars and buses and bikers and hikers passed; I decided to write a letter. I positioned my typewriter on one end of the duffel bag and myself on the other, and proceeded to write to Ermonie. I told her I was God. I had intended to keep it to myself, but such moments should be shared with loved ones. I felt rather amusing, sitting there on the side of the road, typing away on my little portable Royal. One car passed. I heard someone yell and say, "GO FOR IT." I thought it was Ramona Pearl.

I finished my letter and once again held up the sign, LA— lalalala lalala. Other hitchhikers began popping up on the front side of the curve. They kept getting rides. I wasn't discouraged; I did finally move to the front side when it became vacant. No sooner had I moved than a car stopped next to me. A young woman with long auburn hair got out of the car and smiled. "Been waiting long?" she said. She carried no baggage of any kind and was wearing a "Hands of God" tee shirt over jeans and Nikes.

"It's been hours, my dear."

"Where are you headed?"

"LA"

"I'm on my way to Santa Barbara for a party. Do you mind if I stand with you?"

"Hey," I said.

"If I don't get a ride to take me all the way, I won't go."

I felt no need to question anything she said. She stuck out her thumb and a car immediately stopped. I knew a thumb was better than a sign. The rear door was pushed open and I hopped in without question with my gear. My beautiful accomplice hedged momentarily.

"How far are you going?" she asked.

A man was driving, and a woman with a large bubble of silver hair was sitting up front on the passenger side. "San Simeon, dearie, to the castle. Is there anything the matter?"

"I'm looking for a ride all the way to Santa Barbara," she said. "I think I'll wait."

The woman with the bubble hair turned and looked at me. "Aren't you two together?" she inquired.

I was sitting very comfortably in the back seat, alone. "We met five minutes ago. I've been waiting for hours. If you'd rather I get out, I will."

"Is San Simeon good enough for you?" She wore baby blue spectacles with corners.

"Yes, ma'am, I appreciate it."

I winked at my accomplice and said, "Thank you." She smiled and shut the door. We pulled off.

Rupert says, "Positioning is a very important part of life."

Pickles and ice cream—fried herring—potato chips.

"I'm Beatrice and this is Irving." Irving turned his head and smiled, exposing gaps alternating with crooked teeth. He hadn't said a word. He had absolutely no hair. He drove slowly along the winding road.

"I'm Sullivan Duda," I said. Then, I thought, "If I'm God, why can't I tell anyone?" I decided to play it safe in ladies' lingerie for a while, at least until I got used to the role--Everything in its own time. And time passes.

"There are so many poor people hitchhiking," Beatrice said. "Isn't it awful?" Her tone was condescending.

"No, ma'am, I've been enjoying myself," I said. I thought and then chuckled. "Tell me the truth. You wouldn't have picked me up if the girl wasn't there." I matched her tone. But I also managed to catch her eye and smile easing the moment.

She stammered momentarily. "Oh, yes. Irving was just saying there were so many poor people needing a ride, we should help one."

"Thank you, ma'am," I laughed. They were both smoking. "Do you mind if I smoke?"

"Not at all."

I produced my can of Prince Albert.

"Irving, offer the man a cigarette," Beatrice said. Irving didn't say a word. He held out a pack of Raleigh's. I accepted one.

We drove along the cliffs of Big Sur, winding down Coastal Highway! The fog had disappeared. Every turn in the road presented an ever-changing backdrop of lush green vegetation on the hillsides and dramatic drops to the ocean below. Irving and Beatrice were from New York originally, now living in Las Vegas. They were on vacation in a rented car, experiencing as quickly as possible the sights the coast had to offer. Beatrice offered me a biscuit that was left over from their breakfast at the River Inn. I accepted. "Let them eat cake," she said.

Irving kept me supplied with cigarettes, though he didn't speak. Beatrice shuffled through the few eight-track tapes they had and came up with Boz Scaggs. "Would you care for some music?" she asked.

"Why not?"

"Irving and I don't care for most of the modern music," she said. "These tapes were in the car. Since you're a guest, we'll play this for you."

I began to think maybe they knew I was God already. I didn't worry about a thing; I enjoyed everything they had to offer. They were very sweet, and we had a wonderful time. They dropped me at the intersection where the road led to the Hearst castle on the hill. "A pleasure," I said.

* * *

God, schmod. All of that was then, and easy; this is now and it's not so easy anymore. The thought of any kind of positive energy flow is as far away as Ermonie and her freeze dried marine or husband or whatever the hell he is. The fact is I'm here in a cabin in the woods. I'm out of dope and booze; my bucket of shit has bugs creeping into the lime, and I still don't know what I'm going to do with it.

Dump it over the side, asshole.

I said I've had enough of you. One of the bugs, no less.

I'm so sick of eating fucking rice and all that other crap; I'd give my left nut for a fucking hamburger. The blight makes me nervous. I do wish I had my gun. Pieces of my brain on a sheet of paper would be the perfect ending. HAH. Everything has its own time, when the time comes, as the time comes; time always passes. Maybe I'll settle for a piece of rope and a photograph.

Rupert says, "An *I* without the dot is just a little *L*."

Hamburger.

* * *

Standing on the road with a view of the fabulous castle on the hill, I began to slowly lose my feelings of godliness and eased into a real simple state of being once again.

I was picked up by a man in a VW who had been fishing. He was quiet and pleasant and didn't mind my sleeping all the way to San Luis Obispo through no fault of my own. It must have been a cosmic reaction; I couldn't keep my eyes open. He dropped me in San Luis Obispo, where I used a telephone in a restaurant near the on-ramp to call Carla Smersh in LA

I caught her at her home in Venice Beach and told her I would be in LA sometime that night. She informed me of previous plans to be out and said the key would be under the mat.

Once more, overwrought with anticipation for my destination, I took a position at the on-ramp in the hot sun. I waited. Finally a beautiful young woman with ozone eyes and a heavily drugged smile picked me up. I sat in the other bucket seat of her compact car and released my fear of frying. The young woman was called Anna; she carried the same presence that Regina at the Country Fair had carried, but she was a little older. Anna wasn't wearing a toga or a wreath around her head; she was wearing a long soft dress that clung to her thighs. She was also not wearing shoes. "Call on the Lord" bumper stickers were piled on her back seat.

"Jesus loves you," she said as we pulled onto the highway.

"An apple this big," I answered.

She spoke softly with singing words. Gospel music played over her cassette player. My carnal desire convinced me of my mortality; I didn't mention that I had been God a few hours earlier. I could have dealt with a relapse. If she wanted to call on the Lord, I was willing. But Anna was perfectly happy with believing in the other guy. She didn't preach to me, so I didn't preach to her. She spoke of the love of the Lord without any demands.

Rupert says, "I know where I'm at, but I'm not always sure when I'm there."

Hamburger.

I felt comfortable with Anna driving along being pure. We stopped behind a supermarket; she checked the dumpsters for food.

"Seven-Eleven's and anywhere they sell prepackaged sandwiches are good also," she said with a dreamy swagger—and she was one of the meek. "Once the bread is soggy, they throw the package away."

Such a journey it was, with so many vehicles and so many faces and ways. How privileged I felt to be given a taste of the sweetness and magic there is and the choices offered.

Anna dropped me at an on-ramp near Grover City. I waited and watched and held up my sign, LA. My next ride was in a laundry truck with a happy driver who had finished his route for the day. He wore a hat with a shiny bill; it fit his white uniform and reflected his smile. He took me to Santa Maria, where I called Damien Rumsford.

"Call me when you're close," he said. "Whatever time, I'll come and get you."

After speaking with Damien, I copulated with a Coke machine, leaving myself with 20 cents in case I should happen upon a mad crap game or a disconnected hooker. The sun was falling low in the sky and there were no apples to be seen anywhere; I was too busy looking two hundred miles down the road for my friend Damien and dear Carla Smersh. Such a love affair we had had, Carla and I—fiery and passionate and short—and whenever she wasn't with her husband or other lover it was actually fun.

Rupert says, "Sounds like a pattern to me."

Hamburger.

Each of the few times I had seen her on the screen in one of her movies, I dreamed of the moment when I would have the opportunity to become a groupie without the relationship with the insane woman. Soft porn seemed to go well with her, I recalled--So did hard.

I was also looking forward to meeting for the first time the immortal Dominic Rodriguez Sepulvida, the man responsible for opening my eyes and mind to Easy Now.

The on-ramp was occupied where I was in Santa Maria. The blockade was in the form of a pair of escapees from an orange orchard.

"Hey, mon, you can tumb wit us, we goin du San Diego," said

one who was wearing tomato stains down his front.

"It wouldn't work. I'm headed to LA—lalalala lalala," I said, being a snob and walking up the on-ramp, pressing the legal limitations.

* * *

Maybe if I stick the hollow point up my ass and fart, I'll blow my brains out. There's always a lot of shit; I could possibly stick my head in the bucket. On second thought, I think I'm immune. I've been wallowing in it for 41 days now.

Rupert says, "Everybody is an asshole—in some other asshole's eyes."

Hamburger.

* * *

I began pacing at the top of the on-ramp, not sure whether I wanted to risk a trip to the police station by edging out onto the freeway or perhaps spend the night watching a pair of greasers cause the traffic to slide by. I carried my sign while I was making up my mind. A car yanked off the freeway onto the shoulder.

"I saw your sign," said the driver. "I'm on my way to San Diego."

Like a turnstile at the World Series, the miles clicked off. The driver was a sailor headed for the sea; I was a passing fancy headed for wherever he wished to drop me. How we got there, I don't know. We left the freeway and drove across mountains in a 280Z lost in a maze of determination for destinations differing. He took me to a taco stand in Glendale, where I became confused reading the map of Beverly Hills. I called Damien and he came for me driving a red Corvette with a blonde at his side. I felt a tremendous surge of joy and love seeing a familiar friend after so long a journey. The blonde was called Trudy; she had enormous boobs and an empty head and a red jumpsuit.

"I gotta take a crap," Trudy said while we were loading my gear into the Vette.

"A lady doesn't say, 'I gotta take a crap.' She says, 'Pardon me, I need to powder my nose,' " said Damien, reprimanding her. His handlebar mustache did all the talking. "She's gotta good body," he mentioned. "She's one of Dominic's models."

I was in LA. LALALALA LALALA. It was 11:00 on Friday night and the 14th day of my journey.

"Can you take me to Venice Beach?" I asked.

"What? Don't you want to come to Dominic's? Trudy's not the only model."

"Dear Carla's expecting me," I said with an exhausted smile.

"Is that the broad you said was the porn star?"

"Soft porn, Damien, soft porn."

"Hard porn, soft porn, popcorn, hey?"

Trudy returned and the lady in red sat in my lap all the way across town. Carla's apartment was modern leopard skin, facing the ocean and the circus of Venice Beach. We found it easily enough and the key was under the mat as she said it would be. We made plans for getting together and Damien and Trudy went about their business.

I relaxed with a glass of single-malt scotch and waited, listening to Vivaldi, for my movie star. It was after midnight before she returned. She had shaved her head. I wasn't surprised. I wasn't shocked. Her dark eyes flashed at me like two lit matches in the dark. I was lost in a dream. We hadn't seen each other in years. We had had contact, but with the safety net of a wire and great distances. There was a surge of silence when she entered; even the record ended. We embraced and I felt her head. It was smooth and eerie, being so close to her brain.

"Sullivan," she said.

"Carla fucking Smersh," I said.

"Take a shower first. You smell like a bear," she said, and laughed a wonderfully cynical laugh.

I had seen her in a movie with a bear, but she had hair then. Now she was beautifully bald. "Why did she do it?" I thought. It was so--animalistic. I became aroused, and a bit curious.

"Carla, are you. . .you know. . .are you. . .completely hairless?"

"Sullivan," she said in a seductive tone, "life is filled with many mysteries. The answers belong only to the daring—and the clean!"

"My journey. I gotta tell you about my journey," I said. I don't know what came over me. She poured herself a drink and refilled my glass with scotch, and I told her about my marvelous journey and how I had been caressed by a gentle breeze and passed from hand to hand like a diamond at an auction. I rambled and shouted and laughed to my bald-headed audience until I finally passed out on her leopard skin couch.

DAY 42

Rupert says,

> Got that old time drip and burn
> When will I ever learn
> You gotta sniff
> Before you cut the pie.
> Fill out a questionnaire
> But show them that you care
> Cause life is just a breeze
> Less you got Social Disease
> Show me that you care
> And change your underwear
> And be choosy
> Bout with whom you go to bed.
> If you've been sleeping with the masses
> In that endless line of asses
> Forget the JAZZ and just give me some head.

Rupert likes to rhyme.

Dump him over the side.

* * *

So it goes. When I awoke surrounded by leopard skin on a Saturday morning I knew my journey had ended. I walked to the bathroom to relieve myself to find it was no relief at all. Those all-too-familiar symptoms of a burning sensation and my penis having the sniffles caused me to laugh that the joke was on me. I could only laugh. I looked in on Carla. She was lying naked and hairless in a leopard skin bed with a body fulfilling its desires to stay eternally young.

"Carla," I cried.

Her nipples were erect. Her eyes peeking out of a perfectly formed head like some alien with great sexpectations and a perfect body—a porcelain work of art. She glistened from her moist lips. . .lips.

"MMMM, good morning," she oozed.

"I've got the clap," I said, with torment bursting my jeans.

"What?" she screamed.

"Gonorrhea," I repeated.

She began laughing a wonderfully cynical laugh. "A souvenir of your wonderful journey." She was hysterical.

"Part of the road," I reasoned.

"Thank God for long stories," she said. "I go on location in three days."

It was absolutely disgusting. We could do nothing but talk the entire time. We rekindled an old friendship that had been ended by sexual jealousy and growth in different directions. She took me to her personal doctor where I was tested and treated and punctured.

Carla spoke of her career and her road and her dreams. I spoke of Ermonie and my dreams.

"What do you have to offer this woman?" she asked.

"Me," I said.

"What do you have to offer?" she repeated.

"What more can I offer than my willingness to accept the responsibility of being with another person and continuing from there?"

"The dreams of a child," she said.

It was clear. We played for the next three days on the beach and in the ocean. Damien and Trudy joined us in watching the skaters and bikers and the circus of Venice Beach. With all of my hair and none of Carla's, we fit right in. Her leopard skin outfits were kicky.

But. . .but. . .now.

No, then. We spend the days. . .we spend the night. . .

We. . . Now there is no Ermonie.

Carla left on Tuesday morning. She dropped me in Beverly

Hills. Dominic Rodriguez Sepulvida, the supplier of Easy Now, wrapped up in ladies' lingerie, was the host. I had pictured him many times in my imagination. I thought him to be some sort of god wearing long flowing robes and a wreath of flowers. By him, I was shocked. He was short and fat and smoked a big green cigar. His jowls wiggled when he spoke. The place he lived in was a palace.

He was King Henry the Eighth. "Der's money in drugs," he said.

"But. . . Easy Now. . . I mean, easy now," I was pleading.

"In New Orleans, they call it Night Train," he said.

I was fucking shattered.

"Dis is America," he said. "Land of opportunity. Better living through chemistry. It's gotta purpose. It keeps a certain segment happy and sedated so dey can go about der business a survivin'. It also makes a few bucks."

"But. . .but. . ."

"Easy Now," he laughed.

* * *

Easy now, he laughed and I sit here in the woods. I have no more booze, nor drugs, and my last bit of tobacco burns my lungs. It's funny, my sticking t has become a way of life. Certain disabilities have to be accepted and dealt with, I guess—as does the fact that I have no money and I'm alone here with a three-legged dog. Ermonie is married. There are trees and birds and flowers and peace.

And one bucket of shit, you asshole.

My friend, I've just finished dumping it over the side, and you are my friend, if only for a moment. For now, we talk and communicate if only for a moment. You see, this doesn't happen a lot. It couldn't. It wouldn't be real. I'm tired of surface relationships. I have a lot to offer and a lot to learn. I'm always willing to learn. That's important to me. Tell me about the mountain you crossed yesterday. Was it high and covered with rocks? Were the turns such that you had to slow down? I may never cross that mountain. I may have crossed one like it. I probably have. Then we have something in common.

This is important to me. How did you feel? I see you lived through it. SO DID I. Look down the road a piece. It's hard to see what's ahead. Would you like to know? I wouldn't; it doesn't matter. I'm sure it will be the beginning or the end of another county. The liquor laws are funny in some. So are the people. It's sad I won't to get to know everybody there; then again, it would be too confusing anyhow. I do know they've crossed similar mountains. Even on the salt flats they must have rocks.

I was with a pretty young girl yesterday. It was nice. It was a sustaining moment. I felt the joy of pleasure. So did she; we communicated. I didn't feel deep love. My heart is too valuable to prostitute itself for but a moment. . .but moments are important to me. Even if they don't last long. They have to be. Right now, that's all there is that's real.

* * *

RING. RING. RING. You have reached the hollow point of man's theory as you listen to the wire connecting focused sound between a machine and you. If you decide to hang up, I'll continue speaking. It doesn't matter if you're there or not, wherever you think you are.

"When the music's over turn out the lights," says Jim Morrison.

Rupert likes to rhyme.

I left in a hurry--with no place to go.
I discovered this--Once I had left.
And now--I'm there--Wherever I am.
Still unsure--Of where I've been.
I left in a hurry.
Goodbyes are such a trauma.

Lalalala lalala, says Rupert.

Easy Now.

About the Author

Ken Piaskowski has worn the following hats:

Altar boy, writer, football player, Social Security Administration clerk, bartender, bouncer, band manager, doggerel writer, gardener, door-to-door salesman, dishwasher, cab driver, real estate salesman, construction worker, firewood cutter, shopping mall Santa Claus, night watchman, food handler, stage actor, pari-mutuel clerk, movie extra, plasma seller, narrator, typist, substitute teacher, fisherman, boat waxer, migrant worker, water man, producer/director, documentary filmmaker, founding president of Ocean City, Maryland Friends of the Library, entrepreneur, census taker. And so on. . .

www.ingramcontent.com/pod-product-compliance
Lightning Source LLC
Chambersburg PA
CBHW071949040426
42447CB00009B/1296